The
Birthmark Scar

By
P. E. Berg
&
Amanda Hemmingsen

Photography Credit to Willym Brown

For permission, serialization, condensation, adaptions, or for our catalog of other publications, write to Ozark Mountain Publishing, Inc., P.O. Box 754, Huntsville, AR 72740, ATTN: Permissions Department.

Library of Congress Cataloging-in-Publication Data

The Birthmark Scar by P.E. Berg -1970-
Amanda Hemmingsen -1988-

The Birthmark Scar originated as a way to psychologically record and process the death of a father and how coping with death introduced concepts regarding psychics, past-lives, and synchronicity.

1. Coping 2. Past Lives 3. Metaphysical 4. Synchronicity
I. Hemmingsen, Amanda, 1980, Berg, P.E., 1970 II. Metaphysical   III. Synchronicity IV. Title

Library of Congress Catalog Card Number: 2021946338
ISBN: 9781950639083

Cover Art and Layout: Victoria Cooper Art
Book set in: Amatic SC & Times New Roman
Book Design: Summer Garr
Published by:

PO Box 754, Huntsville, AR 72740
800-935-0045 or 479-738-2348; fax 479-738-2448
WWW.OZARKMT.COM

Printed in the United States of America

CONTENTS

Chapter 1
The Green Man

The green-painted warrior sat, his breathing labored and his skin soiled. Spots of blood matted his curly red hair and marred the mossy-green of his paint. The man's sword lay near his wooden chair, carrying three new chips from chopping at bones, blood still smeared and streaked from the lethal wounds he created and the death he brought to the fresh bodies that still lay on the battlefield several miles distant from the village. The blood was now dried. He sat in his sturdy but makeshift chair of wood logs and animal skins, reflecting on the tough victory of his clan on the wet, cold grass fields of the Highland valley.

His breath shuddered as his gaze fell upon the sword. It was tradition to let the blood of your enemies rest on your blade for some time after the battle so you could capture their souls and prevent them from going to

Valhalla, the majestic enormous hall of the fallen of those in combat located in *Asgard*. The land of Asgard was ruled over by Odin, and all the people of the Highlands shared stories of those who died in combat led by Valkyries to Asgard. Such a noble death's reward was the envy and true purpose of every warrior. Today, many souls had been barred the honor of Valhalla. And many souls now sat in those halls, feasting and boasting with the great heroes of the land. The Green Man hadn't taken off his coat of rich animal furs and headdress of deer antlers before sitting. They, too, still wore stains of blood from yesterday's battle.

Fighting began just after dawn. Icy dew droplets drenched the field, typical of an early autumn on the mountain of the clan. Drums and bagpipes echoed far and wide in the heavy cold air. The sonorous reedy sounds of the bagpipes filled their souls full of bravery, courage, honor, and tenacity as they readied themselves for the clash. As the music leapt to its frenzied peak, the two groups of warriors closed upon one another. The close combat fighting on the field was quick. Over in a few long and bloody hours. The Green Man's plan had worked very well against the unorganized clan. Their warriors had rushed the field with no thought to their hold on the high ground. Simply by having the bagpipes continue for a few counts while the enemy began its rush exposed the overeager enemy clan.

The clan called this man the Green Man in their Celtic dialect. He earned his name from leading spiritual rituals around the communal fire inside the looming standing stones, fully carved by the ancient ones from the dawn of their oral histories. Every ritual, every change in season, every battle, every birth and death, green pigment from soil and plants colored his body, making the runic tattoos along his neck and arms particularly lurid. The green washing over his body marked his transition from a single soul seated in a body to his soul/body acting as a conduit for the gods and spirits of his people and of the land.

Many years ago, a holy person from across the farthest oceans and eastern lands visited the village. In her hood and black robes, tattoos spiraling across her entire body, she followed the will of the gods, traveling ever onward, trading food and shelter for herbal remedies. She never charged for predictions. On the night of the first full moon of the flowers, when the Green Man was on the cusp of manhood, sitting with the other children as the adults welcomed the goddess as she gave birth, Chira called across the fire so all could hear, *Gana Kirtumukha.* Upon hearing the sounds of the unknown words, he found himself walking to stand before her.

The holy woman Chira spent weeks with the boy she called *Gana Kirtumukha.* As they sat with the goat herds in the mountains, their conversations wandered from the properties of the roots and flowers to the portents of breezes. As summer began its descent into winter and fog began to creep along the mountain, her lessons turned to ways to speak with the gods and the spirits of the East, and most of all the ways of magic spells and chants.

The morning's battle would add kindling to the myths and stories that twined around his life among the peoples of the mountain in the Highlands. He heard the whispered edges of the tales of how the spirit of a madman, a man who sacrificed himself to Odin long ago, possessed his body with the donning of his antlered helmet and his hands grasping the broadsword and makeshift hatchet with its curved blade. He rammed his antlers with the strength of his back and neck. Three weapons, to hurt and stab as many enemies as possible. Many kinsmen mistook him as dead in some battles, drenched as he became with blood. They thought the blood was his life bleeding away from him. Their start of surprise at his blade or hatchet swinging with ferocious strength and quickness never crossed the Green Man's awareness. Some would flee from him because they said he had the wild demon spirit eyes of a madman, one touched by Odin himself. Before their minds could catch up, their bones and their guts knew that once he targeted you, his eyes could see nothing else, nothing could touch him. Their bones and guts would send their bodies fleeing before their minds could catch up. Many a man had attempted to cut him down as he pursued a target; many had seen the wild demon in his eyes, but none who had made direct eye contact ever walked off the battlefield. That no one lived to tell the tale of what lay in the depths of his eyes on the battlefield only fed the dread and horror of the telling of the stories. Word of his battlefield actions spread throughout the lands and he was feared by many leaders of clans that might otherwise clash with his people. His makeshift metal armor was still on his body while he sat in his chair because he did not have the energy to take them off.

As his breath calmed, the Green Man sat composing and ordering the pivotal moments and actions of his people's fight in his mind. Later, he would translate his mental pictures into Sanskrit and also in Celtic runes because he knew both, one of few of any of the clans who did. He knew he had to write down his memories to create the history of the clan to pass on to the next generations. Oral storytelling kept the clan in rhythm with its ancestors; the act of writing kept the orators in harmony with the sacredness of their task of remembering for the people.

Though the clan now gathered for the evening meal and ritual fires, the Green Man knew no foot would tread to his door reminding him of the time as they did for the elders and revered ones. Nor would sibling, child, or parent walk from a room with readiness to leave. The Green Man lived alone. In the prime of adulthood, he was brought before the council to be exiled. The king, being a man, let emotions rule his head in matters of family pride. The Green Man bowed his head before the will of the council, refusing to sully the proceedings with protests of his innocence. *Explanation empties your soul of conviction. Conviction is the vital force that connects you to the spirits*, Chira had said before she walked out of the village. He'd pondered those last words for years; that moment before the council, he knew was Chira's final test. He had never imagined the cost—his honor before the clan—and he didn't know what exile would bring, but nothing could sunder him from the spirits. *Gana kirtumukha* in the holy tongue of Sanskrit translated to "face of glory" for the people. If the king chose to cast out the face of glory, all the more reason to stay at one with the spirits. Those years of exile and wandering between villages on the mainland were filled with hunger and uncertainty, the miseries of existence without a people. Eventually, the message reached him. The king had died, one of his last wishes was his return, for this man's wrongful accusation to not pass with him as a weight on his soul. The Green Man's innocence and honor before the people had been returned to him.

But such a loss leaves marks in the soul. When he returned to the village, he never trusted anyone again. He kept to himself, returning to the poverty of his adolescence, tending the goats as they wandered the grasses. While he'd wandered the mainland, he'd been forced to master the art of a steady mind. As he wandered the meadows following the goats, as he had done with Chira in his youth, he applied that steadiness of mind to remembering her lessons and studying the secret properties of nature, as the spirits revealed them to him. Within a few weeks of his return and new life, he began to have visions. Sometimes they would be of the future, sometimes they would be of the spirits or gods. He never spoke of them, content and at peace with his understanding of the value of explanations. Gradually as battles were fought with other clans, he began to earn respect for his warrior skills. After years of this, he began to be accorded leadership and asked to guide the rituals before battle. Once, he felt himself become a channel for the gods of the people during a pre-battle ritual. The king of the clan understood what was happening, and after that battle, the king asked him if he could conduct the rituals before the fire between the stones. Their people had not carried out those rituals in almost a full generation. He felt the spirits of the land answer yes with his voice.

Eventually, he built himself a home in the woods. No one visited him unless they were invited. There were rumors by the people that he conducted ceremonies in the country with large fires and singing but such was the way of the clans on the Highlands that those with the ability to act as a conduit between the gods and the people before the fires between the stones were accorded the respect due to them. It never would have occurred to the people to gossip or wonder at the Green Man's secluded rituals such was the trust and sacred bond among all the peoples of the Highlands.

The Green Man would spend weeks in nature and return to the village with messages from the gods, the trees, the animals, and the seasons. The village would all listen and when he talked to the entire village, he would paint his body green. He had been given a message in one of his spiritual journeys that the color green was a powerful natural color and would help him communicate the gods' messages to the people. The truth for this man's latest message to his people was that respecting nature was the key to being connected to the gods. The Green Man lived a simple life with no luxuries because he was humble and wanted to feel the emotions of the natural world.

This night after the recent battle, the Green Man stood among his people with green clay on his face and his arms and legs with green leaves and on his coat and he spoke to them about their history of their clan, about how their gods were pleased with their victory, and that they should give back to nature and always with their entire being respect nature. If we hurt our mother Earth, it will bring drought, poor crops, poor weather, and other horrible things.

This special night the Green Man spoke to his people in a calming, patient voice, knowing what his warriors had done, knowing that some of the men died in battle, and knowing the families of the fallen were present. The bodies of those who followed him that day were wrapped in cloth and laid individually on mounds of logs. The burning of the bodies returned the spirit back to the earth so they could go to Valhalla and then after a time of rest and feasting come back again in another glorious life.

The twelve bodies all lay in a row and one by one the Green Man took a torch from the bonfire and laid it on each of the bodies to start their own ceremonial incineration. When all twelve bodies were burning and the wooden pyre fully ablaze, the tribe started singing and chanting their ancient songs, wishing their fallen warriors, fathers, and husbands a good spirit ride to the higher divine because of their sacrifice today. The songs were a blend of spontaneous soaring outcries and ritualized repetition of ancient phrases and benedictions. The outpouring of spontaneous and ritualized grief and gratitude honored the dead for fighting and defending their families and their clan. The songs were simple phrases of ritual honor. The better for the hearts of the people to pour forth their pride in the noble courage of the fallen. The elders kept time with their rhythmic chanting of the lists of names of all who had offered their life to the clan in battle. Next time, these twelve names would take their place on the list, to be remembered and cherished.

As the elders' chant began to fade back into the ancient songs, the Green Man started dancing slowly around the bonfire, beckoning with his eye contact and ritual gestures for first the mothers and children of the fallen, then wives and fathers to join him. The dance began slowly, a gentle transition from grief, softly melting into a celebration of their spirits traveling to the next world. The dance of celebration at its peak was wild, free, arising from the movements of the children. People joined and rested as they were called. The Green Man, his ceremonial role over, moved toward the men's fire. As one of his kinsmen slapped his back with joy, the Green Man twitched. He had been wounded there in battle; with the fires' light one could see a small line of blood slowing moving down the skin.

CHAPTER 2
THE READING

The northern gusts split time with muggy summer breezes. The steadily cold, violently temperamental winds from the north would soon dominate and Kansans would know winter had arrived. That Saturday morning when Paul pulled into an antique store parking lot the chill was ascendant. He put the truck into park, but his hand hesitated on the keys, the engine purring gently. His eyes stared unseeing at the nineteenth-century buildings lining Main Street. New signs and modern advertisements decorated most of the original structures. The street was empty except for his car. He had an eight o'clock appointment with a psychic.

Paul sat there doubting why he kept this appointment; he had had a difficult night. His mother called. His father had passed away just after midnight. Out of sheer habit of punctuality, he'd kept the appointment. Three weeks ago, in a blaze of excited curiosity, he'd let his amazement at one of his dear friends of many years admitting to getting Tarot readings spur him into peering across the curtain with curiosity. The thought of scheduling a psychic reading had never occurred to him before Jamie had glowed with passion as she revealed this new side of herself. Jamie, the young department secretary who was also training to be an Ashtanga yoga teacher part-time, had always been around psychic readers and Tarot card readers, though Paul had only just learned of it when she announced she was pregnant. Discovering this normal person invested so much in this stuff had spurred Paul to give it a try. As he sat in his truck still debating if it was worth it, a hand in the antique store flipped the sign from closed to open. He stared at it, his mind still in a daze. Some force from inside himself that he couldn't explain drew him to open the door of the truck.

That first inhale of cold air woke him up. His mind accepted that he was going through with this. He stepped out, pulling up his coat zipper and covering his head before walking across the street toward the antique store.

Paul opened the door, the smell of the old wood furniture reaching his brain before the chaotic sight of the crowded-together chairs and tables that filled the front of the store registered. A bell rang as he opened the door. Some of the pieces had been sitting awhile, from the thick layer of dust on the furniture. The store smelled like his grandmother's farmhouse. He slowly walked into the store in the hundred-plus-year-old building that had been a guesthouse to some Civil War Union general at one point in its life.

An older woman sat at a small table by the back wall. She was in her late fifties, short and large, with a bright blue bandana around the crown of her head, in jeans and a t-shirt like any person on the street. He wasn't sure what sort of clothes or appearance he expected of a fortune-teller, and he found himself reassured by the everydayness of her look and dress. She said, "You must be Paul. Please come and sit down." Her name was Lena and she was sweet and had a calming voice and continued shuffling cards as Paul began to walk to the back of the store.

He walked through haphazard aisles, with old desk and chairs as obstacles, and realized they were the only ones in the store. He took off his coat and placed it by the chair. A round table was covered with several intricately decorated scarves of purple and teal. Lena stood up to shake Paul's hand. Paul smiled, mind still churning with doubt and uncertainty. He was tempted to make some excuse and walk back out, but something inside him told him he needed to follow through with this appointment. He reminded himself he was supporting a local business owner, which was one of the ideals he carried with him in his business decisions. That fact gave his mind something solid to cling to as he sat in the chair across from Lena.

Lena said, "Paul, I was about to cancel this morning's appointment with you but my spirit guide told me that someone close to you had passed away and traveled through the astral worlds already and I had to relay to you that he had passed away, is fine, and not to worry about him."

Paul felt shock as the blood in his face dissipated. He had never seen, met, or heard of this woman before. How could she have known … ? He only told his friend, Robert, after he received the call from his mother. There was no way she could know. He dropped into the chair, stunned, his mind racing in circles too wildly to formulate a response.

Lena said, "I have a spirit guide that talks to me since I was a little girl. She is a voice from a Native American shaman and her name is Tinoma, and she has been communicating with me since I was nine.

"She has been talking to me my whole life. I'm not crazy. Tinoma talks with spirits who are transitioning or stuck in this world and have not moved on yet, but your father passed away recently and as a spirit has quickly moved on to his heaven or nirvana due to his actions during his last and most current life."

Paul sat there confused, stunned, and so wanting to believe in this woman whom he had never met. Her eyes told him he could trust her and she had nothing to gain to make something up that was so true. Her smile was true with her wrinkles around her eyes. He usually trusted his gut to steer him through new or uncertain situations, and it had gotten him out of many places that were speeding down a crevice right toward trouble. He was usually good at reading people through their physical reactions from the facial expressions, their dilation of their eyes, and looking at movement of fidgeting fingers. Everything in him told him to trust her. It felt right.

"Lena, you are right that my father died last night a little after midnight … thank you for letting me know that he passed on to heaven already." He continued talking, sharing about his father's life starting in poverty as the oldest of ten children, and how he was drafted into the army for the Korean War then joined the army to avoid a second draft and served a career with another combat tour in the Vietnam War. The details spilled out of him once he decided he could trust her. It felt good to share. He ended by telling her that his father was a good man and a fair man. All that his father wanted was to pass away in his sleep because he had recently been diagnosed with Alzheimer's. He died on his terms, the way he wanted to with no pain.

"Your father sounded like a good father and friend." Lena suddenly stopped and closed her eyes, head tilted slightly as if she was listening intently to someone. Her hand went up into the air to pause their conversation. She was nodding her head as if she was receiving a message. Then she opened her eyes with a smile.

"Your father wants me to tell you this … please don't fuss, tell everyone at the funeral not to fuss. Tell them I lived a full life. Tell them I am with my brothers and sisters and my mom and pop. Tell the good folk that I am with Willy, my father, who died when I was two years old. Tell Mom that I am proud of her and she will be fine. Tell them that the church was my stability. Tell them kindly not to fuss, I am fine, it was just my time, and tell them Ma says not to fuss either."

Paul pulled out the notebook he always had on hand. Any important meeting or event, he had it on him in easy reach. He never thought he would be taking a message from his father, who had died less than eight hours ago. He scribbled furiously, striving to transcribe every word, not to miss any part of the message. The message was so true to his father. The words Lena said were exactly how his father would have said them.

And yet, part of Paul's mind was still in complete disbelief. The rational analytical side of him that defined the universe according to the rules of causality he'd been taught as a child could not assimilate what was happening. But his gut vehemently knew these words were from his father. Paul felt a wave of peace wash over him, simply happy to be receiving a final good-bye and send-off from his father. It was true to his dad's character to leave a message for a son seeking some closure.

Lena said, "That is all that I have from your father's spirit … He has gone away to his heaven and can't be communicated with." She shuffled the cards in front of her and said, "Shall we begin the session?"

Paul had never been to a psychic or had any readings done before so he was shocked that the real session had not begun yet. "Lena, is this the way sessions start usually?"

Lena smiled gently. "No, never, that is why I am

excited to see what the cards say for this session. I have never had an astral message to a client before a session in my thirty years of reading cards. I am all goose bumpy with what will happen next, so let's begin."

Paul sat there, slightly out of breath, trying to make sense of things, then mentally decided that he must continue on this path of discovery. As she shuffled the deck, she explained they were Oracle cards, not Tarot cards, and there were dozens of different kinds of Oracle decks, but she trusted Oracle cards overall and used a special custom deck made for her by an old friend. She spread the deck in an arc across the table, asking Paul to pick five cards. She pulled the five from the rest of the deck and flipped over one at a time in an inverted V shape.

Lena studied the cards over and over and kept looking up at him. Feeling her gaze, not having any clue what was going on, the remaining eddies from the first shock latched on to this new discomfort, and his mind started questioning the whole process all over again. Her fingers kept touching the cards and he could tell she was communicating with her spirit guide again by the way she was trying to listen attentively like a hearing exam with headphones trying to listen to all the tones.

She said, "Are you ready for me to tell you what the cards say?"

He just nodded at this point, picking his pen back up, not knowing how fast the words would come out of her.

"Has your left shoulder blade ever been injured?

Any scars or birthmarks there?"

He paused and a small chill crept across the base of his neck. Paul did have a small birthmark there. And a one-inch scar from the American occupation of Iraq, when a mortar landed near him at Mosul airfield and exploded a fuel truck. Some hot shrapnel lodged deep into his skin between his protective armor. The field doctor did not know exactly how the piece of hot shrapnel got sent through the small opening in the armor. His mind stayed intent on taking it out and sewing him back up, rather than idle speculation at a minor mystery. The doctor stopped the bleeding and sewed him up in the dirt with no painkillers. The scar was rough and deep and about an inch long on his left shoulder blade. It still hurt once in a while due to loss of some nerve endings and scar tissue. The scar and the small birthmark in the same location were vividly on his mind. Once again, his mind grappled to answer how Lena knew. He finally said, "Yes, I have both on my left shoulder." He also recalled how he had met one of his future most-trusted university professor friends that evening in Mosul after the explosion and they would reconnect many years later in Kansas once he became a professor at the university where Robert taught.

Lena only smiled and said, "In a past life that you experienced, you were mortally wounded by a spear or sword in the left shoulder blade in the same spot and that is why you have a birthmark there."

Paul was stunned again by her remarks. How could she know these things? All he said was, "Please continue."

She closed her eyes, "It was during the Dark Ages, around 1500, you were a soldier for the Scot-Irish military, and there was a conflict between the Protestants and the Catholics. Witchcraft was somehow involved ... or just the Catholic Church accused someone you knew of witchcraft, which started the initial conflict. You also had a conflict—more like an inner conflict about witchcraft. You knew it was not what the political and military leaders thought it was. You were in the battlefield among the chaos on a wet grassy field in dawn with the temperatures right above freezing, and you fought well until an enemy soldier drove a sword into your shoulder, scraping between your bones. You ended up dying on that battlefield. You were content because you fought for what you believed in ... you had no wife or children to mourn you, but your loyalty and duty were remembered among the military and the town. You saved many of your friends that day but they could not save you. You are buried on that battlefield with your friends. The name of the clan was—" She paused. "The name of your clan back then was Gregor or MacGregor."

Paul looked at her again with amazement blazing from his eyes. His mother's family was a MacGregor from Scotland, who had lost their name when they rebelled against the king and the king outlawed their name. His family left Scotland and came to America after the Revolutionary War and changed their name to McGehee, to start a new life.

How could this woman know that? The scar on

18

his left shoulder started to tingle with a painful burning sensation ... maybe simply because he was paying attention to it, or maybe because he was making it psychologically hurt. Why should he believe this woman? He could not wrap his mind around this new layer of revelations. Paul had walked in just an hour ago out of curiosity and habit. He'd walked in in a fog of delayed reaction to his father's death. Deep in his core, underneath all those other layers, though, it felt like an alignment of him spiritually. He wanted more but was scared to ask. He started to get up from his chair.

Lena said, "I think we should continue the reading."

Though he wanted to be afraid of what else she might say, he readjusted the chair, ready for more. He was a well-educated adult and taught at the local university and had researched the science and psychology of adult learning with emphasis on the brain and this past hour with a simple woman had flipped everything on its end. Paul had learned through graduate school to use his mind and break the parts into smaller parts and not try and see the problem as a whole but to see the linkages between the problems and their components. His doctoral professor, who had served in the Korean and Vietnam War, would show him on a chalkboard slowly how to see a problem and pay attention to the details, because the human relationship details always tell the rest of the story, and slowly reveal the solution to the problem if you have the patience to see it. As Paul thought of his professor, he wondered what his scholarly and academic friends would think of his true and honest acknowledgment that he truly believes in fairies, witches, and the metaphysical. They would most likely kid him about him believing in the Easter bunny and Santa Claus.

So, without any sense of certainty or clarity in his mind, he said, "Please, continue the reading," to Lena. This simple woman with a past-life reading had just confused a logical and methodical mind. He was afraid but needed to have the rest of the reading.

With anticipation, Lena smiled and continued to look at the cards again. She said, "Many people walk in here and expect nonsense when I do a first reading, but you are different. You only need to believe what you need to believe for your growth. All of this process does not have to make sense right now. Just let it percolate like coffee and you will find meaning when it is time."

At that moment she sounded like one of the Buddhist monks he had met almost twenty years ago in Tibet, when he was studying abroad in India. The monk almost said the exact same thing. Somehow that caused his body to relax for the first time since he woke up this morning. He waited, calmer than he had been all morning as she finished flipping the array of cards.

Paul readjusted his chair and took a breath, feeling his heart rate rising inside the bubble of calm. His mind couldn't rest. He had not really comprehended everything Lena had told him. His mind began to ping around, searching to analyze, comprehend. Clearly, she had some ability psychically to know things about him that no one else knew. But nothing made sense, still, somehow. So, he took a deliberate, calm breath and relaxed and focused his eyes on the cards as Lena began looking at them over in a V shape again.

Lena kept touching two cards over and over again and having an internal conversation with her guide that lasted several minutes before she nodded and looked up. "Paul, are you involved in the church? What about your family?"

Paul said, "I grew up Catholic, and we went to church every Sunday and holy days. My father and grandfather were extremely devout, and my genealogical research of my Germanic ancestors found that there was a nun and a priest every generation. Even I thought about being a priest for a short while when I was eighteen."

She smiled, "Would you believe that in a prior life you were a high priest or bishop in the church, and you had power and wealth in your region? You were a powerful but fair bishop and took care of the poor." She turned her head slightly like listening for a whisper from her spirit guide. She then said, "There is a woman, with brunette hair that you already know or will meet soon, who was with you. You will be friends with her now or might be in the future." She paused again, "This woman was a witch in those days in your past life." She paused again with a puzzled look and said, "She is also a witch in this lifetime!" She continued, "This woman, in your past life as a bishop, she was a dark arts witch, but you protected her, and even lied to the governor to save her.

You risked everything to protect her. She also trained you privately in her craft in your quarters. You would meet out in the country privately. She even initiated you into the craft secretly, you knew the risk if the church or authorities found out about it, but you did it anyway because of the inquiry of knowledge. This woman, she died young of a tragedy, but you died of unexpected causes and still very wealthy and no one ever knew you were secretly being trained a witch while you were a bishop." Lena began flipping cards over and shuffling them again.

Paul's mind was spiraling, because he had faith in her first past-life reading—he did have a scar and birthmark on his left shoulder and had noticed in grocery store horoscope tabloids that birthmarks were marks from past lives, with nothing scientific at all in his reasoning. But this new past life that a woman he knew today he also knew in a past life and she was a witch in a past life and was also a witch today? Paul did not know any witches. How would he meet a witch in his simple life in a small university town?

As he was thinking, Lena had laid down another set of cards on the table for the next reading. She could tell he was thinking, and she looked at him a moment before asking if he was ready. Paul caught his breath, hoping he could handle another reading on a past life that he didn't believe in just an hour ago. He could not help but want to hear another.

Lena started flipping over the cards with authority and stopped in the middle of flipping the fourth card and froze, the card was a figure dressed like a holy man with an infinity symbol over his head. The word magician was written on the bottom, but Paul couldn't see any other details from this distance. Lena kept turning over the rest of the cards but her finger went back to the magician card. She asked, "What does the word Hermes or Mercury mean to you?"

"Well, Mercury is a planet ... is it the name of the Roman god with wings on his feet? No, that's Hermes. My last real study of mythology was over twenty years ago."

She said, "This card represents the magician who is the planet Mercury and is also Hermes, who is a messenger to the gods through the worlds of metaphysical reality. This particular card means you have a mastery of the imagination's conscious and unconscious process." She paused and asked, "Do you ever get voices in your head with messages?"

A voice in his head? ... Well, he did not think so ... other than the voice he called conscience—that figment of good and evil on both sides of his shoulders like a cartoon talking to him and having a conversation. He was always talking to himself, but never really thought he had messages or was never a messenger to the gods. What a confusing new development to this strange morning.

Then she turned over the last card. Her body became intently still as she focused on the card. "That's quite interesting. My, you are a unique customer! I don't ever get these exact cards with a customer on their first visit with me." The last card she flipped over was the knight of swords with a knight riding a white horse with his sword raised high. Paul merely thought it was a soldier card.

She started to explain his last past life with this card first. He was a soldier again but this time it was in America before the revolution, probably late 1600s. She said he was a soldier in the British army with valor that he used for notoriety. He spent over twenty-five years in the military and retired with no job afterward but with wealth and land. He lived in the northern New England area. Lena slowed down. Paul could tell her spirit guide was talking to her. Lena then said that the brunette woman who was a witch with Paul in the first past life is back again in this past life, but this time he married her and had no children. She explained that he married late, in his forties, and he was well traveled and did not have need to boast about adventures like most younger British officers. His wife died young and he mourned her, staying a widower for quite a while, but did find happiness. "No, wait, you watched your wife die," and she pauses sadly before continuing, "She was accused but never convicted of witchcraft because she worked with herbs and plants or watched someone work with herbs. She died of the smallpox young—not even thirty—but the people just thought her witchcraft spells suspiciously backfired on her and that was why she died."

Her right hand returned to the magician card. Her index finger rested on it as she stared at it before turning her gaze to Paul. "Well, we have already gone past the hour, and I have another customer in shortly. I'll explain more next time."

The thought of a next time hadn't occurred to Paul until she spoke. With the cliffhanger card after being hit with all the other profundities, he decided he agreed. He would see her again.

Lena stood up. Paul appreciated her gentle courtesy of escorting him to the door of the store. As he stepped onto the pavement an elderly man in a fedora walked up. Their eyes met. Paul felt like he knew him but he had never seen him before in his life. The man nodded at Paul, "Excuse me, sir," then clasped hands with Lena with genuine warmth in the gesture. They seemed like old friends. Paul kept walking as he buttoned up his coat. He was totally confused at what had just happened the past hour and needed a cup of coffee down the street at a local coffee shop to let things comprehend. He started walking down the street as he pulled up the collar on his coat. Paul walked past the yoga studio into the mostly empty coffee shop.

CHAPTER 3
THE NEXT DAY

Paul sat with his coffee at a table by the window, trying to contemplate everything Lena had said to him. His rational mind wrestled with itself; how could he feel such a strong sense of belief with so many unexplainable facts? He knew he needed to trust his gut, to trust that strong inner voice speaking to him. He left the shop still unsettled. Still in turmoil the rest of the weekend, he kept directing his mind back to the work at hand: preparing for a week of teaching and research.

Paul was a professor in education at the local university and enjoyed seeing his students light up with excitement and curiosity more than almost anything. That joy normally made it easy for Paul to fill his weekends with his work. More than teaching, Paul loved to research. Once he got a new subject, he would spend weeks in the library finding all the books, journals, and oddities about the subject and then do a full analysis. He was afraid this was going to be his next topic to research, and that was part of why his mind struggled to focus on the task at hand this weekend. Even though his mind was still in turmoil, Paul looked forward to the challenge of working piece by piece through this mystery. Placing this puzzle at the top of his research list helped Paul find those last reserves of focus to finish lesson prep and to catch a decent night's sleep Sunday evening.

Paul was walking on campus on this fall Tuesday in his traditional tweed coat and scarf. This early in the semester wasn't time to pull out a t-shirt and raise the eyebrow of the dean. He walked up the steps to Knowles Hall, the College of Education building named after the father of adult education, Malcolm Knowles. Paul noticed today's group of students trying to study for a test or complaining about a test or paper. The steps were the ideal height for sitting in a group, and there were always some students enjoying the fresh air and the mutual stress. The freshman classes were on the first floor and all the faculty offices were on the fifth floor of the education building. Two days after that odd experience in the antique store, Paul's mind was still busy trying to analyze Lena's words about his past lives. He had come in early today with the intent to focus his energy on preparing for his father's funeral. He had scheduled the Catholic service, written a check for the priest, confirmed the grave site in the family plot, worked with the funeral home for the viewing tonight, decided on flowers, called everyone, ensured the obituary was published. He'd worked out all the details for his father's funeral except for the eulogy. He still didn't know what he was going to say tomorrow to all those people from his hometown.

As he walked through the hallway to his office, he thought of the words that Lena had told him during their session about how his father did not want anyone to fuss over him and so he found his office and fixed himself a cup of coffee as his computer warmed up. He stared at the genial clutter of papers, pens, and knick-knacks on his desk, trying to let his mind go blank. He knew he needed to go over his always-full e-mails before he could calm his mind about writing his father's eulogy.

As he was going through dozens of e-mails from students and education book publishers, with the occasional bureaucratic announcement from the university, there was a particular e-mail that caught his eye. The subject line said, "Editor here, ready to help you with your book." It had been on his to-do list to find an editor for his book that was about half complete, but Paul hadn't published the need or mentioned it in the usual circle of professors. There was always a young graduate student or a recent master's student from the English department who needed a quick $500 to use their talents before they land that better job. His first book he hadn't hired an editor, and the publisher's editor sent several snippy e-mails on how much work Paul created for them before outright stating that early editing is always best.

So, with interest he opened the e-mail. Nera was new to the city and her husband actually worked in the College of Education as the new graduate student hire. Paul did not give the e-mail much credence, because most people say they like to edit but editing is the hardest part of writing. It's the analysis of every sentence and the tedious examination of the endnotes and references; his belief was most people would rather have a root canal over such fine-grain scrutiny of thousands of words. So, as he recalled Nera, she was a brunette, slender, young and attractive, always in high-quality makeup and high-quality attention to her clothes. She acted smart and used the correct words, but her master's was in sociology and her bachelor's was in history, so really, he did not think it would work.

Paul sent her a quick e-mail back, asking her if she was serious, and saying that he would send her a sample chapter to edit. He felt certain he would have to discourage her from pursuing editing with him. To that end, he attached the roughest chapter in his book and told her to get it back to him in a week. Within seconds after he hit send with the e-mail, she replied that she could have the chapter back to him tomorrow. Paul merely chuckled to himself and continued with the rest of the e-mails.

He then took out his leather notebook that he had taken notes on during Lena's session about what his father had conveyed and laid it on his desk. This would be the initial note. He took a breath and started a new document on his computer, slowly writing all the thoughts in his head and using Lena's comments about what his father had supposedly said. He started typing around 10 a.m. and kept wrangling through the eulogy for the next couple of hours.

Paul sat back in his chair, trying to stretch the tension out of his fingers and wrists. He let out a tired, contented sigh. It was an excellent eulogy. He was proud of the words he had put together in honor of his father. But he could never share with anyone at the funeral that he had spoken to a psychic about his father ... the Catholics would have him burned figuratively. The little town in Kansas where his father grew up and where he retired was full of devout Catholics and religion ran deep. He would speak this eulogy composed from the words of a middle-aged lady in an antique store who passed on his father's words—but absolutely never tell a soul where he received his father's guiding and consoling words. As he sat there, slightly bemused at this turn of events, Paul decided he would explain it as his last conversation with his father a week before he passed away. With that decision made, Paul returned to the draft for one final edit and review of the language. He was proud of himself; it was short and exactly what his father would like, especially the comments of no fuss over his death because he lived a full life. Paul thought it would be an effective reading in front of a packed church.

As he finished the eulogy, he received an e-mail from Nera that she was done editing his most difficult chapter. It had only been three hours since he sent it to her. Very odd. So, he opened the e-mail. She said she had the time and edited quickly. Paul looked at the work and the comments and it was the finishing touches that he needed. She even did the endnotes, with only a few errors. Paul wrote her back, thanked her on her speed of editing, conveying that he was impressed. He asked her if they could meet personally because that is the way he worked and she requested the sooner the better and to meet at Casaneta's, his favorite high-end bar. Paul had adored this bar from the first time he set foot in it almost ten years ago. The back room was lined with bookshelves from floor to ceiling along three walls. All of the seats were easy chairs with gorgeous side tables, carefully arranged for little bubbles of privacy. The university professors that visited there had a tacit agreement—conversation and hob-knobbing stopped at the entrance to that little library sanctuary. The building the restaurant occupied was built on Main Street in 1865 during the Civil War and had been famous as a hotel for over eighty years, boasting that Lincoln had stayed there. It was also infamous for being a speakeasy during the prohibition years and had reports of ghosts throughout the last fifty years from various guests at the hotels. Whether a marketing plan or good advertising, the bar was always full leading up to Halloween with ghost tours of the building now a yearly social event for the business. Paul sent the location and time for Thursday night. Within a few minutes Nera confirmed the appointment.

Paul felt very lucky to find this particular person

in this time frame to help him finish his latest book out of the blue. He wasn't quite sure what luck meant. Maybe the stars were aligned for him today. He chuckled quietly to himself. The stars? And yet, somehow, his mind tentatively conceded this might be a valid theory to explain the strangeness of the day.

He decided to read over the eulogy one final time. He still could not fathom that he had seen a psychic just six hours after his father's death and that she gave him an effective message from his father, that was so clear and accurate that he was using it as the frame and substance of his eulogy message to the family, friends, and community that would fill the church. Paul wanted to believe in Lena; he could say he did believe in her even when there was no logical rational reason to believe, but something about this meeting made him trust her and her motivation to convey a message from his father. Paul felt there was something else going on with all of this about the message and his father. There was something deeper that he could not comprehend, yet it felt familiar and known. It felt like an old dear friend that he had not seen in twenty years or that favorite uncle you remember from every holiday and event as a kid, but somehow never see again once you became an adult. This emotional connection with the metaphysical just felt right but Paul still resisted it.

He laid the completed eulogy on his desk and called a professor friend in philosophy to see if he was available for a quick chat. Finding that his friend was free now, he quickly picked up his coat and left the office and went over to Smith Hall where the philosophy and religious studies classes were taught. Paul found his good friend Stan, or more properly called, Dr. Stanley Franklin Gray, a renowned world philosophy researcher and religious artifact expert, who had worked part-time for the Vatican as a consultant and there were also rumors among the faculty that he had worked for the CIA. Stan had a subspecialty in ancient religion, the occult, and anthropology. His office was the typical old philosophy professor type with the tweed jacket carefully hanging on an antique coatrack, books to the ceiling on shelves, piles of books on the floor, and the key-note messy desk with twelve books open with tabs. The office smelled of mothballs and coffee. Stan was almost seventy years old but loved to talk one on one; unlike most professors, he dedicated himself as much to passionate extroversion in the classroom and public events as he did to intensive introversion in his research. As Stan shook Paul's hand he said, "Paul, great to see you on this cold day. What can I do for you? You sounded distracted on the phone."

Paul was about to speak, but Stan interrupted him with consolation for his father's death. Paul accepted with the courtesy his mother and grandmothers trained him in before describing his encounter with Lena. Stan made Paul include all the details about what Lena had said and then had Paul explain the eulogy. Their discussion lasted two hours and two cups of coffee each with both being intrigued by what they were saying and hearing. For Paul, it felt like the therapy meetings that he'd participated in over the years he was battling post-traumatic stress disorder after his time as a human terrain research advisor in Iraq. He would say something, and the psychologist would merely ask more questions. Stan was pulling the same move on him. Paul was ready to hear what this world-renowned philosopher and psychologist had to say about what had happened. Paul leaned forward in his chair, "So, Stan, what does this all mean?"

Stan looked puzzled and replied, "What do you think it means?"

"That's not an answer."

"Well, my friend, that is the best answer I can give you. The events have many high-energy connections to coincidences and facts, but I can't prove what Lena told you was right or wrong. Only you can believe. What I can say is, she knows things about you that only you knew so that means there was a third force—call it psychic, metaphysical, what-have-you—there is some intangible variable in the equation. She had nothing to gain from lying, but if she is right, then she could and will be right again. As we've wrangled over in many of our discussions, there are many phenomena and questions that we can't answer scientifically as yet. Carl Jung did the most discussion and research on the metaphysical, and it actually caused him to end his friendship with Sigmund Freud. Jung once said, 'Your visions will become clear when you can look into your own heart. Who looks outside, dreams; who looks inside, awakens,' so the best answer I can say is trust your heart and pursue this further—follow your intuition."

A young student gave a hesitant rap on Stan's door, peeking in with eyes beaming a sense of peril over stress over some paper or deadline. Paul took his cue and started to pack up his briefcase. It was time to be professor again and do some more homework. As they were both getting up from their chairs, Paul noticed a Jung phrase in an old frame on Stan's wall.

We should not pretend to understand
the world only by the intellect,
we apprehend it just as much by feeling.
Therefore, the judgment of the intellect is,
at best, only the half of truth,
and must, if it be honest, also come to an
understanding of its inadequacy.

Paul looked back at Stan and smiled.

Stan said, "During my dissertation writing, years ago, I used that quote to motivate me, because it reminded me that the intellect does not hold all the answers, we have to trust our imagination, our dreams, our heart, and our intuition to find the answer as individuals."

Paul just laughed. Such a psychologist and philosopher answer of nonmeaning. The two men shook hands one last time and hugged each other with polite gesture and promised to talk more, since their offices were just across the campus lawn from each other, but each knew full well that students would fill out time for the last month of the semester with finals due and papers to grade and department meetings and functions to attend.

As Paul was leaving the building and heading back to the education department building, he knew the answer to his question. He knew that Lena was correct and she had connected to his father and relayed his father's intent for his eulogy. New questions arose out of the solidness of the answer to his first question: What else does this woman know? How do these past lives connect to his current life? Who is this woman that he knows in this life that was with him in a past life? The questions swirled in his mind as he got to his office, shutting off the lights and tidying up the space before heading home. Paul would battle with the unknowns of these questions as he traveled home and prepared himself for the evening's visitation in a small town just hours away.

ɞ ɞ ɞ

Paul was never going to remember everyone who shook his hand and expressed fond memories of his father during the visitation that evening. Paul was the only son still living. His mother and older brother had passed away years ago, so he was the last of the family still alive. It was a distant comfort to be embraced by the community, swathed as Paul was in the sensation of realizing his whole family was now gone.

The people of the town and the local church knew the circumstances and because of that they came out in droves the next morning for the funeral church service. The hearse arrived exactly on time to the church and Paul was to follow his father's casket to the front of the church. Paul kept his eyes glued to the US flag draped over it in honor of his father's service in the Korean and Vietnam Wars. He walked alone behind the coffin. Behind him were the last of his father's brothers and sisters and a few cousins. The Catholic service started and his uncle read the readings as required and then it was Paul's turn to stand up in front of a full church and talk about his father.

Paul walked up to the podium, taking a moment to survey the room. From behind the podium, the church felt more silent and still than he'd ever experienced. In the quiet, he could hear a few people sniffling. He could even hear one or two people starting to cry. He said, "I am Paul, the youngest son of William, my father, and I would like to thank Father John for allowing me to speak at my father's service. I am a little nervous but I will do my best."

His body was charged with nervous energy, but he had written everything down to the exact word of what Lena had told him and had read it many times to be sure each word was in its proper place. He took a breath and started reciting his speech, using his professorial voice to make sure everyone could hear him. "I was able to talk to my father one last time about a week before he passed away and we had an excellent talk; he knew his health was going and I gave him my word that I would relay his message."

It was a cloudy morning and the church was somewhat dark from the stained-glass windows. As he was talking the clouds slightly parted and the sun shone through the vibrant reds and blues and greens of the glass windows, filling the church with some warmth. Paul spoke about his father, how he did not want anyone to fuss about his death, that he lived a full life, he served in wars, raised a family, lived all over but most important he returned to his hometown and continued to go to church and served in the Knights of Columbus to give back to the community. Paul spoke of how his father missed his mom, his own dad and brothers and sisters that had already passed. As Paul was finishing the eulogy, he could hear more crying in the church pews. He did not know how effective his eulogy was, but he felt right, the church was warm with the sun, and the speech was over. Now it was time to finish the mass and go in procession to the cemetery.

When the mass ended, the priest started to move down the aisle and the pall bearers took their positions and followed the priest to the hearse waiting outside. As Paul walked alone behind his father's casket, the last of his family, there was great sadness in his heart, but he knew his father was in a better place. While the casket was being loaded into the hearse, mourners made their way to their cars with their families, calmly lining up between the police escort cars. A long line of cars, lights on, drove together across town. As the cemetery came into view, Paul could see the military color guard waiting to receive the hearse.

Everyone got out of their cars, making their way to the priest standing under a tent with the casket. The color guard did their rounds, the flag was given to Paul, and "Taps" was played in the cold quiet morning air, while the surrealism of the moment kept reality clouded for Paul. After it was over, everyone gave him condolences and said what a good man he was, and several folks told him that the words he spoke were exactly what Bill would have said and they were exactly what they needed to hear today. Paul heard that from dozens of people. Dazed as he was, he felt from each handshake and hug how it positively affected the families and how it made everyone who attended the funeral feel better and not grieve or fuss. These words from Lena from his father gave peace to the community, which validated them even more and which gave him more conviction to pursue this psychic connection with the other side and the past lives that Lena had also mentioned.

Paul sat in the chair facing his father's casket, still in a haze from the funeral, knowing he would never remember everyone who shook his hand. He bent his head in silent gratitude for everyone who joined him that day. Paul sat there, holding his flag the soldiers had folded and just letting his mind calm. The people were visiting with one another and gave him space for the first time this morning to just sit in peace. People started to trickle away from the cemetery; the sun again was trying to break from the clouds to give warmth to the cemetery and burn the last of the dew off the ground. Paul didn't notice when the last people left.

Paul said his final good-bye. In his heart, as he stared at the box covering his father's body, he spoke to his father. "Dad, I relayed your message. It worked. People accepted your loss from Earth and were comforted." Paul got up from his chair and touched his father's casket one more time. A small charge of static electricity ran up his arm as he touched the casket. He bowed his head one final time before turning around and walking toward his car.

Paul then noticed a young woman standing under a tree looking at him. She was tall, slender, brunette, wearing a black dress and fashionable sunglasses. She did not look familiar and the elegant cut of her dress did not fit with the rural midwestern town. She looked out of place. As he continued to walk over to his car, she started to walk toward him. Paul reached the car door, and she said, "That was a beautiful memorial for your father. Your words moved me."

Paul looked back at her, "Thank you, it was a tough day, but the words were inspired and I hope they affected everyone who attended." He then paused and asked, "Do we know each other?"

She extended her hand; Paul shook it as she spoke. "We have met, but not in this lifetime. My name is Nera."

Chapter 4
The Handshake

Paul stared blankly at the elegantly clad woman. He had just walked away from his father's grave, his final good-bye. Why was this woman here? She was shaking his hand right now, and his mind couldn't pivot from the experience of grief and closure to this new mystery.

She must have noticed something, she took the initiative to continue speaking, smoothly moving right past his silence. "What a beautiful funeral for your father."

Paul only half listened as she kept talking.

Nera was trying to tell him to connect the dots from her e-mail yesterday about editing. After explaining a little about herself and interest in that skill set, she paused and smiled expectantly at him. Paul looked at her a moment, realizing he needed to say something. "Nera, ok, the editor." He realized their hands were still touching. Right as he noticed, Nera let go of his hand, as if she thought shaking his hand would help him connect the dots on who she was.

Paul grasped for something further to add, "Thank you for attending the service. My father was a good man."

Nera smiled with her dark sunglasses on and said, "I really want to be your editor."

Paul said, "I know, but this is not the time." He put together his first coherent thought of this entire conversation. Is this persistence? Or is this some kind of stalking? She tilted her head and turned slightly toward her car, but her smile didn't lessen. Paul knew she knew the conversation was over. He'd made it clear he was not in the mood for this game right now. She turned back toward him, bringing her head toward his, intending to kiss him on the cheek, and whispered into his ear, "It's nice to meet you again, but we are not in Boston." She turned around and walked away, like she also knew that she left him more puzzled and looking at her as she walked away.

Paul turned toward his father's grave and stared at the clouds on the horizon as they gently moved across the sky. After a few moments, he felt able to drive and a yearning to be home. As he started to turn on the engine, a white sports car shot by his truck, and he could see this Nera with her designer sunglasses driving by. Paul wondered why anyone would want a small editing gig enough to drive to a funeral in another town.

Paul slowly started his truck and suddenly shifted to drive. He checked his rear-view mirror for any other possible stalkers who wanted to be his editor. After everything that had happened this week, it seemed a reasonable thing to do.

Paul meandered through the streets of his town. He'd lost the interest to go home, but he didn't really want to be anywhere else either. He drove through all the local spots in the town, enjoying the scenery moving around him and the music on the radio. Eventually, he decided to go back to his office to just take in the day and check e-mails. He got onto campus and parked in the faculty's mostly empty parking lot and started walking to the education building. As he started up the steps, Paul thought he saw a white sports car in his peripheral view, but why would this Nera woman follow him to work? It made no sense.

Paul walked into his building, contemplating his father's death and funeral and seeing Lena and then using her message to write the eulogy for the family and friends who attended the funeral today. Now he had this attractive female stalker who wanted to edit his book. What was happening to him? Was he falling into some espionage scenario like in a movie or a spy book, where everything turns upside down because of one event? Paul wanted to laugh, but the strangeness of it all kept churning inside.

His office door was dotted with a few post-it notes from students. He barely gave them a glance as he unlocked the door. Right now, he just wanted to sit in his office and relax behind e-mails and work for a while. He would get to their stress and concerns once he had a little peace of mind back.

As Paul sat down, he immediately started to feel a sense of ease from the comforting presence of piles of books and papers all over the office. He believed, like Einstein, that a messy desk meant a complex thinking mind. He liked his corner office with a window view of the campus. Paul turned on his computer, waiting for it to boot up. He pulled out his coffee mug from its home in a drawer. Turn on computer, make coffee, his routine of over a decade. He paused with his hand on the coffee bean tin. Yes, today was a good day for a cup of the special coffee. He turned back to his desk, opening the bottom drawer and pulling out a bottle of Irish whiskey from the back of the drawer. He thought he was safe because the building was almost completely empty and since his father's funeral was that morning, he didn't think any dean or chairman would fault him for drinking in his office on a day like this. So, he pulled the whiskey out and poured the coffee cup half full, and then said to himself why not and poured it full.

Paul sat with his mug, checking his e-mail and letting the first drink calm his nerves and burn his throat. The sun was setting, and soon his office was the only one with a light on. Fully immersed in reading e-mails and sending responses, Paul was startled out of his reverie by a knock on the door. He thought it must be the cleaning lady or a security guard checking for something so he got up and went for the door and opened it. Nera.

Paul was shocked and fully thinking of a first-class

stalker now.

Nera said, "I apologize for interrupting, but could we talk? I would like to apologize for my actions."

Paul's first thought was to not let her in his office. Apologize again? She could have done that at their meeting Monday; it felt like an excuse or ploy. He opened the door and gestured her toward a chair, because he was always a gentleman at heart, "Ok. Please come inside."

Paul left the door open as he always did when someone else was in his office.

Nera sat down across the desk from him. She kept her head slightly bowed, staring at a pile of books between them. "I know this looks like I am stalking you but I am truly not." She continued, "Paul, I needed to come to your father's funeral, which was not the best time, but I had to personally meet you."

As Paul listened, he studied her hazel eyes. There was something familiar about those eyes, like he had met her before … but, Boston? He had only been there on a layover once, years ago. This time, she seemed shy and sincere.

"I completely understand if you do not want me to be your editor due to my actions." She looked up at him for a moment, stared directly into his eyes, and said, "Do you remember me?"

Paul said, "Today was the first time we have ever met. I do not think we have ever talked before today."

She asked again, "Are you sure you don't remember me?" Nera ran her fingers through her hair with an air of frustration. She leaned forward in her chair for a moment, then abruptly stood up and walked to the door. "Well, it was nice meeting you." Pausing for a moment, gazing into the hallway, she turned around toward Paul. "I have something for you," and she put her hand into her fashionable blue-suede bag.

Paul panicked like she was going to get a gun out, but she pulled out something small wrapped in old white linen and placed it on his desk.

Nera whispered, "This is for you and from your past. I am so sorry about everything." A cord was tied around the object wrapped in linen. Nera quietly closed the door behind her as she left.

Paul sat back down. Then stood up and locked the door. He sat down again, looked at the linen wrapped with an old cord, and before he started to untie the gift, he drank the rest of the whiskey in his coffee mug and welcomed the burn.

What a day ... what the hell could this be? With this new turn of events, Paul found himself curious and intrigued. He slowly pulled the twine open and started to pull the linen apart to see what was wrapped inside. He pulled away the corners of the cloth to find an antique dagger—like a knife almost, about eighteen inches long. From his amateur history experience, he was judging that this piece was three to four hundred years old. He picked it up by its wooden handle. He felt like this dagger was made for a smaller man or a woman to use; it felt too small for his hand. As he held it, he could feel its metal and heaviness. If a woman used it, she would have to give a straight-in thrust to be effective. The blade smelled like sage. The inscription on the blade was Latin or Celtic; he did not know what language it was, but it was not a language he knew.

He felt the blade. It was worn down with use and it looked ceremonial. He admired it. It looked like it had been used for years because there were small red stains, tiny speckles of blood, on the blade and the wood handle.

CHAPTER 5
THE KNIGHT

A knight with worn and battle-hardened armor rides into the outskirts of a small village. He dismounts from his horse as a gaggle of children swarm him. The crest of the Knight Templar adorns his chest. After tending to his horse after the long ride, he leads his horse through the houses toward the main square of grass in the middle of the village where sheep and goats grazed. The children stay with him. He touches their heads and gives them smiles, advice, and tosses them a few coins to be good and get something for their mothers to put up with them. This village cherishes him and has for many years. The Knights Templar have spoken for the people at the king's court many times. Every few years for several decades now, he and many of his compatriots have passed through this village as part of their circuit through the land, speaking with leaders and simple folk, listening to the tales of their lives and livelihood.

His name is William. Today, he doesn't stop in the village, remounting his horse at the opposite side of town and calling his farewells as the children shout their good-byes. He rides a mile on his horse through the forest and then walks the last mile, enjoying the touch of the grass and the smell of nature; his hand and demeanor toward his horse is steady. Neither words nor gesture ever too hard to hurt, but his horse bore as many scars as the man, and they are good friends. The forest, dense with trees, has a small trail winding through it, breaking off from the main road about a mile outside the village. As William walks through the gloomy and shadowy forest, he hears animals, and a deer crosses the path a dozen feet ahead of him, meandering peacefully toward a nearby stream. The knight knows the way like the back of his hand and he keeps moving slowly into the darker forest.

The knight stops cold as he enters an open meadow, hidden in the dense forest. The sun shines playful warmth on the colorful wildflowers abundant among the grass. At the top of a gentle hill stands a small stone house. It is a warm house with smoke rising mellowly out of its chimney, plants and herbs and crops growing in variously sized and shaped plots dotted around front. The stones of the house are irregularly shaped and colored, but their edges are smooth and gentled by time. The big wooden door had a star burnt on it to remind people who lives here.

William knocks on the door. No answering stirring of movement comes from within. The door remains as silent and unmoving as the house inside. As William walks along the side of the house toward the back he touches a set of metal chime hangings that make sound with the wind. There are over a dozen on this side of the house alone, and William is comforted by the musical medley of sounds as the breeze plays with the metals. Behind the house is a larger plot of tilled earth filled with rye, olives, tomatoes, and other food crops, along with an old stone well. As William rounds the back corner, he sees her. His heart stops. He stands in silence, watching the sun dance through her hair as she leans over a plant, her movements graceful, sure, and elegant.

A small beautiful woman, crowned with a mess of dark amber curls, fussed with the well's pulley system. She was talking to herself; William could hear the charming voice that he has been dreaming of grow louder as he approaches. A brown shaggy dog barks at him, jumping out from behind a row of corn. Distracted, he turns around, and the woman bounds toward him with the bucket nearly about to hit him over the head. A few paces away, she gestures at him with the bucket, blowing a curl from her face and says, "Well, William, it's about time, the dreams and visions told me you would be here last week." She gives a hasty welcoming curtsy before folding her arms across her chest. She stands there, waiting for him to give a sad face and before he can make another movement, she jumps on him and gives him a hug, murmuring, "It's good that you could visit me. I missed you so, dear one."

Her name was Anna, and she said with laughter in her eyes, "Do you need any healing? I think I might be able to heal you," because she was a spiritual healer, and William always needed healing. Some of the village folk still joked that she had special powers. But Anna had a warm genuine charm with the people and no one ever disliked her, softened by her ready smile, gentle wit, and generosity with herbal tinctures and salves. Upon meeting someone distrusting, suspicious, or otherwise cut off from their heart, she would tilt her head and without seeming to use any words at all, draw out their story and ability to share a joke. Often as not, the joke was a piece of sage wisdom that lingered in their minds and earned respect from the soundness of the point. She had a special smile reserved for men, and a way of teasing them that left them in a dazed state of their teenage years. She made them feel young and the grace of their manhood; there was no grasping or clutching or power-grabbing about her charm. Even the stoutest of those of the church found nothing to hold against that smile.

They finished their hug, and she grabbed his hand, tugging him playfully into her stone house. The shelves and floors had a thin layer of dust, but inside was warm and the log stove burned merrily, a pot of stew bubbling and wafting delicious odors. Books lay in stacks and piles everywhere, interspersed with charms and bottles of herbs and plants drying, dangling from the eaves. She had been writing earlier, as a sheaf of paper and an ink quill lay on a partially cleared space on her writing desk. The house was so comfortable; slightly cluttered but the warmth brimmed with affection. She gestured toward the tea kettle and raised an inquisitive eyebrow. He shook his head as he flopped back into a chair, "Whisky?"

Anna smiled, pulling out two pewter mugs and a glass bottle. She handed him his mug before curling up on some pillows. As they toasted and took their first sips, two cats sauntered up to William, inspecting their new visitor. In time, the cats sat on William's lap, fully expecting affection.

They talked as he gave her word of his latest travels and they laughed liked old friends and she caught him up on her latest adventures. Their first drink of whisky ended with several more until they were both slightly drunk. It was getting late and she got up from her chair and asked, "Well, before you ask, I can heal you tonight if you need."

William laughed. "Three hundred miles by horseback, Anna. My bones are weary and my nerves flayed. The world is eating me away. Three hundred miles by horseback, Anna."

His people were at war, and he was a leader, his life dedicated to service. After all the battles he had been in and the trauma to his body, it would only take a couple of healing sessions from Anna and he would almost be like new.

Anna tilted her head and looked at William's shoes. He laughed as he sat on the floor to unlace and remove them before pulling off his shirt. As he did so, she lowered the oil lamps in the room and lit some incense. He lay back on the dark green woven blanket, and Anna began lighting the white candles at each corner of the blanket. After bowing to the lights Anna made her way to the north-facing window to open it. As she walked back to the blanket, William could hear the gentle chimes of shells and metal wafting into the room with the wind. At the foot of the blanket, Anna raised her arms up and started breathing and singing slowly, awaking the spirits. William felt his eyes closing and tension beginning to melt from his shoulders. She knelt next to William on her knees and touched his bare feet and closed her eyes.

William felt his entire body relax and start to hum with the energy beginning to course through his body. Anna chanted in a foreign language as she moved her hands near his body awakening the muscles and clearing the wounds and the stress. William was a battle-hardened knight. His body ached most of the time. Even when you made it through a battle without bleeding, the jarring of horse and sword took its toll. And it was rare to walk away from a field without your own blood spilt. The doctors could not do much medicine for him. One of the mothers in the nearby village with sons now grown, watching him struggle off his horse years ago, had pulled him aside to tell of a young woman in the woods nearby. The gesture was advice and warning in one breath. Nobody in the town visited her home in the dark woods. Nobody knew for certain what she did or who her people were. They never spoke of her to outsiders, for though they didn't understand her, they loved her for her generous ways and kindnesses, as one loves a child playing. The mother who pulled him aside likely saw her sons in him, the ache of imagining her own sons' pains in the king's war must have arisen in the impulse to speak of the rumor that this woman practiced uncanny healing arts, in spite of the village's unspoken agreement to not mention her to those passing through.

Anna had male visitors from across the continent, to include Catholic priests. Such a thing, in the eyes of the wider world would have spun viciously into accusations of prostitution. Maybe the villagers initially had such suspicions when she first moved into the stone house in the woods, but such was her way with people that the village folk quickly became her staunchest protectors. Over time, many priests, men of noble dress, and women would pass through the village on their way to Anna's for their ailments and medical matters. And she always seemed to be in town, with a little gift or two of teas and tinctures, on days where some grievous illness or injury struck in the village. William had met her almost eight years ago and made every effort to visit her on his routes to get spiritually healed. He would travel by horseback over several countries just to spend a day or three with Anna. He secretly loved her but never let her know.

As Anna was healing William, he could feel the energy clean his body like the searing pain of fire on an open wound; the results were extraordinary. They were dear friends and could tell each other anything, and they had a bond of total trust. Tonight, she kept healing him and the house became exceedingly warm and at the apex of the flows of spiritual energy, she laid on him so that their hearts touched, and they held each other. At this part of the healing, their hearts beat as one and they exchanged energy. They fell asleep on the floor with the two cats curling between their legs.

ℰ ℰ ℰ

The floor creaked under several pairs of boots.

Dozens of torchlights flickered through the windows on all sides of the house. William's horse gave a loud noise, annoyed by being woken. William awoke instantly. As he started to puzzle at who was in the house and who was outside, a large tree limb swung down on his skull, and he fell to the floor with the rush of people coming into the cabin. As he went unconscious, he saw was several men taking Anna forcibly out of the house.

ℰ ℰ ℰ

Paul suddenly woke up from his dream, all sweaty, drenched, and struggling to realize where he was, a stone cottage in a forest, or a two-story ranch house in a college town. He knew he was in his bed in his house, but the dream was more vivid and real than anything he'd ever experienced. He could still smell the fragrance of Anna's hair and her touch was so real. He was there but he was here, it could not have been just a dream. It just could not. He turned on his light and he was in his bedroom in his house. What was happening to him? Why did he have such a vivid dream?

Paul's first thought was that this must have been one of the past lives that Lena had talked to him about. He went to his desk, grabbing his notes and thumbing through them. None of the past lives she explained were like the dream. He winced to himself, and the thought crept in that maybe he was going mad. So, he walked into his kitchen and went to his bar and poured himself a drink, Balvenie Portwood twenty-one-year-old single whisky. He had tried many types of whisky, but this brand and this particular taste brought him a little back to his roots. His family had come from Scotland and had immigrated to America before the American Revolutionary War. He promised himself he would visit, but he had never visited his homeland and this whisky was his simple connection to his homeland, plus who does not like whisky?

He drank his whisky slowly on his back porch, listening to the gentle sounds of the night, and the wind danced gently in the wind chimes that his father had given him a few weeks before he had died. The sound was soothing, and he watched the sunrise as he sipped his drink, awash in awe at how small he was in the world and how beautiful the sunrise was today through the glow of colors in the sky.

Chapter 6
The Dagger

On Friday Paul took the dagger to his friend Dr. Robert Anderson, an eccentric anthropology professor. His office had little figurines, artifacts, and antiques as well as silly souvenirs from all over the world that he had dug, found, or bought. Whether or not it was bought or excavated, they all looked like ancient artifacts. Robert was a gentle eclectic, almost hippy, he loved what he did and never minded the poor pay that the university gave social science professors because he would probably do what he did for absolutely free. Robert loved human and anthropological research that much. He really loved to find the stories behind artifacts so Paul could always call on him with a puzzle. Paul had left him a voice message before midnight that said, "Robert, I have a challenge for you!" and as expected Robert was full of anticipation.

Paul walked up to Robert's office and knocked on his door, and Robert yelled, "Paul, is that you?"

Paul replied, "As always, the education professor is on time like a good student while the anthropologist would always be late or lost on campus because they can never find their classrooms and they get lost in museums."

Robert laughed and shook his head as he opened the door. His mind was too busy anticipating Paul's historical artifact challenge to come back with a witty retort. Paul bowed and pulled his hand out of his coat and slowly gave Robert the wrapped linen package. Robert unwrapped the linen with a deft and careful touch. Once completely opened, he paused, eyes locked on the dagger with utter quietness. Robert paused for an unusual amount of time, holding in his built-up excitement. The extraordinarily long pause was something Robert always did and he could never keep a secret long, but this one object puzzled him and he did not want to tell Paul what it was quite yet.

Robert looked up at Paul and asked, "Paul, where did you get this exquisite artifact?"

Paul said, "You are not going to believe me, but a strange woman handed this to me. I just met her yesterday. She reached out about editing and then showed up at my father's funeral. She said this was mine and she was sorry about everything. Really confusing stuff, especially on the day of my father's funeral."

Without pulling his eyes away from the dagger, Robert opened a desk drawer, slipping on a pair of cotton gloves with practiced ease before picking up the dagger and inspecting it with a magnifying lens like Sherlock Holmes. Paul loved watching his friend while in his element.

Paul asked, "Robert, what are you doing? It's a knife or a dagger because its sharp on the point side and dull on the edges and probably a woman's, look how small the handle is."

Robert looked up and had his reading glasses low on his nose like he would give a student who gave a quick answer without looking into details in one of his classes. Robert softly and like a tenured professor said, "So that is what you think it is? A dagger? Paul, well, I would believe the proper term to use would be athame or a ritual knife." Robert kept looking at Paul waiting for a reaction.

Robert looked up and then raised the athame in his hand and said softly, almost chanting,

Aradia and Cernunnos, deign to bless and
to consecrate this tool,
that it may obtain necessary virtue
through thee for all acts of love and beauty.
Aradia and Cernunnos, bless this
instrument prepared in thine honor.

Paul was completely confused, "Robert, what are you chanting and most important *why* are you doing that?"

Robert took a breath and said, "Well, my dear friend, this is more than likely a historical magical ritual knife also called an athame. This athame could be used in current modern-day witch, pagan, or Wiccan rituals. In the Garderian Wicca folklore, athames are associated with the element of fire and in the Golden Dawn tradition are influenced with air. Most knives like this have a painted black handle. If you look closely, this one was painted black once a long time ago. The Golden Dawn is part of the Hermetic systems. This is good historical occult stuff. What a unique find."

Robert flipped it over and said, "You can tell it is old witchcraft folklore oriented, due to the inscription here in the Theban alphabet, yes, this could be used in casting magic circles or the folklore and tall-tales believed to be magical.

"The inscriptions look done before the rise of modern Wicca. In folklore, it's said that athames could control spirits and in the 1950s Gerald Gardner described an athame as the 'truest Witch's weapon.' In the whole Wicca movement, they claimed to connect to historical witchcraft, but that's been largely discredited. But still, it is nice to believe a little of these magic possibilities, and it makes for such a great story."

Robert paused for dramatic effect before continuing, "The term athame under the Wicca or witchcraft terminology means the key of Solomon and also 'arthame' to describe a black-handled knife."

Robert was giddy, pouring knowledge out of his years of study. "This lost Theban alphabet is a writing system with unknown origins, first published in the sixteenth century. There is talk, and purely talk, that it was originally a runic alphabet but all that exists is rumor— no archaeological or historical evidence—that this is also the famous so-called witches' alphabet. That is another borrowed folktale and story about the start of the Wiccans back in the 1950s. It is close in style to the old Latin alphabet in the vertical strokes and capitalization, as you can see." He whipped the blade in front of Paul for a few seconds, before his excitement bubbled back into words.

"Another quite funny story about the Theban alphabet is that Ozzy Osborne, the crazy rock-and-roller who ate the head off of a bat in the '70s in a concert, used the Theban alphabet on one of his record cover albums called *Diary of a Madman* (1981). It was probably used as a publicity marketing tool, that was the way to be rebellious to parents in the '80s. So, let's try and translate what this Theban inscription says on your so-called dagger correctly named an athame, which is much more curious now with all this discussion we have just had."

Paul so felt that Robert just schooled him on something that was so new on knowledge for him, he felt like an old undergraduate. Paul's thoughts turned to wondering why he received this athame from this strange woman, Nera, and why did she tell him it was his and why did she apologize for something. He sat there in anticipation and really felt like he was opening up Pandora's box as Robert kept telling him more and more about the athame.

The letters to Paul looked between Old English or

Latin or more Celtic and he watched Robert look at the inscription, and letter by letter, look through his translation book and write down the English equivalent on a notepad. He kept squinting through his magnifying lens to make sure the letters were correct. As he was translating, Robert kept the teaching session going, "The Theban alphabet was first published in Johannes Trithemius's *Polygraphia* (1518) and discusses Honorius of Thebes, which could be a mythical character from the Middle Ages. No one really knows, but the rumor—unproven of course—implies that it could go back to the Catholic Church as this Honorius and the two most favorable identities would be Pope Honorius I or Pope Honorius III. So, this Honorius of Thebes was the one who claimed to have created the Theban alphabet in *Polygraphia,* but the more fun connections are that the witches and occult tag to connect to Heinrich's Cornelius Agrippa's *De Occulta Philosophia* (1531). The book is one of the oldest existing medieval grimoires. And before you ask, a grimoire is also known as a 'book of spells,' which included instructions on how to create magic, how to perform spells and summon angels, spirits, and gods and demons. Remember the TV series *Charmed* from the 1990s? The books the girls would use to create spells, well, that was a book of shadows or a grimoire."

Paul was somewhat dumbfounded again like on a spiral wondering how he was connected with all this occult, this athame, and some strange woman, Nera, who gave him this with a secret codex and said she was sorry.

"I got it!" Robert looked up with the grin of a little

kid figuring out a puzzle in front of a parent.

Paul moved next to him toward the desk. Caught up in his own thoughts, he was not fully paying attention anymore and on information overload while Robert was trying to tell him what the code meant.

Robert pointed to the inscribed notes and said, "Well, are you ready for the translated inscription on the athame in the hidden Theban alphabet—

Thee who own this tool will have power to inner temple.

Robert then paused and flipped over the athame and read:

Beware, do not conjure spirit, may curse you, warned you are.

Robert and Paul just sat there and looked at each other with disbelief. Paul, overwhelmed with questions and unknowns, Robert, like a kid on Christmas morning wanting to know more. Robert asked, "What do you think it means?"

Paul couldn't begin to methodically recall, let alone analyze everything that had happened, he could only think *why him*, but a part of him was curious in this new path that had come to him and for once in his life, he was going to take the risk and come out of his shy personality and fully pursue this new mystery. What was happening to him and why?

Robert waved his hand and said, "There is also another inscription on the base of the handle. I did not see it at first. It is not in Theban language but rather Gaelic, but I know what it says."

Robert slowly said with a Scottish accent, "Suil Dhe na gloir, which means 'The eye of God of Glory,'" and he continued with "A ghnus Dhe nan dul, which is 'Face of the God of Life.'"

Paul was totally confused on why a dagger was linked to the ancient occult and also had an unknown origin language and also a Gaelic phrase. What could this all mean? They both just sat there in Robert's office for a few minutes in silence. Their eyes met, each quietly smiled, and then laughed for no reason, it was one of those laughs like what else could just happen to them on this unique day.

Robert looked around the office and said, "This is too much. Let me close the door and let's share a drink. This is so much fun. It's almost 5 p.m. and the building will be empty soon, no one will know. Let's have a thirty-year-old whisky, some expensive Scotch whisky, in celebration of your unique discovery. I think I even have some druid figurines around my office somewhere. Please tell me more about this mysterious woman."

Robert closed the door and left the light on, which would tell the other people in the building that he was still here but did not want to be disturbed because he was working late. He then quietly said, "So no one will bother us. Let's have a drink together. I'll grab my whisky from its puzzle box from my travels in Iraq. You grab the glasses."

So, the two professors were now going to break the rules and have a drink on campus and contemplate what it all meant. Naturally, they got off topic and talked about life. Eventually Paul turned the conversation back around to the athame.

Robert just laughed and said, "I will have a plausible solution tomorrow; that is usually what happens in my PhD mind once I have twenty-four hours to think about things and plenty of whisky."

Drinking always helped Paul with opening up the mind; if they had been at his house, he would have pulled out his marijuana because he still believed the shaman way and some natural drugs helped him contact the spirit world and converse with the subconscious mind, or so he believed.

They both drank a little more than expected and started to depart with no final solution but with their brains storming exhaustively, mulling it all over. The real discussions would have to wait until tomorrow. They toasted once more, loudly clinking their glasses to both of their fathers' lives. Paul so needed this break from reality with a friend and to have happy drinks in private to talk. He really had not talked to any one of his friends about his father's death so it was more like a drinking therapy session, which are always the best. They knew they could not sleep in their offices but they lived only a mile from the campus so they walked home together to assure each of them got home. They were happy that no one saw them as two professors stumbled along holding each other up drunk like the young college students they were almost thirty years ago.

CHAPTER 7
NERA

As Paul woke into awareness it was morning, his skull let him know its opinion about too many Scotch whiskies. It was a Saturday morning and there was no work today.

In no hurry, Paul stretched and loosened his joints before rolling out of bed and heading to the coffeepot. Every morning started with coffee and greeting the sunrise. He gave up sleeping in years ago, and his body was accustomed to sleeping right up to sunrise, waking up to its own well-regulated internal alarm.

Paul got his coffee and sat outside on his deck. There was a slight chill to the air and he watched the steam come off his coffee cup in the cold air before his gaze became drawn to the gentle pinks and oranges of the sky. It was one of those things that humbled him and kept him simple and aware how small everyone was in the world.

His mind was sequential; as his thoughts loosened and expanded with the light of day, they returned to the beginning: Lena's words about his father, how his father's message gave meaning and peace to those at the funeral, and how that gave credibility to Lena's actions. He still had his notes on his three past lives, and he was slowly leaning into the validity of it and the possibility. The one thing that puzzled him was Nera, this beautiful woman who gave him the athame. Why did she give it to him? She was the additional curve ball that sent the bowl of logic flipping on its side. It was like having a jar of marbles all aligned in the jar and then having someone spill your marbles all over the porch causing disarray but in the chaos of the marbles there is a system of chaos theory waiting to be solved.

So today he was going to try and figure out this Nera thing and how she just came into his life right at this particular moment. Paul kept mulling it all over as he went back inside and took a shower.

He finished drying off, putting on a pair of blue jeans and a vintage Tom Petty t-shirt before sitting down at his computer and checking his e-mail. The first e-mail was from Nera. Paul sat there, contemplating what he should ask her. He wanted to bring up the athame, ask one or a dozen of the questions swirling in his mind. He decided to just offer her the job editing his current manuscript with possible future projects later on. He needed to create a contact and a line of communication. He constructed the business-like e-mail, expressing how he approved her skills in editing, sending the e-mail out before he changed his mind, hoping for a quick response.

Nera's response took almost an hour: a request to meet in the evening at Casaneta's, where not many would notice two people doing a consultation. He quickly agreed. They scheduled for 6:30.

Throughout the afternoon, Paul continued to struggle with the last four days, trying to take it all in, stare at the marbles strewn on the floor, in order to find the origination and causation of all the events and the meaning in their sequence. That was how he solved complex problems in his research: dissecting the problem and rebuilding the events to find the themes and commonalities. Paul worked this out during his dissertation, and he had been using it ever since. The mental work had challenged and satisfied him for over a decade now. Somehow meeting Lena triggered these new metaphysical and spiritual events. A new question entered his mind: Did Lena and Nera know each other? The answer might help him make sense of things. It was plausible they did, and that could explain why Nera wanted to meet him and gave him the athame. His mind kept going back to the three past lives Lena told him about. None of them talked about the athame. Paul felt like a good quarter of the marbles weren't even in the picture.

Paul reread his notes of past lives. Lena had said he died of a spear in battle. Paul touched the scar on his back, reminding him of where all this started. His thoughts returned to the athame; where had it been for hundreds of years? He massaged his head; another dull headache was starting. Time to let the problem go until he met with Nera and could ask some of the questions circling his brain. He needed some kind of solution.

☙ ☙ ☙

Paul entered the high-end bar in the quiet downtown just a block away from Lena's store promptly at 6:30. The bar was on the main floor of a historic hotel built in 1895 and converted into business offices twenty years ago.

Nera was sitting in the library exactly where she said she would be. As before, her outfit was stylish and chic, tight-fitting jeans and high leather boots. She clearly liked money for clothes. As he walked into the room, she glanced up casually, "Get yourself a glass of wine and I will be waiting."

Paul walked to the bar in the adjacent room, selected a merlot, and brought his glass to the library, taking the lounge chair next to Nera. They sat there in a quiet awkward silence for a few seconds before she spoke first, "Paul, I want to apologize for coming into your office after your father's funeral. I needed to give you the knife, it was just something that called me to do it."

Paul said, 'You mean the athame?"

She looked up at him with confused but cold eyes and almost in distress she looked around the room and was at the moment at a loss of words as if a secret was let out. He could tell she had to catch her breath. "How do

70

you know it was an athame?"

"As a professor, I like to get my facts straight and when a beautiful woman puts a dagger wrapped in linen on my desk and say it's mine, well, my professional curiosity gets the best of me, so I did some research," he said as he smiled back at her.

Nera collected her words and asked, "Were you serious about letting me be your editor or was it just a way to talk to me?"

Paul said, "Both, but if you want to be my editor, I will have work for you tomorrow morning in your inbox and it will be steady for the next couple of weeks if you are up for the editorial challenge?"

She smiled and he could tell she loved editing and the challenge of conquering a manuscript. He stretched out his hand and wanted to shake her hand to finalize the deal. She looked up at him with her green eyes before shaking his hand and then something curious happened.

He was looking into her eyes and felt very familiar, like he knew her but he could not place her, but then it was gone when she took her hand away.

The rest of the evening they talked about editing, slowly sharing a small part of their lives that they wanted and allowed to share with someone they just met over a glass of wine.

After a longer pause than normal, Paul asked, "When will you tell me about the athame?"

"It will take time," Nera said then sighed. "I will start in two days when you meet me again right here for another discussion. We will also talk about your manuscript and then we will talk about other very important things I will need to slowly tell you so that you can understand."

At that moment, he was amenable to that compromise. He really did not need the whole answer tonight and slowly having the facts come to him might be the best option and he logically agreed.

Paul said, "Ok, in two days at 6:30 right here."

They both got up to depart and he walked her out of the bar to her white sports car. She asked, "May I give you a hug?"

Paul said, "Sure," as a natural response, and they hugged and there was a connection again for a short time like something familiar and then they went their separate ways.

Paul was almost thinking these small touches of handshakes and then the hug was Nera trying to bring a memory out of him; there might be some familiarity, but he could not recall.

He drove back to his house thinking about the day, knowing that he was moving in the right direction in trying to solve this athame challenge. It seemed like it was not a challenge but more of a penance for Nera.

At the cemetery she'd said, "Sorry for everything," like there was some remorse. Maybe she is trying to send him a message of something that happened, and then he just smiled while he drove. Paul bet some of this was from a past life like all these other things were. What on earth had happened to him? It was like the psychic had opened up some damn spiritual channel and all these metaphysical things started happening to him. Something was trying to give him a new perspective or give him a message like the message he received from his father. Paul took a breath as he drove into his driveway and there was Nera's sports car again.

Paul just smiled, a mix of amusement and frustration. He got out of the car, and Nera started to walk toward him. He said, "Lightly, or now heavily stalking me?"

She said, "No … I want you to wear this tonight when you go to sleep. It will help you find the some of the answers you are looking for." And then she lightly kissed his cheek and departed.

He looked into his hand and there was a bracelet, more like a charm bracelet but all of the stones were white with some type of cord entwining them. It looked older, not modern at all. Definitely made by hand. He took the bracelet and put it on and walked into his home.

He changed clothes to get ready for bed, and brought out his good alcohol, the Scotch whisky and poured himself a double. Paul sat on his back patio and contemplated the day. He looked at the bracelet and then decided to look up on his iPad what it was. After some quick internet searching, it turned out to be a white Howlite bracelet. Several articles described that Howlite opens and prepares the mind to receive the energies and wisdom of attunement to the seventh chakra and Light. Purported to reduce anxiety, stress, and tension, it also can be used to facilitate awareness, encourage emotional expression, and assist in the elimination of pain and stress. He further scrolled with his thumb and saw one article describe it as a calming stone, an excellent antidote to insomnia due to an overactive mind. Howlite teaches patience, tolerance, and a positive outlook on life. Howlite also promotes kindness and peaceful coexistence.

Looks like this might actually be good for him. As he finished his glass of whisky a wave of emotional exhaustion swept over him, so he went to bed. Paul stared at the bracelet on his wrist for a few moments before climbing into bed and falling instantly asleep.

CHAPTER 8
MISSING

As William opened his swollen eyes and tried to turn over, he felt the bruises the midnight guests had given him during the raid. In the early morning sunlight, lying there on the floor of Anna's house, William felt dried blood on his face and chest.

He slowly made his way to sitting and gently probed the knot on his skull. He called out for Anna but there was no response. The house felt empty and cold. He gingerly made his way to his feet, still shaky, and started to look for Anna. He went outside into the sun and saw the horse and wagon tracks and knew that they had taken her—whoever they were—they took her for some reason.

Before he had visited Anna's house, he hid his armor and blade in the wood line for safekeeping. With every fiber of his being, William knew he needed and must find Anna. He did not know if they took her because of who he was as a Templar Knight but he doubted that because the surrounding villages had always been grateful for the support of the knights. William assumed they took her for other simple village-rumored reasons. The other possibility was some political men she had rejected advances from. Such men always hated being turned down and always wanted their way; their reputation could survive, but a woman's reputation was forever tarnished. Such power-hungry men would always say they could not be turned to the woman's advances due to the devil or some witchcraft paranoia. At court and in local fiefdoms, William always laughed at how these notable and political leaders blamed witches for lust because it could not be their fault. He loathed men like that.

William knew this was a time for business and if necessary, he would use his power as a Knight Templar. Most days, William got to be a humble servant of the land, but sometimes pulling rank was necessary. William grew more upset as he thought it over in his head, and he walked into the wood line and retrieved his armor and slowly put on his chain mail and silver worn-steel armor and lastly, solemnly, put on the red cross armor before strapping on his long sword and extra daggers. One particular dagger had etched carvings and looked out of place with the other ones and this one he put in his boot.

He was ready to get on his horse—only the worst type of scum stole horses. His horse being there lent credence to the idea that Anna's capture was political.

William started riding toward the village slowly, holding his ribs as he rode to not cause them any more pain.

After a half-hour ride, he came upon the small village. He rode in at a sedate pace to assure everyone could see who he was, and so he could observe the glances of the villagers at the imposing, formal figure with the Templar attire. They cleared space for him and his horse, instinctively knowing where he was headed. William tied up his horse outside the small building of the local law of the village.

Inside, William asked for the leader of the town and for who was in charge of the raiding of the small house in the dark forest. The sheriff cockily called out from a back room, without seeing William, "We found our witch and our intent is to hurt her. We found her with a poor fellow that we gave a bad headache," and as he walked out, he saw William and stopped his story immediately.

"Sir Knight, what can we do for you?"

William with his deepest voice said, "On whose authority did you take this woman?"

A female voice rang imperiously from the back room, "It was my authority."

Everyone turned around to see an elegant brunette with a side of ego dressed in honor and royalty. William knew exactly who it was, Lady Margaret, a spoiled niece of the king. Spoiled rotten she was, and conniving. William had met her in London and turned down her advances. Their paths had crossed several times in France and Spain. William had absolutely no interest in such a self-absorbed woman who only sought money and power.

Margaret cooed, "Well, Sir William, why are you here in this simple town? Were you the one these men beat up when they grabbed that witch Anna for me last night?"

All the men looked at William and also made the conclusion that he was indeed the one they had beaten up.

Margaret just chuckled. "Sir William is with the Knights Templar but last night was sleeping with a witch. Your taste in women is beneath you."

William was calm and observant of his next response as he said, "I would rather be with a good genuine poor witch than sleep with a spoiled classless bitch."

Margaret slapped William. It was a futile gesture; they both knew she had no authority over him, but he was worried about Anna. Margaret could use this situation to hurt William since she now realized he just might love her.

The men in the room were confused and knew the power of the Knights Templar and also knew the power of the king's niece. So, William claimed, "The woman is working with the Knights Templar and is protected by Rome and the Holy See. I must know what you accuse her of."

The senior village authority person said, "Sir Knight, we accuse her of witchcraft."

"Does she get a trial to provide some justice as required by law?"

The town leaders had not thought that far ahead and assumed the king's niece would take full responsibility for their leaders' actions toward the witch. There was confusion, and one of the men started to say something and Margaret, in her most spoiled voice, said, "She is a witch. She will be punished and burned."

William said, "The law of Rome and the pope protects this simple woman from death. Anyone who kills a representative of the pope shall also be guilty as acts against the pope and the church."

So, they both challenged each other's authority because the king was the king but the pope was the leader of the Catholic world and politically, they were equal. The spoiled Margaret was livid for she always had to have her way and hated to lose at anything and how dare she not get her way. She desired William but he had denied her multiple times. Margaret's vanity and spoiled nature made her even more irritated at the rejection because all men should love her. She couldn't handle the truth about herself. William called her honestly a "spoiled girl" on most occasions and in public to piss her off on purpose. It only redoubled her mad desire to have him. Apparently that love had morphed and grown to where her mad jealousy had her concocting elaborate schemes. It fit with her nature to be a vengeful woman to any woman that William could and would love and she would punish poor Anna because William chose a poor woman who lives in the woods over her. How dare he! She was truly vengeful beyond reason and she was enjoying hurting Anna to spite William.

The room full of leaders of the town agreed to a

trial immediately because the last thing they wanted was to have either the king or the pope mad at them; they relied on both to survive economically and politically. So, within an hour a trial was formed and the local judge, who was not included in the taking of Anna, was called into the middle of it. He knew this was a lost scenario for him because someone with powerful connections had to lose … unless he could find some way that both sides could win.

William first asked to see Anna in her cell before the trial. Everyone in the room except Margaret flinched because they had hurt Anna severely last night when they took her and the men now knew if William saw her in that condition, the knights would forever be vengeful on all of them. The lead judge, after taking a look at the guilty and fearful faces, finally drawled, "Well, by the law we must let the knight see her," and so they led William to her cell where they had severely violated her. Anna was on the floor with an old blanket, kidney-sized bruises everywhere, blood in her tangled hair, and a black eye. William took her into his arms and held her and he could feel the blood on her forehead where they had hit her and when he touched her, she flinched from the bruises and the pain.

Anna looked up at William. "I knew you would come to save me. My visions came true about you. Please don't let them hurt me anymore." Her voice was weak with exhaustion and pain, but no fear.

William became determined and promised he would

help her get out of this situation. She touched his hand and said, "Don't sacrifice yourself for me."

He only whispered back to her, "I will do the honorable thing."

She softly smiled and said, "That is what I was afraid you would say."

William stayed an hour in the cell with Anna tending to her wounds. He knew that Margaret was a vengeful woman and would do anything now to hurt Anna. She was willing to throw her political clout around solely for the mad pleasure of causing William pain. William sat with Anna, thinking about it, until the late evening light hit, and the guards came into the cell to take him away and take Anna to another place. William demanded to know what was going on and they would only tell him to be quiet.

It was close to dusk and the town was fully awake with torches and the people were in the town square. There was a post in the center of town with chains on for whipping, and a pole with wood being laid underneath it and William knew exactly what they were going to do try to do to Anna. They were going to claim she was a witch and burn her tonight and William would be her only defense.

As he walked toward the town square, he could imagine Margaret's joy in seeing Anna chained to the whipping post and William's personal suffering. In Margaret's mind, she was powerful because she wanted to be a queen someday, and William's public comments about her character were hurting her chances to marry a man of power that would let her walk all over him.

The authorities put the frail Anna in the whipping chains and ripped off her dress to expose her bare back. The square was full, the milling crowd turning violent and hungry for blood. William demanded in a loud ringing voice on whose authority and what right were they doing this. The judge said the authority was with the king.

"I do not see the king here."

The judge said, "The king's niece is representing the king."

William said, "By whose authority could a woman replace a king?" and the crowd looked puzzled. William knew that women did not have such claim or authority. The judge was being bullied by Margaret to punish Anna on weak accusations, and William stood proud and said, "What has this woman, Anna, done to be carried out of her house and put in jail and abused by her authorities?"

The crowd was listening to William, which sent Margaret into a spoiled fit. The judge said, "The charges have been discussed and the witch will be whipped and burned."

William stood proud and slowly revealed his armor while he took off his cape so everyone in the crowd knew he was a Knight Templar and what it meant. William asked, "How many lashes is she to receive?

The judge said, "Twenty lashes."

William then said, "I will take her punishment for her, then you may burn me."

The crowd went silent. William declared in public, "The blood of a Knight Templar protecting an innocent woman will be on your hands."

It was a rule in the country that another person could take punishment for an accused witch, a decree instituted by the king several decades ago.

William repeated, "I will take the lashings and then we will see what happens next."

The judge, who did not expect this at all, quickly agreed and the tables were turned on Margaret's plan. Margaret wanted to destroy Anna not William. She loved William. However brutally furious at him she was, she did not want to see her love whipped and burned. But she knew the law and there was nothing she could do but be dangerously upset.

William asked the crowd, "The law states that another person can take the punishment for an accused person. Do you not all agree to that?"

The crowd quietly agreed. So, William went to the pole where Anna was bound and released her and picked her up and laid her clear of the whipping pole. She said in his ear softly and sweetly, "You said you were not going to do anything silly." And with a smile that tore in his heart, he winked back to her, "I know I said that but this will be ok, you have to trust me. Trust me."

William took off his armor with a proud deliberation to every movement. He'd positioned himself with his back to the crowd and judge. He meant the initial show of quiet confidence to be interrupted by the reveal of his back. He wanted the crowd to see the dozens of scars there from battles and wars across Europe. He wanted everyone to see what kind of man was about to be whipped. The executioner assistant was going to bind his hands but William said, "I give you my honor that I will not let go until after twenty lashings" and the assistant stepped back.

William yelled, "Go ahead." The justice agreed and nodded to the whipping authority, who struck William hard across the back, opening up his back deeper with every lash, but William just stood there. The whips continued until the blood covered his back and the tears of skins were horrifying. The crowd was shocked at how much pain William could endure. William purposely looked at Margaret, seeing tears in her eyes as he looked at her with total disgust and finality.

As the final lash hit William's back, he was near collapse. His body wanted to pass out. As he was released from the post, he swayed weakly, but stayed standing. He looked at the crowd and said, "Have you seen enough blood tonight?" Blood pooled along his boots on the platform.

The judge said, "The Knight Sir William has received the punishment for the accusations against Anna and the matter is closed. There shall be no burning of this noble knight while I am the judge."

Then Margaret like a spoiled child yelled, "No! It is not over!" and walked over to William. As he stood there, empty of energy, she pulled out the special knife he always hid in his boot. Margaret drove the knife deep into

William's back, while she smiled and said softly to his ear, "I am going to burn Anna tonight and there is nothing you can do about it." Then she kissed William on the cheek and said, "You should have loved me."

☙ ☙ ☙

Paul woke in a scream in his bed in the middle of the night, fully exhausted and sweating profusely. He frantically talked to himself, mumbling over and over that he was in his bed in Kansas in his house and safe from that horrible and vengeful woman. He must be going mad. What was happening to him? Why was this happening to him? He sat on the edge of the bed and put his feet on the ground, feeling the hardwood floor beneath his soles. Paul was not losing his mind; his rational mind was taking over and he knew he might be emotionally unnerved from the continuing strangeness, but all of this was happening to him for a reason, all of this was a process. He calmed himself down and used breathing exercises he had learned during yoga classes. Breathing was the key to lowering his heart rate and calming the situation when the chaos wanted to run amuck. He sat there in calm. He walked to his bar and poured half a drink, just enough to calm his nerves. He went over to his desk and picked up the wrapped athame. He unwrapped it and studied the blade in the light of his desk lamp.

There was something about this blade, something familiar about it, but why did Nera have it and why was she sorry about it? He could feel, deep in his mind, a growing familiarity and recognition of it, but he did not know why yet. He started to play with it and flipped it in his palm, twirling it on his fingers. When he realized what he was doing, he was struck by all the problems this athame had caused him in the last three days. In a moment of anger and disgust, he threw it toward the table and it stuck hard upright on his coffee table slightly vibrating. Thoughts rushed his mind about the action he just did. He had to calm his mind and he quickly finished his drink and turned the air conditioner down to make it colder, which always made him sleep deeper. He went back to bed exhausted, blood pressure rising, heart rate up, and hoping to fall quickly back to sleep.

CHAPTER 9
LENA'S SECOND VISIT

Paul woke up exhausted and physically tired. He looked at the nightstand and realized that he had two strong drinks the night before, plus two glasses of wine. As he reached for the glass, his eye caught the Howlite stone bracelet. Paul couldn't remember many details from his intense dream, but knew it ended with severe pain. He had a few fuzzy images from the dream of a woman and then of a whipping post and that was all he could recall. His mind was not letting him recall the rest of the dream.

He spent the morning slowly waking up over a strong coffee and enjoying the sunrise. Paul was sore for some reason and felt aching from the dream last night but the details of that dream hid at the edges of his conscious memory. It felt like at any minute, the details would pop into his mind. After the sun was over the horizon, Paul walked with his coffee to his desk and turned on his laptop. Maybe checking work e-mail from home would be helpful to get his brain clearer. As his computer was booting up, he went back to pick up the athame that was still embedded into the table and thought he would do his own research on the so-called dagger while he finished waking up.

As he drank his coffee, he slowly started searching for information on athames. He surfed the internet, and more and more witchcraft websites came popping up regarding athames. He read that an athame is usually black handled and double edged and one of the magical tools in traditional witchcraft ceremonies. As he continued to read various blogs and articles, he observed that every athame historically had a black or white wooden handle with its original owner or region engraved on it. Engravings on the blade told the story of the knife and its power. Such inscriptions could be anything from astrological symbols to ancient druid to other magical languages. These symbols were codes to gods and goddesses, spirits, and other divinities. He sat back in his chair confused and wondering what all this meant and continued to read and search the internet.

He looked up the etymology of the word. Athame is a derivative of the Latin word "artavus," meaning a quill knife. The oldest known use is found in the medieval grimoire, *The Key of Solomon.* Compiled in the 1500s, it was likely the distillation of a long oral history, but there is no way to verify that. In the grimoire was an ancient drawing of a knife that looks like a sickle called *artavo*. The blade was shaped like the fingernail moon or a bowline.

The athame was used to direct divine energy into sacred ritual. Gerald Gardner, who founded Wicca in the 1950s, claimed the athame was the most important ritual tool of all of witchcraft. Today, the athame is part of the four primary tools of modern witchcraft and Wicca, along with the pentacle, the wand, and the chalice. The knife was used to cast circles by tracing the circumference or to cut and reseal a ritual circle and to consecrate objects. The last thing Paul read was that touching another person's athame without permission was considered an intrusion upon the owner's property and sacred space and a violation of the code.

The article continued on to say that if anyone stole another person's athame, that person would be cursed until they returned it to their owner with an apology. He stopped and reread the last sentence: if a person stole someone's athame, that person would be cursed until they returned it to the owner with an apology.

He instantly connected the sentence with Nera and her comments, "This is yours; I am sorry for everything." Could this have been his and Nera stole it? But he had never seen this knife before, and he had never met Nera before. A new thought popped into his head: what about a past life?

Paul realized he needed to meet Lena again to help him make sense of this. Lena was becoming more and more important as a key to information and the cornerstone of insight and clarity. Paul dug her business card out of a folder and texted her, asking if they could meet today. Lena replied that the soonest she could meet was 5 p.m., and he agreed, anxious to find out more about everything.

Paul worked all day in his home office. All day it was a struggle to stay focused on the research material of his book; he kept anticipating the evening and somewhat obsessing about the athame. It sat next to him while he worked. The blade refused to give him any hints, or perhaps he was unable to receive any messages. All he really knew was that he hoped that Lena could assist him one more time. He felt like she was the gatekeeper to this other unique dimension of metaphysics and past lives.

Even though he'd only known this blue-collar, kind woman a short time, Paul realized she was one of the most generous women he knew and was the key to all these unexplained events. As he walked into the antique store one more time where the sign said closed but the door was unlocked, he hoped that she could help him again and give him the messages that he needed to find the meaning in it all.

Lena was sitting in the back of the store at her table with her Tarot and Oracle cards ready. She smiled and asked how the last couple of days were going. He spent the first ten minutes catching her up on the funeral, Nera, and especially the athame. She only smiled kindly. It was like she knew the events were going to happen and that he'd be returning with questions but did not warn him because he needed to be in charge of his own journey.

All the while that Paul described the twists and turns, Lena kept smiling on the other side of the table. Paul was somewhat frustrated and asked, "Did you hear everything that has happened to me?"

Lena calmly said, "Yes, very clearly, it was all foretold."

Paul sat there, expecting nothing more than a generalized, obscure philosophical saying. He didn't think concrete answers were in his cards today. Paul said, "Lena, by the way, I have a surprise for you."

Lena's eyes gleamed with excitement as Paul handed her the wrapped linen package, which contained the athame. He watched how gently Lena held the object and the great care she gave to setting the bundle on the table and untying the old string. As she opened up the cloth to glimpse the athame, Paul could see the respect and care she gave the object before even seeing what it was.

Lena asked, "May I hold it?"

Paul chuckled. "That is why I brought it here to you today. I need you to help me with this mystery object. I need your opinion on what it is. I've learned the historical side, all the academic research and theories, and now I need your opinion. It seems your opinion could be more accurate."

Lena carefully tried to find the right way to pick it up. She gently raised it off the table into the palm of her hands and started to move her fingers across the symbols on the blade and touch the black handle over and over again and turned the athame over and over, studying the blade extensively. The she said, "May I try to read it?"

"Yes. Please."

Lena quietly said, "I am not going to decipher the words, I'm going to psychically read it." She took the blade with both hands and held it in between her palms and closed her eyes. The spontaneity and fluidity of her features as she sat there conveyed something real was going on, unseen. After a few moments, her features shifted as if in conversation with someone to her right. Lena was having a conversation with herself—or wait, Paul remembered she had a spirit guide. Paul thought about how enthusiastic Robert was over reading the inscriptions. Lena's reaction and manner were completely different: almost calm with only a hint of excitement as she felt the blade and the energy inside it.

Lena continued to hold the blade and kept talking with herself with her eyes closed. It looked like some kind of spirited debate was taking place. Then she smiled a great deal with her eyes closed and slowly opened up her eyes and looked at Paul. She put the athame back on the table with the blade pointed toward him.

Lena smiled and said, "So what do you already know about this blade?"

Paul then explained to her that he had taken it to a professor and knew about the possibility of it being a magical knife or ceremonial blade, possibly with witchcraft and not just a dagger and about the language on the blade and really how the evidence he had did not clearly define what he had. He was exhausted by all the energy he had held in about all the information he described but could not put it all together. He then said, "Well, this woman I just met gave me this athame, Nera."

Lena stopped Paul immediately. She asked, "Was she dark haired, tall and slender and well dressed?"

Paul nodded yes, and then Lena's face was saddened. She was heavily saddened. Then she softly said, "You need to be careful with her. Be aware, she is not what you think she is."

He agreed, "I do not know what she is but someone who wants to be my editor."

Lena softly spoke, "That is enough for now about her, just be careful." Paul was already confused and then he described what little he remembered from his dream that he had the night prior about an innocent woman and a knight and a whipping and an evil woman. Lena took it all in and then said, "Let's see what the cards say today for you. I think that is where the answers lie. May we begin?"

Lena stopped shuffling the cards and set them back down. "What happens when you touch the athame?"

Paul said, "Nothing. I don't feel anything, plus the handle is small and I have large hands. I have touched and handled it, but I do not get anything from it."

Lena said, "Before we do the cards, do you mind if I purify the athame and re-consecrate to cleanse it? Maybe it might reconnect with you."

He nodded yes, feeling he did not have a choice. She

walked over to a small cabinet and grabbed some candles and some incense and some sage and water. On a separate wooden end table, Lena carefully set a small bowl of water in the upper left corner. She sprinkled three inches of salt diagonally across the center of the table. Then, at the head of the table she set a lit white and black candle. She closed the ceremony with burning sandalwood. Lena took the blade and told Paul to watch her. So, Paul got up and joined her. Lena said, "Paul, I will need you to do what I say when I say it, ok?" He nodded and put the blade in his hand. "Since this blade was given to you, you must say the words and hold the blade for this ceremony."

She told him to run the blade over the flame of the black candle. After he did, she handed him a piece of paper and said to read it.

He read,

All negative thoughts to be banished,
all unwanted vibrations be gone.

Then she told him to pass the blade over the white candle and he followed her guidance.

She handed him another piece of paper and he said,

Let only the forces and power
I wish be within from this moment.

Then she told him to pass the blade across the

incense smoke, while she sprinkled salt over the blade, which caused sparks on the heat of the blade, and he read another passage,

> *Elements of air, fire, water, and earth,*
> *To this tool of the magick now give birth.*
> *Blessed and consecrated in this hour*
> *Be thou athame of strength and power.*

Lena took the blade from his hand, wrapped it in the cloth, and retied the original twine around it. She handed it him as she instructed, "Paul, you must hide this athame in a safe place and from now on only use for magick."

Paul nodded, confused—it was an entirely new experience. And yet, he knew the athame was now spiritually cleaned and ready to be stored. He did not comprehend what she meant by "only use for magick," but Lena was getting up and moving back to the table with her cards. She paused and asked Paul if he was ready for a reading. In response, Paul sat back down across from her, athame wrapped up neatly next to him on the table. Lena laid out her card deck and asked Paul to pull seven cards. She laid them down on the table in a V shape.

At the apex of the V lay the magician. The card pictured a man holding his hand in the air with his other hand pointing to the ground, and on the table next to him lay all the suits of the Tarot. An infinity sign floated above the man's head. Lena turned over the second card.

Hangman. The third card was the knight of swords astride his horse. The fourth card was the lovers, a man and a woman walking along a path together with angels flying overhead. The fifth card showed three swords piercing a heart in the rain. The sixth card was the king of swords sitting on a throne pointing his sword upward. The seventh card was death riding on a horse with a black flag bearing a white pattern.

Lena took a deep breath, touched each of the cards with her fingers before she started and then paused again, like she was having a conversation with her spirit guide. Then she looked up at Paul and said, "Are you ready?"

Paul nodded with cautious anticipation.

Lena then described the cards before her. She said, "I want to start with the hangman's card, which is very powerful, but it also means letting go and surrendering ego, and virtually turning everything you know upside down, which I think is happening now anyway."

She continued, "It also means some type of martyrdom." She stopped and then went with her finger to the knight of swords card and said, "Paul, what this card means is once you set forth your goals there is absolutely no stopping you from finishing. You may become blinded by your desire to solve your challenge. It means you must be careful by your strength in accomplishing your quest. You may charge into dangerous territory, which could lead into actual danger."

She then touched the lover's card and paused. She said, "Paul, this card does not mean a physical lover but a companion that you have not met yet in your current life, but you have spent at least one past life with. This woman will help you with your personal beliefs system and will help you stand for what you believe in, and she will help with your philosophy of life, the life which you were meant for. This woman will help you uncover what you find important and unimportant in your life. She will help you bring out your true self, so you can finally be genuine to the people around you."

She paused again. "You will find the angel Raphael, who is the angel of air, and he will guide you. He will help you with your mental process, and also this future love, this future love will be friends with you for years before you go to the next level."

She touched the three of swords card and looked up at him with a smile, "You have picked one of the most iconic cards of Tarot. This card shows that you will have or have already had great grief and loss in your life, and severe heartbreak, and you have recently had a low point in your life. Paul, the journey you are on will lead to rejection, betrayal, hurt, and pain, but you must go on it. The way you think will save you. Your logical, methodical way of thinking will reduce your personal pain. This pain and grief you are about to receive will help you in your future life. They are teachings that will bring joy later in life.

"Through pain you will learn, a necessity of human life. This process will make you stronger and more vigilant. This future pain will knock you down, but your choice after that will determine your future, to rise again; this means you will be prepared for the next stage of your life. This pain and grief will hurt, but you will be enabled to forget your past and focus on the future. Don't worry about the past. Focus on the future. In the end you make your own fate."

Lena then touched the death card and had a conflicted look as she said, "No one can destroy death, death does not differentiate. This is one of the most misunderstood cards in the deck. I am not surprised you picked it. It is a powerful card. This card today means that one major phase of your life is ending and another is beginning. You have a new start coming soon; you will go through a transition, a major change, the old version of you will die but a new version will rise out of the ashes. You will be scared and uneasy, but the most important thing is you should welcome the change, you are opening the doors to life events that will bring you joy, a well-deserved joy."

She then touched the king of swords card and tapped it a couple of times. She said, "Paul, you must remain objective on your future situations. You must stick with the facts and use logic. You must use your intellect to solve your problems and to attain your goals. Your experience and education are an asset. Be observant. You must keep your mind clear." She continued, "You must consider all the possible consequences not just the physical world. A mind that is clear is the best tool, leave emotions out of your judgments because it will fog your objectivity; you must look at the situation and make a clear impartial decision."

Lena then went to the last one, the magician's card. She said, "The card is reversed and sits at the top of the layout. The magician means it is time for you to make changes, when right side up but in reverse, it means there is a master of illusion near you, there is someone near you or soon to be near you, who is trying to trick or deceive you. Please do not be lured by the showmanship or be fooled. Someone near you is trying to manipulate you for their selfish gain. Someone is trying to pretend to have your best interests at hand when the opposite is true.

"Well, Paul, that was a lot to take in one sitting. Do you have any questions?"

Paul just sat there trying to comprehend it all between the lover's card, the magician's card, and the death card. He was dumbfounded; he had reached his limit on all these theories of metaphysical items occurring right now in his lifetime which he paid no attention to just days ago, but now was neck deep in all of this chaos. He just sat back in his chair and said, "I think I just to need to think about all of it. It is quite a lot to comprehend so much so fast. I have your phone number so I know how to get ahold of you if we need to meet again."

With that response, Lena smiled and accepted his answer and started to pick up all the cards and laughed a little also, knowing how much she had given him to comprehend. She encouraged him to think about each of the pieces and then put the pieces together, and she reminded him to take the wrapped-up athame home. She quietly said, "Remember, the athame is clean now and should only be used for ceremonies."

Paul picked up the wrapped athame and started to get his coat on to leave while his brain was a little foggy from the information overload. Lena walked him out and patted him on the shoulder and said, "Everything in the universe is connected, the past, the present, and the future. Everything effects everything. Do what you have to do."

Paul walked outside. The air was biting cold and it was dark. The only lights were the store lights and the streetlights. The sidewalk was empty and it felt so quiet. Most of the nearby stores were already closed and the open bars and restaurants were a block to the south.

Chapter 10
The Future Priest

Xavier Tommaso de Francesco was the son of a farmer from a poor village in southern Italy. His father had to leave the farm and move into the village when Xavier was twelve, leaving Xavier without any future. He joined the Italian military at sixteen. After years of valorous service, he specifically transferred and was selected for the Pontifical Swiss Guard that was recently established. Having Swiss heritage, and having served with Kaspar von Silenen, Xavier was permitted the honor of helping protect the pope. Fit and athletic and strong as an ox, but more importantly, Xavier could fight when needed, he was ruthless in a combat if needed, but he personally did not like to be violent. He was, and felt like, a mercenary, a man who fed and clothed and housed himself from cold skill with violence. He began at the lowest ranks and quickly rose due to his loyalty to the church and to his military leadership.

Xavier was at his best militarily in 1527 when Emperor Charles V's army tried to sack Rome and diverted to an attempt to invade Saint Peter's Basilica. Xavier and his tiny Swiss army held back four times their forces and killed as many of the enemy as they could to give Pope Clement VII time to escape through the secret tunnels inside Passetto di Borgo to Castel Sant' Angelo, a large military fort near the Vatican. The pope was able to hold out for eight days before surrendering to end the onslaught of the Swiss Guard. Out of Xavier's group and his guards, 150 of the 189 died to save the pope that day. Xavier was one of the few survivors.

The brave stand of the Swiss Guard defined who they were and their devotion to protecting the Holy See. Afterward, Xavier became a personal security guard to the pope on his travels. One day the pope asked him what he would like to do and Xavier said he would like to be a priest. The pope applauded his desire, but decided he had to wait a year to properly make such a meaningful life decision. He requested Xavier to take leave and take time being a representative in his local village back home but not tell anyone he was working as a Swiss Guard and especially never divulge that he worked for the pope. He would be on official orders to be a guard for the region for the local church and priests. The pope said, "I want you to tell me what is happening in your local village because I am hearing rumors from the cardinals and bishops but

I want you to tell me directly. Here is a letter from me if you ever need it, but I do not think you will need it with your certain abilities to take care of yourself. Come back in one year, and I will send you to the seminary of your choice. There are certain human things you must explore and decide before you commit to the priesthood."

Xavier departed the next morning wearing common clothes and leaving all of his Swiss Guard uniforms in the garrison. He looked common, which was his intent. Xavier knew no one really knew him back in his village, the poor were ignored, and he had been a quiet shadow to avoid trouble before he left at age sixteen. He thought no one would remember him.

He had two letters in his pocket, one from the local bishop officially transferring him from guard duty in Rome back to his hometown to finish his enlistment—all he wanted anyone to know about his background. He had the letter from the pope safely tucked away. He thought he would die before he used it—unless he needed his life to protect the pope or the church somehow. When he arrived, it looked like there had been little change since he departed over fifteen years earlier. His only attachment here in the village was to his parents, but they had both passed away while he was in the wars fighting. He was not able to attend either of their funerals, and his parents were too poor to have anything of value to leave him.

No one noticed him as he entered the village. He went straight to the church cemetery to visit the grave sites of his parents. He walked over to their tombstones and knelt down and touched their stones with tenderness. After a prayer, he apologized for missing their funerals and had a quiet conversation with his departed parents. He knew in his heart that they both understood that he had to depart the village to make any success. He had to leave because there was no future for him in the village. No future other than being always half-starved and worked to the bone—when there was work. As he was giving his respects to his parents a voice said, "Who are you, what are doing?"

Xavier looked over to the fat bald short priest as he stood up and said, "I am paying my respect to my parents, I was not able to attend either of their funerals because I was fighting wars for our country."

The priest touched his crucifix as if to remind Xavier that he was a priest and said, "You should say 'father' because I am a priest. Don't you respect the priests of the Catholic Church and the pope?"

Xavier smiled confidently and said, "Father, how may I help you? By the way, who are you?" Xavier stood almost a foot taller than the short priest, which quite upset the short priest to have to look up at Xavier.

The priest stood as tall as he could, pushed his chest out as much as he could. He looked frustrated and annoyed at Xavier. Xavier was just waiting for the right time to tell the hubris-laden priest that he was going to be a security soldier for the church and worked for him but he just waited for the priest to embarrass himself some more.

The priest stood proud and said, "I am the assistant priest of the village church and hope to work in the cathedral someday. I have met the Monsignor and the bishop several times … my position is temporary due to my high priestly potential."

Xavier smiled, took it all in, and said, "Father, thank you, but you failed to introduce yourself, you just told me who you know. What shall I call you?"

The priest said, "Oh, my name is Emilio. You may call me Father Emil."

Xavier shook his hand. "Father Emil, it is a pleasure to meet you, and I will be a part of the security force to guard your tithes for transportation for the church here for the next year, I have been transferred here. My name is Xavier." He took out the letter, showing the priest without letting him touch it.

Father Emil pretended to study the letter. It was obvious to Xavier that Emilio was trying to comprehend who would send a security force person here to his church; he assumed someone was sending this man to his parish to spy on him or maybe this new person was incompetent, which was highly unlikely. Father Emil could not comprehend all the options but was happy to have new and stronger security. Muscle had its uses, after all. In fact, Emilio already had a way he could use Xavier in his favor with certain issues he was having.

Emil looked him up and down and said, "Well, if you are assigned to the church then you better follow me to the church and annex where you will be living." Emil started walking out of the cemetery, and Xavier picked up his only bag of items and followed.

As they walked, Emil said, "I may need a man of your occupational skills for other security measures as I protect the parish against certain evildoing."

Xavier walked along in silence. He did not know exactly what Emil meant but knew he would be introduced to it sometime.

As Emil and Xavier walked into the village toward the church, many of the villagers who acknowledged the Father looked at Xavier but could not place him. Xavier recognized most of the villagers since he grew up in the village but he was so poor a child here, he knew why they did not remember him. After all, he was just a part of the background here when he was a child, he had no potential, no connections, and no family help. Xavier just smiled and knew that each of villagers knew him but did not recognize him. Since Xavier had departed the small village, he had grown almost nine inches and gained seventy-five pounds of muscle and his hair was longer. He walked down the streets with a solid quiet confidence.

When they turned the corner, Xavier was slowed by the view of the church in which he grew up. His family would all sit on the back row and when they gave tithe it was so small compared to other parishioners. The money could have bought food, but his father was such a devoted Catholic that they were accustomed to not eating on Sunday because they gave their money to the church. Xavier remembered that vividly. His father would never tell anyone how much giving to the church hurt his family and never asked for help. It was a silent devotion to God and to sacrifice. His father would always say, "The first shall be last and the last shall be first." Xavier did not understand the meaning until much later, when he experienced war and power. In Xavier's belief system, humility and penance were what God sought in people and that was his motivation. His actions to God would be his life.

As Emil and Xavier walked behind the church to the annex, there was an older friar in his eighties carrying a large basket of vegetables that he had just taken from the church garden. He had dropped the basket and was trying to pick up the vegetables. Xavier stepped down and started to help the friar. The friar said, "Thank you so much. I am getting clumsy in my eighties."

As they both put the last of the vegetables in the basket and stood up together, the friar dropped the basket again and yelled, "Xavier, my son, I am so glad to see you after all these years!" The friar gave him a hug and Xavier also gave a hug back and they smiled at each other.

Xavier said, "Friar James, how did you remember me after all these years?"

Friar James smiled and said, "I would never forget my young boy, Xavier. I knew you would become something and that you had to depart to return. I also know who you are under orders for." As he said that statement, he winked at Xavier.

Xavier immediately remembered when the friar

would come by his family after mass and hand him an apple or fruit to take home with him and he would always wink as an assurance it would all be ok.

Xavier just smiled and was thankful that one person in this village had remembered his poor young life. Friar James said, "You should visit me in my house when able, we can talk about Laura. She is still here, but she is in trouble."

Xavier had not thought of Laura in so many years. Laura was his only friend growing up. She was from a wealthy family and wanted to play in the woods and play with swords, which her parents refused so Xavier would meet her in the woods and teach her boy things, like tracking animals, bow skills, and wrestling. They knew each other and shared personal stories with each other along with a friendly competitive spirit and a drive for excellence. When they were in the woods, they teased and bantered freely, but they both knew when they walked back to the village they had to act like the children and parents they came from. Laura was not allowed to talk to Xavier in public due to her social status, but she would always look into his eyes and smile and wink at him.

As soon as Father Emil walked over, Friar James put his finger to his lips to stop talking about Laura.

Father Emil said, "Let Friar James pick up his vegetables because he is such a clumsy friar and should be retired. Friar, please have my things ready for mass tomorrow morning. Xavier, I need to show you your room and discuss a task I need you to do for me."

As they walked together and left the friar, Father Emil walked with Xavier and asked, "Xavier, what do you know about witches and witchcraft?"

Xavier said calmly, "Well, Father, I have not experienced many trials of witches or witchcraft, and I have not been aware of any issues with the church."

Father Emil said, "If you had formal education with the church and not just soldiering, you might have the expert knowledge I do about the threat of witches against the church. They are evil, these wicked women, all of them are evil and set in their ways against the church and our entire establishment. They all need to be burned and sent back to hell."

Xavier was confused. He knew full well the rumors of witches and witchcraft, but the pope's stance on the matter was of the necessity of scientific reasoning to establish evidence. He knew the pope's opinion, which required evidence to prove a witch, not just an opinion or a hysteria by the ignorant, but Xavier was not going to let Father Emil know that he knew the pope's opinion on the matter, or any other matter.

Father Emil showed Xavier to his room and told him to unpack and to meet him after dinner because there was something he wanted to show Xavier after the evening meal.

Xavier sat in his small room that he expected to live in for the next year, under directions from the pope to gain a deeper understanding of humanity, before he would start seminary to be a priest. He knew that he could still fully trust Friar James but he fully acknowledged that he could not trust Father Emil. He knew this type of priest was only in it for the power and prestige of the position and not to truly help the people. Xavier could not tolerate self-centered arrogant people who used others to get ahead. Xavier had dealt with such men throughout his years serving in the military.

Father Emil knocked on the door and asked Xavier, "Xavier, can you come with me? We have business tonight." His voice was different and quite unemotional.

Xavier got up and went to the door and opened it to find Father Emil was in almost farm gear, nothing of the priest about him. Xavier was instantly suspicious on what Father Emil needed him for tonight on his first night in the village. Father Emil had two horses that were ready outside for them to take on this errand for the priest. Xavier asked, "Where are we going and what are we doing?"

Father Emil just said, "Do not ask such questions, just do what you are told. You are just a stupid soldier sent to do my work for me, you will not disobey me this night. I am the authority in this region. I am the appointed one from God. If you do not follow my every order, I will send you to a much worse assignment than this village."

Xavier was cautious and was heightened in anxiety and guarded because the tone and actions of Father Emil had changed to outright commandeering arrogance. They rode side by side along the darkened road and they continued to go farther from the village until they turned onto a smaller trail toward a house deeper into the woods.

Emil gestured for Xavier to get off and tie the horses up. As Xavier was doing so, Emil lit two torches and said to follow him down the small road deeper into the woods. The moon was not out, and it was also cloudy, so the torchlight was even more difficult to see. Father Emil led the way down the darkened road and Xavier quietly followed him. They eventually came to a small house, which was completely dark. It looked abandoned in the shadows of the torchlight. Father Emil looked at Xavier and said, "What happens in this house, you are forbidden to tell anyone, do you understand?"

Xavier was concerned now but fully guarded on what Father Emil was up to in this abandoned house in the dark away from the village. Xavier reached behind him to assure himself he still had his knife and dagger if there was any danger approaching. Father Emil said, "Xavier, stay outside and I will bring you a witch. You will help me take this sin against God to the village jail and we will put her on trial tomorrow. I know as a fact she is a witch. I have personally witnessed her evil acts. She is a demon. Do you understand?" Father Emil pointed his finger at Xavier using as much power as he could pull over him.

"I understand."

Emil turned around and went into the house, and Xavier could hear a woman scream and heard furniture being turned over. Emil sounded like he was getting hurt, and Xavier could hear Emil say, "You bitch!" Then the door flew open and a small woman tried to leave the house, but Emil was hanging on to her leg and would not let go of her. Emil yelled, "Xavier, stop this witch from leaving! Grab her now!"

Xavier grabbed the struggling woman quite easily due to his strength and agility as a soldier.

The woman screamed, "Please let go of me! This bastard is trying to rape me! He is a monster!"

Xavier had both arms around her, and immediately knew that voice, it had changed a little, but he knew that voice. The voice of his only childhood friend, Laura.

The woman struggled again and again trying to be set free. She yelled, "Only one person knows how to counter my moves. Who are you?"

Xavier grabbed her hard and whispered into her ear, "This is Xavier. Please cooperate. I swear on my soul that I will help you, but I need you to trust me now. Please ... Laura."

"Xavier, is that you?" and she looked into his eyes and immediately stopped struggling. He shook his head to acknowledge not to divulge his identity.

Xavier looked over to Father Emil, who was struggling at the doorway, and said, "Laura, kick me hard and I will let you go, right now. I will come looking for you and will find you. Kick me now, hard like you used to, now. You know how to take me down, now!"

Laura kicked him hard into his groin and he moaned out loud and he dropped her from his grasp and she started running into the woods.

Xavier fell on the ground, and Father Emil yelled, "You idiot, go after her!"

Xavier got up and started to slowly chase after Laura into the woods holding his midsection in great pain.

Xavier started to run into the woods, and his familiarity with the woods came back to him as he ran in the moonlight and his childhood memories came rushing back to him. He knew where Laura would hide. There was a cave not far from here where they used to meet and talk as kids. He turned left and recognized a rock formation and knew he was close. There were some changes in the terrain but rocks that large weren't going anywhere anytime soon. He turned left and found the cave entrance. He stopped immediately. He walked slowly to the entrance. He talked slowly, "Laura, it's me."

There was a quiet voice from the cave, "Xavier?"

Xavier slowly walked into the cave into complete darkness, and he felt a hand reach out for him and instantly the two hugged and Laura cried on his shoulder and he held her strongly and safely. She cried and said, "That bastard tried to rape me. That man hates me. He has been trying to hurt me for the last couple of weeks."

Xavier said, "I need to bring you in to the church, and I need for you to trust me. I have a plan to set you free of him forever, but you have to trust me."

"I am not going anywhere with you because once that bastard has me in custody, he will burn me like a witch. I am not a witch; I am a healer of the old ways and you of all people know that."

Xavier said, "So, Laura, how are we going to get out of this and have Father Emil stop harassing you forever?

You were always the smarter one, think of something."

"Xavier, you just do not know how horrible a person Father Emil is. He's been trying to touch me for months; he has tried to use God as approval to touch me in my private areas. He has even said that God told him to seduce me! And when I turn him down and deny him, it makes him furious like a spoiled child. I hate that man, he is unforgivable. He is pure evil. He has had his way with young girls in the village because the young girls do not want to make God mad at them; that is the horrible things he tells those young girls when he seduces them in the name of the Lord. That man deserves to go to hell, to burn. He is an evil man."

Father Emil was much more horrible than what he initially thought and he was thinking of what final way he could make him stop harassing the women in the village. How could he make Father Emil confess his sins to the village without knowing he is confessing? Xavier said, "Laura, do you have those mushrooms and herbs in your house that help you talk to the spirits and angels?"

Laura said, "What do you have in your mind?"

"I have an idea, but I will need you to trust me. I can't tell you what it is so I can protect you fully. Please trust me."

Xavier stood up in the cave and grabbed Laura's hand and they walked out of the cave together back toward her cabin. "Laura, I give you my word that I will give my life to save you, but I need you to trust me in this situation."

He looked at her in the moonlight and he could tell she was smiling and she said, "I trust you with my life." She hugged him long and deep. He then hit her as hard as he could and knocked her out cold to the ground.

Xavier said, "I hated doing that, dear, but it was for your own good. I promise you will not be hurt." He said this knowing she was knocked out cold and could not hear, but he wanted to say it out loud to himself to assure himself that his plan would work.

He picked up Laura and threw her over his shoulder and started to walk back to her cabin where Father Emil was waiting. Xavier hoped his plan would work and as he got closer to the cabin, he could see that Father Emil had lit a fire in the fireplace and the cabin was lit up and getting warm. Father Emil was very pleased with Xavier as he carried Laura into the cabin and tied her to the chair so she would not fall out of it. Xavier finished tying Laura to the chair next to the chimney and then acknowledged to Father Emil that she was secure. Father Emil was looking for some wine or something to drink in the house and Xavier said, "Let me look for you. I always have good luck finding alcohol."

Father Emil quickly agreed, feeling frustrated in finding anything to drink and too short to reach the taller cabinets.

Xavier knew the wine was kept on the highest cabinet and reached high for it, because he was remembering his visits with Laura before he went off to war many years ago. Laura had showed him where her father had always kept the wine, and the two of them had shared a glass together at the age of sixteen right before everything changed for him once he left the village. He was still thinking out his plan as he was pouring Father Emil a drink of wine.

Xavier walked over to the cupboard and opened up the double doors and saw all the glass jars filled with dried plants and spices and he looked for the right bottle that would cause issues for Emil. He quickly opened it and dropped several drops into the wine that he gave to Father Emil.

"That took you long enough. What shall we do with our witch? You successfully captured her. Shall we have a little fun with her, maybe we just let her stay asleep and do what we want?" He slowly touched her hair as she was still unconscious and tied to the chair.

Xavier said, "I did not tie up the horses and I think they might have walked off; may I go search for them while you do what you must to her?"

Father Emil said, "Why, yes, please, go get the horses. I shall not walk back, that is so beneath me. By the way, please pour me another glass of that wine, it is so well made." He raised his glass and finished the rest of the wine and handed the empty goblet back to Xavier.

Xavier just smiled, knowing the effect would happen soon, and why not put more odds in Laura's favor and give him some more. Xavier went into the kitchen and filled the goblet and put another two doses of powdered mushrooms into the wine and stirred it well. He then walked back into the room and handed the goblet back to Father Emil. "Father, here is your wine. Please pace yourself, so you do not become confused from the wine."

Father Emil just laughed and took the wine. "I can hold my wine. You are just a poor laborer. Now leave me alone with this witch and fetch the horses. Do not come back without them." As he said these last words, he grinned evilly.

Xavier acknowledged the orders and left the house. He hoped Laura would be ok once she awoke and that he gave Father Emil enough herbs to make him sleep soon so that nothing horrible would happen to her. He hoped his plan would work but he had another addition to his plan that he needed to do first. He actually did tie the horses securely but needed the horse for something else, and just hoped the timing of all these things worked out to save Laura.

Father Emil watched as Xavier walked out into the darkness, almost panting with excitement to be alone with Laura in his power at last. As he turned toward her, she began to stir and wake up. Father Emil said, "My dear, glad you could wake up and join me, you stupid witch." He slapped her hard on the face, which caused her lip to split open and a drop of blood dripped down her chin. Laura struggled to work on the ropes but could not untie them. Emil said, "I had my new parish guard tie you well so you would not get out, and he even said it was a knot he learned as a child playing in the woods near this village."

Instantly, Laura thought about the time she tied Xavier up around a tree and he could not set himself free;

she had taught him how to get out of the ropes. She quickly felt with her fingers to determine if it was the same knot and it was. She could work herself out of the ropes but needed to keep Emil occupied as she worked. She needed to deceive him and delay him. She wondered where Xavier had gone. The huge knot on her head ached, and she gritted her teeth in anger. Somehow, she'd get even with him. Her immediate concern was to make sure Emil did not violate her. He was so revolting and unattractive, he was just a terrible human being.

Emil walked into the kitchen, and Laura frantically worked on the ropes, unable to break free while alone in the room. She ceased her efforts when he walked back into the room with a knife. He pulled a chair in front of her, and leaned forward toward her, touching the point of the knife at her heart. Laura froze. Emil moved the knife down to cut off a button on her blouse. This then slowly opened up some of her blouse to him. Slowly, he used the knife to cut two more buttons. Laura noticed he was having issues and kept shaking his head, as if he were trying to stay awake. Emil looked up at her and used his knife one more time to cut the last button, which exposed most of her breasts to him, but he did not look interested and almost looked like he was going to pass out.

Emil said to her, "You witch ... I am going to make you pay for denying me so many times, but I am having issues ... there must be something wrong with the wine that I drank, that wine was having an effect on me ... what was in the wine?" With that last word, Father Emil fell to the ground in a stupor, but his eyes were still open and he kept talking but could not move. He just lay there on the ground looking at the ceiling.

Laura knew this was her chance. She quickly worked on the ropes and soon she released one hand and then another and then she released her feet from the knots binding her to the chair. She stood up and tried to cover up but realized the effort was futile. She didn't spare a second to worry about it. As she opened the door, debating escape, she knew she would never have this chance with Father Emil again. From the absurd rambling from the prone priest, it looked like Xavier had given him a large dose of hallucinogens. It was time to get some facts and have Xavier explain his plan. She smiled and closed the door and walked back to Father Emil and said, "Father, I need you to sit in the chair. We have a game to play."

Father Emil smiled, "I so do love games, but I seem to not be able to get up right now."

"Well, if you can't sit in the chair, we can't play peek a boo with my blouse."

Father Emil looked at her with an evil smile. "Oh, but of course, I must get in the chair to play that game, but I do not feel right … right now, I am dizzy and light headed, and everything seems really slow in your voice." Emil slowly got up on all fours and with Laura's help in which he tried to grope her, she pushed him into the chair where he sat slumped over and impaired.

Laura came up to his ear and said, "To play this game correctly, I must tie you up … it will be so much fun, trust me." She gave him a peck on his cheek and smiled and in his stupor, he smiled and put his hands behind the chair.

Emil said, "This sounds like so much fun, but the room is spinning and I am seeing things in the room that I do not know they what are."

Laura securely tied up Father Emil, fully in the hallucinations.

At that moment, Xavier slowly walked into the cabin not making a sound and was not seen by Father Emil, but Laura saw him as he put a finger to his lips so the conversation would not identify him. Xavier walked into the kitchen and Laura followed while it looked like Father Emil was asleep tied up in the chair. Laura said while she pushed him, "Why did you hit me and tie me up?"

"I have a plan and did not have time to argue about it in the urgent moment and I took a chance, that, well, that you could take care of yourself. I trusted my gut and my instinct, something you always told me to do even when logic does not agree. I followed your guidance."

Laura was mad and speechless and wanted to hit him, but instead kissed him on the lips. "I so missed you all these years, and you have grown and gotten a lot stronger. You have changed for the better. So what is your plan?"

"The first part was to bring you back here, to appease Father Emil, the second part was to tie you up in a knot that I knew you could get out of, the third part was to give him your powdered mushrooms which we had spiritual experiences while kids, the fourth idea was to get the horses and buy time. I thought I could bring a witness back so that under the delusions he would confess to what he has done, but I realized we would both get in trouble if we brought anyone here because of the circumstances, so now I am thinking we use this opportunity to scare him so much that he will never bother you or me again and eventually leave the village. So, can you help me finish the solution?" As he finished talking, he took off his shirt to give to her because he had been looking at her open blouse without blushing the whole time.

Laura smiled. "Well, Xavier, you have seen them before, you have even touched them and kissed them before." She laughed and put on his shirt to cover herself up but now fully noticing his chest and muscular shoulders. She never thought Xavier would have matured so much.

Laura smiled. "I do have an idea, because he is in a euphoric state right now, we just have to trick him to believe in what he does not want to believe. We need to play dress-up a little to scare him."

Xavier somewhat knew what she was up to but she was in the lead of this phase as she clearly had something quite distinct in mind.

Laura went into her room and searched her wardrobe. She pulled out a dark red robe, then put it on, along with an old wolf skin that she arranged on her shoulders; she also went into her kitchen cupboard for a mixture of powders and put them and some water into a small bowl. She looked at Xavier and said, "Take off your clothes and let me smear this red mixture on your body."

Xavier looked confused. "You want me naked?"

"Yes, I want you to let me put this red mixture on your body and make you look dead to Father Emil, so when I wake him up, he will think I brutally killed you. So, go ahead, take them off. If you are naked, it will have more effect. Many priests still believe in the folklore of witches and that they seduce their men and then kill them after sex. We are going to convince him that is exactly what I did. Hurry up, get them clothes off."

Xavier did as he was told. Laura noticed the rest of his body had matured quite nicely. She said, "Now stand up straight, so it looks like you had a horrible death." She was having fun with Xavier while she caked him with the red mixture. she had made multiple trips to his chest, stomach, and butt, which she said needed more dramatic effect, but she really did it for the desire warming up in her body. When he looked absolutely bloody, she said, "Stand still for one more thing and close your eyes." He did as she said and she picked up a nice sycamore log that she was going to put in the fire later and took a huge swing and hit Xavier on the head, knocking him out and putting a nice gash on his forehead, which allowed some real blood to drip down his face. The presentation was complete. She smiled to herself and quietly said, "Well, my friend, now we are even." She touched his forehead to make sure he was still alive and put a finger on his blood and then put it on her lips and cheeks.

She turned her attention back to Father Emil, still asleep and tied to the chair. Time to give a performance that ensured he never bothered her again or took advantage of any other women in the village. Her thoughts ran clear and clean and quick. She dimmed the candles to just one and picked up a bucket of water and threw it on Father Emil.

Father Emil spluttered back into consciousness, soaked to the bone. He shook his head trying to wake up from the jolt of cold water. He caught sight of Laura. He squinted his eyes and looked at her again in her bloodied face and her robe. He looked over at the naked, bloody Xavier with a dripping gash on his forehead, knocked out. Father Emil looked panicked. "How did I get tied up? What have you done? Are you going to kill me? The church will come after you! You'll burn, you bitch."

Laura knew the mushrooms were still having an effect on Father Emil by the way he tilted his head and slurred his voice. She looked at him and said, "What do you think I am?"

Father Emil said, "You are a witch."

Laura touched his face seductively. "No, my dear, I am a demon, and I have come for your life or your soul, it depends on what kind of deal we make." Laura knew by making up a lavish story that Emil would be even more scared.

Father Emil said, "What did you do to Xavier? My God, he is naked and murdered."

Laura went over to Xavier and put her finger on his

dry blood on his forehead and then touched her fingers to her mouth. She knew Father Emil was getting more scared by the minute and so she slowed down. She knew how weak he was inside; he was not a brave man. Laura licked her lips as she turned back to Emil. "You know that I made love to Xavier madly like animals and then I murdered him because I had no further use of him. He has given me his seed and 1 shall use his seed to nurture a demon-witch child into existence. You, well, you could not even get aroused and so pathetically passed out. You have no manhood; you are a pathetic man. I think I shall kill you slowly."

Father Emil was vividly shaken. "Please do not kill me, please, I beg you. I will do anything you want if you spare my life."

Laura pulled out a large knife from her cloak and said, "Anything, really, well, I do not trust you, especially by the way you have treated young girls in our community. I think I shall kill you now so you will never hurt another woman."

Laura pulled the blade out and then pulled Father Emil's legs apart and started to unbutton his pants, "I think I shall fix the thing that causes all your problems and dismember you."

Father Emil was fully and truly frightened. Blood drained from his face. He started to cry. He said, "Please, I will do anything you say. Please do not cut it off or damage it. Please, I swear to God, I will do anything you want."

Laura said, "Well, I do not think I will kill, but I

think I will damage you a little." She had lowered his pants and was digging the knife along his upper thigh near his groin slightly cutting his skin but not causing too much blood loss.

Father Emil was fully crying and sobbing while Laura was digging into his skin near his groin on his inner thigh. She used the blade to draw a reverse pentagram on his inner upper thigh; there was only a little blood loss, but the work was not half bad. The Father now had a sign of the devil marked on his skin. Laura slowly moved up to Father Emil's sobering face and said, "Do you swear to your God that you will never hurt another woman?"

As she asked him this question, she touched the blade on his groin and he said, "I swear, I will never hurt another woman."

Laura then said, "I do not believe you." She then pushed the knife right across his groin pretending to slice him open right there.

Father Emil screamed, "I swear, I will never hurt another woman in my life."

Laura stopped and almost believed him but then drove the knife slowly into his scrotum and said, "Do you know how much blood is in the scrotum if you only pierce it a little?"

Father Emil said humbly and crying, "I swear to my God that I will never hurt another woman in my life and if I do, I will take my own life."

Laura stopped moving the knife. "Do you swear? Speak up one more time."

Father Emil, tears and snot running down his face, said, "I swear to my God that I will never hurt another woman in my life and if I do, I will take my own life."

Laura pulled the knife away from his groin and said, "I swear that if you hurt another woman I will take your life." As she said this, she touched the knife along his throat. Father Emil's eyes rolled back in their sockets and he passed out.

Laura knew she did not have much time, so she quickly woke up Xavier and took him to the kitchen to wash and to put some clothes on him.

He said, "What happened?"

Laura said, "I knocked you out so we are square. How do you feel?"

Xavier leaned on Laura and she helped him clean up and get dressed. Xavier said, "So, what was your plan?"

Laura said, "I scared him so much that he passed out again, but we do not have that long before he wakes up, and we must pretend nothing happened, ok? Pretend you just came back with the horses and we will untie Father Emil and you will tie me back up to the chair so when he wakes up, it will be in the same time frame as when you left."

Xavier said, "That is genius. How did you think of that?"

"I thought of that while I was tied up to the chair and that bastard tried to rape me."

"Now we just have to set the conditions right and make sure everything is believable."

Laura's lips curled up into a devilish grin. "I left a small reminder of the evening on his upper inner thigh."

"No, you did not?"

Laura laughed, pleased with herself. "I just had to."

"Hopefully he finds out about it later."

Laura said, "We will see. Now, Xavier, untie him and lay him on the floor, and then tie me up just like you left me. One more thing, here is your shirt." As she took off his shirt, her shirt was opened up again exposing her breasts. She sat in the chair and told Xavier, "Now tie me up like you used to." She smiled mischievously, thinking about the times when they were young and exploring each other.

Xavier got up after cleaning himself off and putting on his clothes and then saw Laura with her blouse fully open, ready for him to tie her to the chair. What has happened in such a short time together? Quickly, he tied her up and then Laura said, "Go outside and reenter. Slam the door so that it awakens Father Emil from his stupor." He stopped and walked back to her and opened up her blouse some more and said, "Well, dear, we have to put things how they were." He grinned at her and gave her a soft kiss on her forehead and winked to her as he softly walked out the door.

CHAPTER 11
THE BISHOP, AD 1481

The bishop stood at the base of the cathedral, near an assembly of altar boys and deacons ready to start his Holy Sunday service in a village in southern Italy. His name was Xavier Tommaso de Francesco, and he was the youngest bishop in Italy with a bright future in the church ahead of him, an unusual thing for the son of a farmer. Xavier tried not to fidget as he fretted about the details and timing of the day's ceremony. Like every other mass he'd ever performed, he obsessed on the pageantry and the supreme importance of starting on time. He knew what the packed house of parishioners expected every weekend and every mass: to hear the word of God from him and be awed at the elaborate orchestration of the holy Catholic Church mass.

The organ, promptly on time as it had been since he'd

had a discussion with the organist, began the introductory music for the procession to start into the main aisle of the cathedral. The congregation rose as one, turning as the procession passed toward the magnificent altar. Xavier was a bishop of the southern province, well educated and well thought of in Rome and by the Council of Cardinals. He knew the politics of the church and their thought of his potential to rise higher to archbishop or maybe a cardinal. Xavier's obsession with timing and pageantry stemmed from his service as an officer. Xavier was a humble war hero of the people—an unusual occurrence for a member of the church, let alone for one whose potential shone bright in the eyes of his superiors. His personal story inspired many Catholics in the region and country to travel to hear his words of guidance through his sermons. Xavier often spoke with such seekers while working in the fields or other manual labor around the church's holdings. Unlike the majority of the highly ranked church officials, he had always thought God's work started by getting your hands dirty. His congregation seemed to praise him for this every time one spoke with him. Xavier had long since learned to hide his discomfort at such adulation and turn the conversation back to the word of God.

His purple cassock flowed, magnificently catching the midmorning light through the stained-glass windows as he led the procession down the aisle. Red and black pipings accompanied his robe. His cincture cord tied around his waist symbolized to him the virtues of chastity and continence. As was his wont, he'd chosen his purple biretta four rigged hat for the indoor masses because it was more comfortable than his cardinal chapeau. Each step down the aisle was preceded by his crosier crooked staff. He used it to keep his pace sedate and to add the semblance of age to his youthful, soldierly gait. On his right-hand index finger lay the fisherman's ring the pope personally gave him when he was appointed bishop of the region in an informal gathering that took place before the official ceremony.

As the mass started through the motions, Xavier continued to be the center of humbled attention. After the first and second reading and the introductory song it was his time to read the assigned verse from the holy Gospel of John to all of those attending the mass this morning. He stood in front of the congregation, his elderly deacon holding the Gospel. Before every reading of scripture Xavier paused to survey the congregation, seeking to connect their souls to the scripture with his gaze. It was a habit picked up from soldiering that he strove to put to advantage in his ministry. Today, he noticed a brunette woman on the last row. A small black veil covered her face, but even with that and the distance, Xavier felt her to be looking straight at him. He knew exactly who she was, knew her soul to be severed from the holy ceremony. She was not a Catholic, and she was watching the holy mass for observation because she was not a Christian and so did not believe in God. Rebecca was her name, and she was a witch.

Xavier caught his breath, kept his composure,

looked down at the gospel, and then decided to read something from Revelations chapter 6:

And I saw when the Lamb opened one of the seals, and I heard, as it were the noise of thunder, one of the four beasts saying, Come and see.

And I saw, and behold a white horse: and he that sat on him had a bow; and a crown was given unto him: and he went forth conquering, and to conquer.

And when he opened the second seal, I heard the second beast say, Come and see.

And there went out another horse that was red: and power was given to him that sat thereon to take peace from the earth, and that they should kill one another: and there was given unto him a great sword.

And when he had opened the third seal, I heard the third beast say, Come and see. And behold, and lo a black horse; and he that sat on him had a pair of balances in his hand.

And I heard a voice in the midst of the four beasts say, A measure of wheat for a penny, and three measures of barley for a penny; and see thou not the oil and the wine.

And when he had opened the fourth seal, I heard the voice of the fourth beast say, come and see.

*And I looked, and behold a pale horse: and
his name that sat on him was death, and Hell
followed with him ...*

He used his pauses and inflections to advantage in the
timing of the echoes ringing through the vaulted ceilings.
Once he said the last line, he took his regular final survey
of the room as a dramatic pause before the next element of
the ritual: Eucharist. He noticed that Rebecca had departed,
which relaxed him some. All of his attention soon became
engulfed in the holy Eucharist and it felt, as normal, like
his soul was flying and his entire mind translucent in each
small gesture of giving the consecrated wafers and wine
to his loyal and faithful parishioners.

As the mass was winding down, and the exiting
procession started with the music and altar boys putting
out the candles, Xavier relaxed completely, felt tonnage
of pressure melt off his bones. Another example of how
church rituals and the readings of the Bible could keep the
people moving toward an improved Christian faith and
continue their path to peace and love. He looked at the
collection of the morning and knew he received enough
money to keep his church and programs going financially.

Xavier positioned himself at the exit of the church
to greet his parishioners as they left the service. He had
to be fully appreciative of every person who attended
because without them there would be no church for him
to work in and no future for his rising religious career.

As the last of the people left the church, Xavier

would always go to his private quarters in the back of the church and change out of his formal attire and put on his black robe and white collar, what he called work clothes. Before he went into his quarters this time, he went and helped count the collections of offerings of coins from the people. As he looked at the money collected, he knew that they were generous and expected much faith and excellent sermons from him in the future.

Another item his parishioners expected was his protection against the rumors of witches and witchcraft spells. Rumors in the region had been growing greater each year, of witches killing livestock, killing babies before they were born, and the most entertaining rumors were of the infidelity of devoted men under a spell of lust for a young maiden. The older political men blamed the young women that they said were witches for their infidelities, but Xavier knew from the private confessions that men knowingly had affairs to meet their own lust. Xavier had to protect their public reputations through confession, so they would become weak and blamed these young women for the infidelities even though it was the men's fault of act. Xavier knew the women were innocent, and he was going to try and protect them as the bishop of his territory. He had an insider in this witchcraft affair; he knew a witch.

As he entered his private quarters, Rebecca was already there waiting for him. She looked at him in her flirtatious way with her slender figure and her long, rich dark chestnut hair and dark hazel eyes. She was tired of waiting for him and seemed frustrated. Xavier said, "I hope you were careful entering my quarters and used the secret passageway through the gardens like I told you to take." He looked down onto her like a schoolteacher checking a pupil's work.

She taunted, "Why, yes, Xavier, I did exactly as you told, because we can't have anyone know that you are friends with my sort of people. Think of the scandal it would cause and your downfall." As she said this, she grinned with a little evil dancing in her eyes, knowing she had some power over him and his weakness that he had toward her beauty and charm. She knew he could not resist her.

Rebecca was an Italian witch from a long line of gypsy witches back to ancient times. They had kept their witchcraft secret throughout the generations. Xavier was one of the few who knew the facts. Due to his power and influence in the church, it was smart for Rebecca to befriend him and to seduce him for his help to prevent any rumor to be released to the town and the region which would ruin him and hurt the coven of witches. Rebecca worshiped a god and a goddess and would meet during the full moon for rituals to celebrate and dance and make love to Xavier even though it was forbidden to a priest to be married or have sex due to their vow of celibacy made before their God. Rebecca knew other priests had broken their vows, but to get Xavier to break his vows was one of her greatest achievements against God.

Xavier was fully aware of Rebecca and what she

was and did. Well aware he lived a double life between the church and her love. Rebecca was his secret weapon into the witch culture, their relationship would have him excommunicated from the holy church and he would be banished from Italy for having the relationship with her, but he did it anyway because he just could not turn off his affection, love, and lust for her and he knew he was in a horrible place living a double life. He loved her like no other woman, when he knew he should not and he knew he had given an oath to celibacy, but knowing the other priests and bishops that had had relationships with women, the only saving grace was that their churches were largely financially sound and funded the country's cardinal's objectives of wealth. Money was always pleasing to the pope in these times. Xavier bet his entire religious career on the money of his church to keep him safe if his relationship with Rebecca was ever found out.

Rebecca made herself comfortable in her favorite chair before beginning with her ritual attack on the church and the canons and how they got it all wrong. "You know, Xavier, the church was formed to control the people. The divine is already inside us, we don't need the church, we do not need buildings, we do not need priests. If we open our heart, if we open our mind, the divine will talk with each of us. The goddess came first before the god, because only women can produce life, so women are actually better. The only reason men run the world is that one day the men wanted power and changed the rules and used the power over the female divine in their books and women were from then on subordinate to men.

"You even changed your Genesis book in your Bible about the first wife, who was not Eve but Lilith, who chose to not be subordinate to man but equal as man, and then the authors changed the story and claimed she was a sorcerer, a devil, the most famous demonic figure in Jewish faith.

"Even you, Xavier, have an amulet in your dresser bearing the names of Archangel Michael, so really the first divorce of the Bible, in the holy Garden of Eden, was when Lilith left Adam and had sex with an archangel and the infamous incubi and succubi, which none of this information is to share with your congregation. You keep them so uneducated by purpose. You only allow a few to learn to read and only allow so few into the beloved church. You so control the people."

Xavier was always astonished by her religious academic knowledge. She actually knew the Bible—sometimes in more detail than he did. She loved to discuss certain subjects that were never discussed in seminary or even noted. Rebecca had this passion as if she had personal knowledge of these histories, like she had a special book that she learned from. If there was such a book, the church would have to destroy it, to think of what the people would do if they had this knowledge. Xavier would always love their intellectual discussions and how she challenged the church doctrine like a student critiquing a teacher, but in the Catholic Church there was only compliance, any type of resistance to the pope was crushed immediately because he was the closest to God on earth for the church. If there were counter discussions, the discussions would be in private with peers and with others who could be trusted to not repeat the discussions to others in the church because the consequences were dire.

It was getting late in the afternoon and Xavier's duties were complete for the day. He had told the staff, as was his habit, that he did not want to be disturbed because he sought deep prayer and needed to get ready for the next week of church services. His Sunday nights were his only time with Rebecca and his only time that he could relax and just be a man, and not a bishop.

Rebecca went over to his cases of wine from Rome and picked up a bottle and said, "Do you think God would mind if we got drunk on his beloved blood tonight?"

Xavier just laughed. "Rebecca, the change of wine to blood only happens during the Eucharistic ceremonies during mass, so the wine is purely wine right now and we would never store blood outside the sanctuary of the church. So, no, God would not mind that we get drunk off a bottle of wine or maybe two bottles. You are so silly."

Rebecca was insulted. "Xavier, you know that the goddess ceremonies and our altars and prayers are so close to your beloved church's, and your so-called church holidays are really my magical holidays first. Your church calendar is based on the moon and the stars, but don't tell your people, they actually would still not believe it." Rebecca was vividly upset and angry at Xavier, more than he had ever seen.

He opened a bottle and poured a glass of wine and calmly said, "Rebecca, your religion is not recognized and only believed by poor gypsy outcast women like yourself!"

Rebecca poured herself a glass, took a drink of wine, and yelled, "How dare you! How could you say that after all that we have been through? What are you meaning, that if I am not with the holy church, I do not matter on this Earth or your community? You know what I do for you by giving you secrets of the woods and the secrets of the book of spells and the rumors from the working social class in your region. You would never be where you are today without my help the last couple of months. Damn you for those comments!"

Xavier realized he crossed a line with her. He hadn't meant to say those words, but Rebecca had a way to send him from calmness to rage within no time; he thought she actually liked taunting him like that. She was the only person who could enflame his inner rage, which he so calmly suppressed when he wore the robes of the church. He looked at her and said, "Rebecca, I am sorry. I did not mean that. I know I should not have said that. I apologize."

She smiled and sipped more wine. "I will forgive for all the hateful things you just said, if and only if you turn this wine into the blood of Christ, so I can finally taste what it means."

Xavier did not expect that response from her,

had never dreamed of that question arising in their relationship. He had blessed wine before in makeshift outside ceremonies for folks who could not travel to church, but the rules were clear: no one could receive the blood of Christ without being baptized in the holy church. He would be breaking several laws of the church to make the wine to blood in his house and then to give it to this pagan and witch. How could she ask such a thing?—but he so wanted her to forgive him and he knew she put her foot down on the matter and he had gone too far in his claims and degraded her faith. In the back of his mind, he realized and hoped she was not from the line of Stregoneria witches, famous for spells and seduction and outlawed by the church. He did not know why he just realized that his Rebecca could be from a long line of dangerous witches. His situation with his relationship with her went from serious to grave. If she was a part of those witches, they would burn him for helping her. He did not feel well right then, but she asked again, "I will accept your apology if you let me drink the blood of Christ. Or maybe I will burst into flames. This might be fun."

Xavier realized he was walking down a path he could not return from; he could lose everything. He offered a counterargument, "Rebecca, I will allow you to drink the blood of the beloved Christ if I can baptize you in the Holy Spirit first. I will do everything you request, but we need to do it right." Xavier was proud of himself, because if he baptized her in the Holy Spirit first then he did not break any laws in allowing her to take the communion and wine and he would call it her first communion under the laws of the church. He was proud of his invention of regulatory dancing to ensure he did not violate any canon laws.

Rebecca was confused, and she stopped being bored and thought in her head about the ramification of the baptism and the end state of actually receiving the host and wine from the blessed bishop. She countered, "I want the certificate that I am baptized with your signature so that if anyone suspects me of being something else, which I am, I can wave the paper and pretend to be a Christian and my chants are actually loud prayers to God, so they don't get the wrong idea. I agree. Let's do it now."

Xavier did not expect the quick agreeance to his proposal, but the cat was out of the bag and it was his turn to do what he proposed. He led her out of his home and they entered the church through the back door. He lit only a few candles so as not to light the whole church, sat her down on the first pew, and said, "I will be right back. I have to change clothes. Just be patient." So, he went off into the back room and started changing into his formal clothing that he would wear while conducting mass. He even put on his special hat and all the colors and he came out to find her still there.

They walked to the side of the church where the baptismal font was located and he poured water from a nearby glass pitcher, letting the water rest in the baptismal font. He touched her hand gently and kindly. "I need to say a prayer for you, and I need for you to agree to the following statements and realize what we are doing might change the course of your history and your destiny. This baptism might bring you in between two worlds of those of your ancestors and those of the followers of Christ. My intuition tells me that this action will save your life on one of your future travels, so you have to trust me, and know that I will always love you."

Rebecca smiled at him knowing that she loved him too, that they could never be together but they would have this ceremony to somewhat spiritually join them and bring her closer to him. And … it might be good to have this as a trump card.

Xavier told her, "The rite of baptism is the first of the seven sacraments of the church. It is to cleanse away original sin and symbolize rebirth of Christ inside you. It is your initiation into the church."

Xavier brought Rebecca closer to the baptismal font, then he tenderly took off her scarf and undid her hair from her braids. He pulled out his priest prayer book and cited the Gospel of John, "Unless a woman is born of the water and of the spirit, she cannot enter the kingdom of God." Xavier then said a prayer to Rebecca and said, "The new life of baptism welcomes you into his holy church," and then, "Pray for us, Holy Mary, mother of God; pray for us, Saint John the Baptist; pray for us, Saint Joseph; pray for us, Saint Peter; pray for us, Saint Paul." Xavier put sacred oil on his thumb and touched Rebecca's forehead, anointing her with the sign of the cross. "In the power of our Christ our Savior," and he laid his hand on Rebecca.

Xavier then prayed over the water, recalling God's graces at the dawn of creation, at the great flood, at the parting of the Red Sea, at the baptism of Jesus in the River Jordan by John the Baptist, at the flowing of water and blood from Jesus's side as he hung on the cross, and at the call to his disciples at his resurrection to go out and teach and baptize all the nations of the world. He leaned Rebecca's head over the water and took a cup and poured the water over her head, saying, "I baptize you in the name of the Father, the Son, and the Holy Spirit," each time pouring water over her head.

Xavier pulled out his oil again and anointed her on her forehead, welcoming her to the church. He grabbed her hand and lit a candle with the other and said the Lord's Prayer and reminded her that she has been reborn in baptism. Once the ceremony was officially over, Xavier looked into Rebecca's eyes and noticed that she was tearing up a little with emotion through the events.

Rebecca said, "I have never felt like that and never knew that was what the baptism meant," as her wet hair fell into her eyes shyly.

Xavier then said, "I shall fill out the official letterhead and document this baptism in the church records so if you are ever stopped on your travels, you can proudly state that you have been baptized by the bishop. You never know when this may be helpful."

Rebecca during the next few minutes had a change of heart on taking the Eucharist and asked Xavier to wait a week or two because she wanted to think about the simple act of faith that he just did for her. Xavier thought that somehow, he might have converted her over to Christianity but still needed her in the inside of witchcraft so he could receive the latest information to stay ahead of the rumors of witches in his region. They held hands back to his house behind the church after he blew out all the candles in the small corner of the church. They quietly held each other that night in his bed, he knowing that he might have significantly changed her and she knowing that something inside her changed.

Just before dawn, Xavier woke up and felt for Rebecca in bed but she was not there. Looking around the room for her, he noticed the light of a candle flickering dimly through the crack in the door. He got out of bed, put on his nightgown, and walked out into the doorway. He saw Rebecca sitting on the floor praying, and at first, Xavier thought that he had converted her to Christianity but quickly saw the crystals in the four cardinal directions and the salt on the floor and the candles in the middle and that Rebecca was naked and chanting. She raised a knife in the air looking up and then used the knife to cut the palm of her hand to spill blood inside a chalice. His holy chalice that he used in mass. He was getting upset at the sight and was about to move toward her, when she said, "Xavier, stay where you are. I have cast a circle around me and the only way through it is if I cut a corridor. Please do not mess with spirits you are not knowledgeable about, and please stay outside the circle for your own safety. I am almost done, just let me finish my closing chant."

Xavier stopped and listened to her gypsy Italian as she performed her chants and as she was calling out to the Goddess Diana to enter the building and enter the circle with her. Chills ran down the back of his neck. The temperature in the room dropped and he felt something dark was about to be opened in the room. He walked closer to the circle and Rebecca stood up with the knife and warned him again not to get any closer to the circle because she was not done bringing Diana into this holy place. Then something happened. Rebecca changed the way she talked and scoffed at Xavier for being a Christian and murdering so many women who prayed to her and proclaimed that she was going to curse this building and the sacraments inside.

Xavier felt his soldier skills returning quickly. He looked around the room for a weapon or stick and found a metal stoke and walked closer to Rebecca. He walked almost into the circle and Rebecca, in an unworldly voice, shouted curses at him and charged him with the knife and drove it into his shoulder, attempting to go all the way through so that the tip opened the skin on his shoulder blade. But the knife was now stuck in his shoulder and she could not take it out, and he slammed her with the metal stoker across the forehead and sent her unconscious across the room. Standing there, attempting to staunch the wound, Xavier knew there would need to be a rational decision and explanation to cover up the truth.

He started to clean up the salt circle on the floor and picked up the crystals and threw them into the fire along with all other evidence except for Rebecca, unconscious and naked on the floor. He then thought of Abdul, his Middle Eastern servant who fought in the wars with him and could be trusted. Xavier had brought him back from the wars to protect him from his own country and he gave him duty and work for the church as a protector and guard on road trips. Abdul slept in a private room in the barn and could be trusted.

Xavier walked across the yard to the barn and woke up Abdul, a large dark-skinned man and not to be trifled with on the road. He had scars like Xavier did from the holy wars and he spoke many languages. He was a Muslim and non-Christian but accepted by the community for his loyalty to the bishop. Xavier woke him up with directions to be ready to ride in short notice fully armed, like they had done many times.

Xavier went back to his house and looked at the room to assure no evidence remained except for Rebecca; he now had to remove her for good.

Within minutes Abdul was at the house in full armor with two horses ready to ride. He said, "Sir, where are we going?"

"My dear friend, I need the most important favor in my whole life," Xavier replied. "This woman was under the power of the dark evil one and tried to kill me, as you can see by the wound, but I knocked her out, defending myself and the building. I want you to take her to my place in the northern lands in the Highlands to my younger brother. You remember the place. She did not mean to wound me because I just baptized her tonight," and he showed him the certificate, "But the evil had one last stand in her before I took action. I want you to protect her like you would me. I want you to travel constantly and eventually enter family grounds, protect her with your life. I will meet you there as soon as I can depart, a couple days or maybe a week behind you. Your obligation to me will be complete if you do this for me."

Abdul obligated his life to Xavier for saving his life and his family during the war, and to have paid in full and someday go back to his homeland was something he hadn't thought of in a long time.

Abdul said, "I will protect her with my life and she will make it to your brother's place, I know the way. I give you my word."

Rebecca was starting to wake up, and Xavier picked her up and held her. She began crying when she saw the knife still inside Xavier's shoulder. He looked up at Abdul and said, "Please take this out and then warm it with fire to heal and close the wound."

As Abdul pulled the knife out, the pain on Xavier's face was deep and Rebecca, pained too, said full of tears, "I love you and I did not mean to do that. It was not me. I swear it was not me, it was Diana. Please forgive me. I could never hurt. I love you. I love you so much." She continued to cry in his arms, then Abdul brought the red-hot stoker out of the fire and told Xavier to bite on the wrap of cloth and not scream as he drove the hot poker into the wound to stop the bleeding and then touched the back of the shoulder where the tip of the blade just broke the skin. The pain was excruciating, and Xavier was almost at his limits. He then looked up at Abdul and said, "Take her now without delay."

Rebecca was confused and Xavier looked straight into her eyes and said, "You tried to kill me in my church and the result of that in our court is death. If you want to live, you will stay with Abdul and he will guide you to a safe place where no one will look for you. It is the only way to keep you from being burned or hanged for trying to kill a bishop. Do you understand?"

Rebecca nodded, knowing that all the best decisions had been made to save her life, and this was the only option. Abdul put a cape over her and got her on the horse with ease, and she looked at Xavier and said, "I love you."

Xavier said, "I love you too, but you must leave and I will come find you as soon as I can. Abdul knows where to take you. You must leave now."

In the darkness Abdul and Rebecca slowly and quietly rode off into the night, and Xavier knew they would be safe if they could get far enough away before dawn. He had filled Abdul's pouch with gold and a letter from him for emergencies to get them past the borders with the church's seal and orders that they were messengers from Rome. With the church's protection in paper, and gold in hand and a warrior leading the way, he felt safe and now he had to come up with a story to tell the church and the cardinals and Rome and his congregation.

He walked along his room thinking of a story in

his head to tell his church leaders and his congregation of how a witch—yes, a witch, he would use the folklore examples—yes, a witch tried to enter the house and he fought her off and she stabbed him with a wicked knife and then she ran off and he sent his most trusted warrior Abdul to go find her wherever it may lead them or how far it may take them. Yes, that would be his story. There were no other witnesses, so he should be good and the evidence was clear and the blood and the wound were proof that someone else had to have done it.

He practiced the story over in his mind and it turned out to be very believable to himself. He then thought of a twist to create a new threat to the church: they would be Christians who were mixing folk magic beliefs into their practices, and he would add the rumor of the *Stregheria*, these examples would be Catholic witches. The story would work and in the back of his mind, he knew what he had truly seen: that Rebecca had conjured up a spirit— whether it was good or evil he did not give it a chance to decide or show its face, but he knew since there was a magical circle in his house that he needed to bless the place with holy water and give new protections to it.

As Xavier was treating his wound with ashes from the fire that he put out, he saw the crystals that he had thrown in the fire. He looked at the four crystals. He remembered Rebecca's chant to make them protect her house and so he chanted the same one:

I charge these special crystals,

Through the Universal Power,

To bring protection

Into my life and house

So, let it be.

He then placed each of the crystals on the four corners of his house for protection. He did this because he had learned from her for the past several years about protection crystals and he trusted his intuition about this type of protection. He knew there was an evil power, and he knew Rebeca was not herself at the end. He also knew he had to strike her because the spirit that was inside her did not need to get out. Even though he was a bishop, there was always room to have a little more magical protection from the other religions.

At dawn, Xavier informed his leaders of the church and he slowly started telling his congregation. Most were proud of their bishop defending the church from an evil witch and slightly awed at the wounded shoulder. The church leaders were also impressed by his bravery, particularly that Xavier did not boast about it but was humble. Everyone was once again thankful to their church for putting such a capable bishop in their region. The witch story intensified the growing suspicion and the social accusations of women who might also be witches. Xavier's story was aligned to the recent rumors that were growing in the northern territories. Since the truth would never be told, it was so far an excellent story to affirm that the church would defend against witchcraft and assist the people.

The last item that Xavier knew he must do is to get it formally written in history by one of his priest-historians. One of his youngest priests, Girolamo, was on an early draft about the history and stories of witches, *Apologia,* for the church about the Stregheria witches of Italy. Girolamo tracked these Stregheria witches who worshiped the Goddess Diana. Most of the stories that Girolamo had heard were from the Tuscan peasants and gypsies. Xavier wanted to add his recent story to his research to make sure it was recorded in history for future reference if needed. He then commented for Girolamo to not add any other traditions to the writings from Egyptian Isis worshiping, the Hermetic following, or the Greco-Roman traditions, and to write the book as an authentic Italian underground and fully hidden from society that remains in the shadows and will remain in the shadows in the future.

Xavier started to leave the office and then turned around and said, "Girolamo, please include another assumption—that witches could also be Christian—in your discussions. Some people who may be devoted to Christ might practice witchcraft for further protection from the spirits which Christianity does not talk about." He was actually referring to himself but could never fully admit that. This was a way to academically and scholarly discuss it without including himself. He continued, "Please include that the witches will not get along with one another due to the fact of not relinquishing their faith, mainly their belief of what happens after we die, the risk of losing heaven was too great for some witches to walk away from, which then would upset the true witches who do not believe in Jesus or the holy God." Xavier patted his young priest scribbling furiously, excited to put these new ideas inside his book, hoping people would acknowledge his research. As Xavier was exiting, he said, "I want this to all be your research. Please do not include me for any references. I learned those assumptions and beliefs through confessions and do not want it to get out."

Girolamo got up from his desk and went over to hug Xavier and thanked him for believing in him and his writing ability. He asked, "May I consult with you more?"

"As long as you never include my name, I will discuss this with you if you bring the wine." Xavier exchanged smiles with his young priest.

Xavier walked into the sanctuary and over to the baptismal font where he had baptized Rebecca the night before. He prayed that the power of God and a little help of the spiritual would provide safety to Abdul and Rebecca as they traveled to his family's lands in northern England. He knew it would be weeks or maybe a month before he would hear from Abdul about their journeys, but he knew—or he hoped—they would be safe.

Chapter 12
The Answer Is Inside Us

As Paul was leaving the store from his second Oracle reading in less than a week, he passed by the local yoga studio. He looked at a sign in the window that said, "Buddhist monks and meditation limited time only tonight RSVP only." For some reason, the image of a monk talking to him sparked curiosity. Paul entered the yoga studio and got his name on the list of attendees for that night.

He spent the afternoon working in his university office catching up on e-mails and getting his final grading for the semester completed and ready to submit grades to the registrar. He was ready for the semester to be over and to have a much-needed three-week break from work and find some escape for a while. As he looked for a book in his leather satchel, he came across a Scottish family reunion invitation that he had forgotten about. The Clan MacGregor in Scotland had invited him to their 78th International Clan gathering near Dalmally, on MacGregor homelands near archaeological sites Stronmilchan and Tigh Mor, where the clan lived in past eras. Paul remembered the six-month effort to prove his genealogy to the Clan MacGregor to be officially recognized as a descendant. He had forgotten his invitation and now the reunion was only a few weeks away. He paused to savor what an adventure it might be, but his worry about getting late registration, late plane tickets, and not finding a room took over his mind, and he put the invitation back in his leather satchel to decide on tonight.

As the time drew near for Paul to go to the yoga studio, he recollected on the last time he met a monk and had one of those conversations that was more questions than answers. It was on a mountain retreat weekend in Crestone, Colorado, an area chock full of Buddhist, Zen, and spiritual getaway spots brimming with meditation, yoga, and spiritualism. He met a monk who told him that he already knew the answers. The monk did not help him find any answers, and he left the retreat more frustrated than relaxed or enlightened. Paul hoped this evening's visit with a monk he had never met would give him some clues regarding all the alignments and spiritualization he was currently going through. He could use some answers, but he expected more questions as was his fate these days.

As the time for the event drew near, Paul got in his truck and drove to the yoga studio, psychologically prepared for yet another more-questions-than-answers session, but also with an open mind for he still hoped to get some answers.

He walked into the yoga studio and the mood was definitely different from that of a yoga class. There were only a handful of people awaiting the monk and his spiritual guidance, and Paul felt foolish like he just paid for a carnival sideshow. But since he paid, he was going to at least experience a conversation with the monk.

At the appropriate time, the teachers told the waiting group that the monk was ready for them to sit in the studio and listen to him speak. Those who hadn't yet, took off their shoes, and the little group took their seats on pillows distributed in a semicircle around the monk.

When Paul walked into the studio, he saw that the monk was a young man, not more than twenty years old. Paul paused in the entrance, startled. All the monks at the Colorado retreat and all the other monks writing books or giving interviews were gray haired or bald. It felt like a good omen somehow.

The young man sat on his pillow and welcomed everyone. After his greeting, he invited the group to chant together in Sanskrit, accompanied by a guitarist seated discretely in the corner of the room. The mood completely changed within minutes and everyone was in rhythm chanting songs in a foreign language. Anyone who couldn't pick it up orally grasped each chant easily from the handout. The chants were beautiful and simple and opened up the heart to love. The atmosphere was something that Paul had never experienced before. The reverberations of the chant, the voices coming together and filling the space of the studio, echoing around the room and adding to the sensation of the sounds thrumming in his body profoundly affected him.

At the close, the monk invited the participants to stay afterward for a one-on-one session, saying that he would be delighted to speak with each of them. Paul took the invitation and stayed until most of the group had thanked the monk and departed. As he sat waiting patiently, completely at peace inside himself from the chanting, a question popped into his mind: where is the inner temple the athame described? He didn't know if this monk could help him, but he would ask. As the last person walked toward the door to leave, Paul approached the monk and cautiously asked, "Sir, could you assist me?"

The monk said, "I will try. What may I assist you with?"

Paul said, "I seek the inner temple, but do not know the way."

The monk tilted his head to the left and replied, "Are you ready to find the inner temple inside yourself? Do you also seek the tree of life?"

Paul nodded his head.

The monk said quietly, "Did the athame help you access the tree of life and your temple?"

Paul stopped, his mind spinning around upon finding that the monk somehow knew about the knife. He replied, "I have not used it to access the tree of life."

The monk smiled back to Paul and quietly said, "Paul, hold the blade tonight and meditate. Open your mind to seek what you can't find; the blade will give you access."

Paul smiled and said, "How do you know my name and about the blade?"

The monk grinned and winked at Paul. "You came here for me to tell you what you already know. You know what you seek, but you are looking with your eyes. You need to look with your heart and your true eye and trust yourself, and you will find what you seek."

Paul smiled backed and recalled the Gaelic inscription of the blade and replied to the monk, "Suil Dhe na Gloir," and the monk just laughed back at Paul and replied, "Yes, Paul, the eye of God will help you see the face of god of life and show you the inner temple. Use the tool wisely."

Paul just smiled back with confirmation because somehow this monk could understand Gaelic and also understood what he was looking for. It wasn't a complete or clear answer, but the information was useful, and Paul felt charged up and excited about solving the riddles for the first time since everything began with the death of his father.

He shook the monk's hand, bowed respectfully, and departed the yoga studio with a sense of satisfaction in what he had received.

He went through his normal evening ritual, with his mind busy thinking about what the monk had told him to do. Unable to focus on reading, Paul walked over to his desk—he would meditate with the athame tonight. He pulled open the top drawer, carefully taking out the wrapped athame. As he unwrapped the blade, he recalled Lena's words that the athame was clean and should only be used for ceremonies.

He had seen and done meditation when he was an undergraduate and exploring the world. It had been a long time, but Paul felt a quiet confidence growing inside him as he dimmed the lights and lit a few candles for more effect. He poured himself a whisky to help the mood and to relax. He sat on the floor and let the candle light flicker on the blade as he held it in his hand. He continued to watch the blade and the play of light on the metal and the way it felt in his hand. He slowly quieted his mind to just let his subconscious go and to relax and see where his thoughts would take him.

Paul quietly sat on the floor and remembered his meditation classes and started to slowly breathe in through his nose and out through his mouth. He started to mentally count his breaths in with a countdown from ten and to exhale with the same countdown length. His breath was calming down, his mind relaxing, and soon he was at that moment when the conscious and unconscious are balanced right on the edge of falling asleep because of the relaxed condition where the mind starts to wander and the mind starts to dream and the mind starts to explore. He was at the last moment of relaxation right at the moment of sleep.

He was now in a dream state, holding the athame in his left hand, his right hand relaxed on his right knee. As he held the athame, the engraved Sanskrit letters started to glow, but he could not see it because his eyes were closed. Paul was now visualizing himself walking in a forest deep and cool and dark. It was an old forest in Germany with dense, ancient trees and little sun reaching the ground. He kept walking until he came out into an opening in the woods and saw a large open meadow in a small valley. As he came out of the woods, he noticed a huge tree, a tree so huge that he could not imagine a tree so large. The limbs were massive, bigger than the oaks around his house. It looked like a huge building almost thirty stories high. Paul walked up to the base of the tree. Stepping over large roots, he circled the tree slowly. Off to the side was a large tunnel between the roots that led into the ground. Footsteps imprinted in the dirt led into the tunnel. Paul climbed over the large root and entered the tunnel that was as tall as he was.

The tunnel ended abruptly on a massive stone deck. To his left lay a beautiful aquamarine lake with purplish mountains all around. Ahead of him was a lake house. The tunnel led to the back patio of an ancient wooden structure. More mountains rose up in the distance on the other side of the house.

At this abrupt transition, Paul felt slightly confused. Uncertain, he realized there were several people sitting on Adirondack chairs around a fire pit drinking what looked like beer and wine, laughing about some joke.

One of the five looked his way and shouted to the others, "Well, look here, Paul the Great and Humble One has finally made it. We have been waiting so long for him, finally time for us to meet." This man was in his forties with close-cropped blond hair and a leather jacket. His t-shirt had the words "got wings?" in the shape of a Superman shield. He had not shaved in a couple of days and had on a pair of gold Chuck Taylor tennis shoes. His eyes and cheeks were a little weathered and covered with fine creases, but they were the Clint Eastwood type of smile lines. He strode over to Paul and gave him a hug like they had known each other for years and sang out, "Paul, it's a long time that we have been waiting for you—by the way, my name is Merc. It is so good to meet you again."

Paul started to shake hands with all the strangers. There were three men and two women. The scene felt like family and a part of him intuitively knew them all. The women to his left was a brunette with long hair, late middle age but sassy with a long flowing skirt and no shoes and a carefree '70s vintage t-shirt that simply said, "I screwed Zeus, literally and mythologically." Her hair was curly and a complete mess and she lounged on her chair, patently braless, pausing a moment for Paul to look at her before rising from the chair. She simply kissed him on both cheeks and said, "Hello, my dear Paul, I am Diana. Please have a drink. We have been waiting for you. You are an entertaining one but so worth waiting for; we have been watching you for some time." She handed him a goblet with engravings on it that were like the runes from the athame.

Paul took the goblet and hoped it was just wine or beer because he was somewhat anxious and scared but so curious. He had never been here before, yet it was so familiar in his mind. He found the only open chair left and sat down. The other woman was older and more distinguished and she calmly came over to Paul and shook his hand like an elegant diplomat. Her attire looked crisp, East-coast old money, and straight out of an L.L. Bean catalog. With a simple but distinguished voice, she said, "Hello, dear, my name is Lilith. It is a pleasure to meet you; we have met before in another time, but that is for another social event. Please, let's talk. We need new conversations, and we are all excited to meet you again. It has been a long time."

Paul sat with his goblet of some unknown liquid before taking in the other two men. The short man sitting quietly in a 1930s suit with a fedora looked familiar, more familiar than the others; he had seen this man before somewhere but could not place it. He looked a lot like his great-uncle Henry. He quietly looked up at Paul and shook his hand and said, "Paul, my name is Willy. It is a pleasure to meet you. I have been watching your life from here. Your family is proud of you and your accomplishments."

Paul smiled back. It was like looking in a mirror, those eyes and brow were like from his family line but he could not place it. The last man to his right just waved and nodded but did not shake his hand. He was wearing ancient robes with a hood and sandals on his feet; he had a gray beard and it almost looked like he was blind by the way he turned his head when the others were talking to each other quietly, like he was trying to listen. He had a calmness to him and it felt like he was from a long time ago, like a really long time ago, like ancient times.

Paul sat there and all of a sudden, the side conversations stopped and they all looked at him and he could feel their eyes on him so he drank from the goblet. His lips puckered and his eyes watered as he coughed from the fumes. They all laughed at his struggle with the drink. They laughed at him as if there was an inside joke. In his life, Paul had drunk many nasty drinks, and this was by far worse than tequila.

Merc got up from his chair and said, "Paul, that was a bad joke. Lilith gave you fermented alcohol from AD 500. We all bet you would not choke on it, but then you did so you passed the test and now we all owe Lilith money. Please take one of my real drinks. My beer is from the 1400s so it's delicious."

He went to his cooler and pulled out a Corona and even put the lime on top and handed it to Paul with an apologetic smile. Paul looked at the Corona knowing it was not from the 1400s and everyone laughed and Merc smiled, "Ok, ok, 1987, there. Honest. It's really cold, please enjoy."

Lilith smiled and said, "Paul ... well, I have this vendetta against all men, you have to forgive me. It is a long story for another time, but you now have my respect. Thank you for being a good sport about the sour drink."

Paul just smiled and quietly agreed and went along with the joke and then drank a long swig of the Corona beer. He was waiting for another joke, but then they laughed again and together said there is nothing wrong with that one.

Merc smiled and said, "So, Paul, we are happy that you have allowed your mind to wander so you can find your own personal inner temple. All you needed was the athame to start to guide you here. This lake house with a huge back patio next to a mirror lake surrounded by gorgeous mountains is your inner temple and unique to your mind and spirit. We are a collection of gods, goddesses, and family members who are here to help you on your journey in this life. We have helped you in your past lives and most of us will help in your future lives." Paul continued to drink and just listened.

Lilith said, "Merc, if you are going to introduce us like that, please be more formal about it so the truth comes out first then bother to introduce who we are." She looked over at Paul, who was content to nurse his beer and just listen. "I am Lilith, Adam's first wife. Much slandered by the authors of the Bible, naturally, since I was the first woman to stand up to God—he actually liked me much better than what was written by those men. Did you know in ancient times women ran the world until organized religion ruined it for us? Since Merc will not introduce himself properly, his real name is Hermes, the winged messenger. Diana will formally introduce herself; she always does. Next to her is Saul and next to him is

Willy, your great-grandfather."

Paul sat quietly and said, "Why are you all here and who chose you to be with me?"

They all smiled at the same time and Merc said, "We have followed your soul and past lives and some of us have swapped out through different ones. Lilith and I have stayed with you for the longest time. In some of your past lives you never communicated and some past lives you communicated multiple times, so we have waited a couple hundred years and two past lives for your soul to come back and meet us. We are also having a small reunion since it has been awhile since we have all gathered here. Well … a couple hundred years Earth-time, but actually in our time reference it has only been a week. Long enough for a reunion."

Paul finished his beer and said, "This inner temple is exactly how I imagined it. I am glad that I'm here and that I know the way to this place, so that I may come back."

Merc tapped Lilith on the shoulder like a proud parent when a son says the right thing in front of the family at a formal gathering. Merc then said, "Paul, from now on you know how to find your inner temple. Please seek and consult us for that is what we are here for. Know that only a chosen few have access and be prepared for persecution if you tell anyone about the inner temple.

"Now that you know the route, the temple is here to show you what you can't see on your own. All we can say is, when you seek the truth inside you and you can't find it on your own, travel back here and we will help you see what you can't see."

Paul heard a sound in the mountains. It was not a natural sound, more like an alarm to wake up sound, and they all laughed again and said, "Amateur. Next time turn all things off to not wake you, but now you know—you are going to be pulled back through the tunnel and tree of life back to the present in a couple seconds. We are real in your mind; do not forget how you got here. So long, my friend, please return soon." As they all waved to him, Paul's body was being pulled out of the cabin, back through the tunnel, back out of the tree of life, and back into the forest and all of a sudden back in his living room on the floor, where his morning alarm was going off in his bedroom.

Paul sat there on the floor of his living room and smiled. He still had the athame in his hand and he still had the taste of the cold Corona in his mouth so he knew it was real to him. He knew everything was aligning for a reason. He felt more assured of his conviction and knew this path he was on in this world; those gods, goddesses, and family spirits were involved to make him learn a lesson and grow in this lifetime.

He just sat there on the floor and started laughing, one of those funny laughs where you can't believe what happened, but it brings so much joy. Those laughs that sound like a snort through every other laugh, a joyous giddy laugh.

"Suil Dhe na gloir, A ghnus Dhe nan dul … the eye of the God of Glory is the face of the God of Life …"

He now knew what the athame was for, that this athame would help him find his gods through his tree of life and his personal inner temple. Then he smirked. *I guess Nera never knew the power or what it was, and if she used this athame to hurt me or anyone I cared for then she would be rightfully spiritually cursed.* He continued to think of the power of this blade and now he knew how important the blade was to him and his new journey.

CHAPTER 13

BOSTON, NORTH AMERICA, 1692

Colonel George Craig, a British officer who had recently served two years in King Williams's war in North America, was taking leave and temporarily living in Boston with his new wife, Phoebe. The senior British officers gave George a four-month furlough to properly be a newly married man. George, in his early forties but still not showing any gray, had been a bachelor for a long time before Phoebe walked into his life at a general store in Albany while he was stationed at Fort Washington. Phoebe was almost fifteen years his younger but they had a generous and playful relationship and she was the vivacious spirit he needed in his life. George did have a drinking issue but not a problem yet; Phoebe had recently begun to tease him about it, but hadn't expressed any real concern. He was a brave officer in the British army and anticipated he'd die in the saddle of service to his dear homeland. He was content. He had love and an honorable service to his country.

George and Phoebe were in their carriage riding through Boston to their new quarters on the outside of town. George liked to be close to town but not in town because there were too many people for his comfort. He did not like all the gossiping. He liked to be in the country in solitude. Phoebe was a beautiful woman, tall and slender, and he still did not know why she accepted him, but he was financially secure and still not too old for making babies, so he was content with her marriage proposal and the possibility of a family with a beautiful woman always ready with a smile and gentle good humor.

He had purchased several acres outside of Boston with a charming and spacious manor house and a staff of two people to assist them with the acres and the house. As a senior officer in the British army, there were required socials and entertaining and he had to have a respectable house and land for his status and rank. Since his bloodline was more Scottish than British, he thoroughly enjoyed eschewing the strict code of elitism in the British officer corps when it pleased him or went against his own common sense. George had already befriended the bartenders and several of the regulars at nearby laborer taverns—something his fellow officers scorned. He would always prefer a conversation with a common man than the hubris of a silver spoon officer. The topics were more enriching with the common man.

As they made that first carriage ride to their new home, George pulled Phoebe close to him and relived the play of events that led to this day. Their first encounter still burned vividly in his mind. A dark-haired woman in a pink gingham dress leaned on the counter of the general store, discussing something intently with the young clerk. A peal of musical laughter rang in the room, and George knew he had to meet this fascinating woman. He stepped up to the counter and she threw him an inquisitive glance, her eyes still warm from the laughter. George forgot what he'd entered the store for. Years on the battlefield, overseeing the placement of artillery, the effects of the landscape, from tree density to hills to waterways and the emplacement of thousands of men throughout— he'd never lost a detail in the midst of the most horrific conditions or in the midst of his own blinding rage of battle. He tipped his hat then cleared his throat. "Johnny, a pint of whisky." The young man had already lain it on the counter, eager to get this competitor for the lady's attention back out the door. George, helpless to this deft maneuvering in a contest he'd never undertaken before, laid his money on the counter and walked back out the door with his package.

Phoebe came from a common family and not from a line of higher blood. George had heard rumors that she talked to spirits and was a healer; no one ever used the word "witch," but there was something different about her that couldn't be denied in spite of her elegant social graces and knack for brightening the parties of the upper crust of

Albany, which would have made her a popular guest even if she wasn't such a draw for the young officers stationed in town. Practical mothers knew that those rejected from a dance with a beautiful woman were often inclined to look about the room and invite another young lady to the dance floor. Phoebe loved her rocks, her crystals, her herbs, and her journals. She loved being out in the woods and working in gardens and if her mixes of herbs helped relieve a cold or an ache, no one seem to be bothered by it.

Phoebe gasped as their carriage curved around a hill and their new home came into view with vivid reds and pinks lighting the sky. George had surveyed the property, but he'd indulged Phoebe's request that they enter the doors together on their first time through them. They stayed up late into the evening, exploring rooms, marveling over the smallest detail, and stopping often just to drink up the sight or touch of each other in their together home. The delight of that first night lasted throughout their months together before George had to return to Albany and Fort Washington. They would hold hands in the city as a sign of their affection to each other. At parties, they were frequently teased for the way their glances and words would tend to tune out everyone else, even in the midst of the most engaging deep conversations or light-hearted banter.

Laughter, affection, and delight marked their first months of marriage. George loved to take his midmorning coffee with the newspaper on the back porch and watch Phoebe skip up the path from a tramp through the woods.

He loved to see the range of her various excitements and delights of discovery at their freshest moment, a fossil, a bird's nest, berries, herbs. He loved how her pace would quicken when she saw him across the distance, how she sat in his lap to show him her new finds or would try to tug him back out to see her discovery out on their land. Everything was working out for them financially, socially, and even sexually. Even in his forties he had had much more experiences in the bedroom than Phoebe in her younger age. Though on his wedding night, he assumed she was not a virgin.

After their four months of married life, George had to go back to the war with the British army and they would be separated again in their marriage. They were both tearful as his men came by on horseback to accompany him north toward the British campaign with the Indians and the French. His men gave him a hard time about leaving such a young and beautiful woman alone, but the servants were there to give her a hand and to protect her if needed. He did not worry about any infidelities that Phoebe would have while he was gone because she was so young and naïve still about things. The perpetual freshness of her delight in their married life would sustain them both through the separation.

As George returned to his regiment and took command and began again pursuing the enemy through fields and forests, he felt himself slide comfortably into a part of himself that he loved much, much more than the trite social world of the city. He knew that soldiering was his talent and he was good at it; it was a natural thing for him to lead. He would be dutiful and try and write Phoebe as much as he could every night from his private tent, but that averaged about one every three days. His entire being was focused on the skills of war. Phoebe wrote less often, but her letters were luxuriously long. The scent of her perfume lasted for weeks on the letters, and he kept them in his pocket, tenderly placing them under his pillow every night, a reminder of who was back home waiting.

After six months of being in combat, George received a letter from Phoebe that she had been invited to a small town in Essex County north of Boston to accompany one of her new church friends who was related to the minister of the town, Samuel Parris. Phoebe was excited to travel with friends to stop being so lonely missing George. George looked up from the letter, remembering recent rumors in taverns and among the men about that town. He knew Phoebe's herblore was harmless, and he hoped that she was not going to accidently fall into the middle of whatever was brewing in the county. He knew her letters of identification as a spouse of a senior British officer could give her additional protection because no one in those parts wanted British officers snooping in their streets and stores asking questions of any stripe. Colony towns were discernably happier when there was less British military presence on their streets. Most of the British elite were unaware of this, and didn't care either way, but George's connection to the common man, and now his common-blood wife and their future common life made him even more invested in staying attune with the zeitgeist of every layer of colony society.

During the first few weeks of her trip, Phoebe wrote more often, her enjoyment of the town and church with her new friends spilling across the pages. She didn't say it, but George knew she was thoroughly enjoying her spotlight in the small upper social class in the Puritan town due to her marriage to George. George knew this was her first experience receiving instant credibility being married to such a senior British officer. He also could read between the lines that her new role and the size of the town meant she wasn't receiving the attention of all the bachelors in the small town like her single friends were. She so wanted the attention. She also wrote about another odd incident that was new to her. Walking into a store, several women were talking about illnesses among the children and how the town could have witches in it. She did not mean to eavesdrop on the conversation, but she could not help herself. She so liked the rumor wheel when it came to women's talking in a small town. In her letter, she was joking and marveling at such an oddity. George felt it was harmless enough, and it lessened his worry to know how her introduction and time in the town was so closely tied to the church and her husband's military status.

After her early accounts of her adjustment to her new life in a new world, George received only a few letters from Phoebe. She sounded fine but he could sense that she was worried about something regarding gossip among the women and although her words were not alarming, they were slightly concerning. Phoebe had always found a way to get into the middle of the gossip of a situation, and even though she was somewhat into the medicinal herbs and mixtures of nature she would never be associated with witchcraft or sorcery. She was too proper and especially with her new marriage to the established military colonel.

Then one letter came to George while he was on the northern British front. Phoebe was now sick in bed and it was more serious than she originally thought. George received permission to go off the front line and have his deputy command for him in his absence while he attended his wife, who was gravely ill. George was concerned as he traveled quickly to Essex County.

George quietly arrived in town on his horse just two days from being notified. The people in the town looked anxious as he rode by and the women especially looked distraught and nervous. He wondered what was going on in this small village to give so many people a look of distress and worry on their faces. He tried to ask a couple of women where the minister's house was located, but they walked away from him as he tried to engage them in conversation. The main part of the village was quiet. Very few people were walking around or in the stores or taverns. The withdrawn demeanor gave George the impression that something grave had just happened. He looked for some official office, found the magistrate, and got off his horse and walked slowly inside. There were several men arguing about something serious as he opened the door and walked into the darkened room. An older man in a black suit with long gray hair to his collar stood from the table, and George saw the man's recognition of his British colonel uniform.

"Colonel, how may we help you?"

George took off his tricorn military hat and slowly walked toward the man. The sounds of his boots across the hardwood floors were the only sounds in the room. "Sir, my name is Colonel George Craig, and I have just come off the front line of the British fight against the French and the Indians to come here and visit my sick wife, Phoebe, who has been staying with the Pastor Samuel Parris." When he mentioned the names of Phoebe and Samuel Parris, the other four men in the room all looked at George in a puzzled manner like his answer just solved a problem that they were trying to figure out. One of the men shook his head and smiled and said, "Well, isn't that interesting."

George looked puzzled. "Gentlemen, is there something you all need to tell me?"

The older man, whom George assumed to be the magistrate of the county, said, "Colonel Craig, it seems your spouse, Phoebe, is in the middle of some witch accusations here in our little township, which has caused some severe anxiousness and fear, due to your spouse's allegations of some young women, that have lived a pure life until now—until your wife's accusations."

The older man introduced himself as Nathanial Saltonstall, the local judge and also a colonel in the local militia. They had a mutual military experience and in the ensuing small talk discovered were both in the British army at the same town in Newcastle years ago. The comfortability of the room was noticeably eased as their talk turned back to the matter at hand.

Nathanial said, "Sir, we did not know Phoebe was married. She never mentioned a husband to the Parris family or anyone else here in town. Unfortunately, she has come down with the smallpox and is in quarantine. A few days before the doctor was called in, she accused some known pre-innocent young girls of conducting sorcery and being witches."

George looked up at the ceiling then said, "Please explain what you mean that Phoebe did not include that she was married." He kept his manner easy, which assured the men somewhat, but it was invariably an uncomfortable situation, and not all of the grins that crossed the men's faces were kind, though they kept their tones respectful.

"Well, sir, she does not wear a ring and she was courting several men in town up until the time she came up with the pox."

George said, "She has been married almost a year to me, but the life of a soldier keeps me at a distance with the latest war going on with the French, and thank goodness the colonists were not uprising against the crown."

Everyone chuckled and said, "God save the king."

Nathanial said, "Well, sir, I hate to inform you, but she acted like a single girl looking for a suitor, and there were at least three known young men who were trying to court her until another young woman named Bridget took the attention of all three men from Phoebe. The children of the pastor are also taken ill, though it's been established it's not the pox."

George said, "Excuse me, sir, I thought you said Phoebe had proclaimed that she was single looking for a suitor here, well, that is upsetting." George's initial feelings while he was courting Phoebe before they were engaged resurfaced. That small voice inside reminded him that she was only using him for access to his connections and his financial security. His love for her, her vivacious attitude, and her youth had impelled him to quiet those voices. These actions that Phoebe had done affirmed that she was not in love with him, but only wanted to luxuriate in his status in society. His friends were right about her; his circle of friends warned him about her motivation, but he wanted to believe that he could fall in love and find happiness. His emotions dropped to a new low realizing that he had been used like no other woman had used him before. He had believed her charm and her words, but they were all fake, her actions were all manipulative, the whole scheme. The color of his face was whitening, and the men looked concerned as he looked for a chair to sit on.

Nathanial said, "Sir, are you all right? You do not look so well."

George just gave a hand signal to give him a minute more before further discussion.

George said, "Gentlemen, I ask on your honor to not tell anyone, especially Phoebe, that I have this information before I see her. I do not want her to know that I know the full truth. I ask you as honorable men to give me that much knowing my new wife lied about being married to me, a dutiful soldier, while she was pursuing other men while visiting this town." He stood up and looked at each of the men in the eye to confirm they would not say anything to anyone because they all somewhat felt sorry for him for serving on the front line and having his young wife then pretend not to be married to him for attention of younger men. The men all nodded their heads as George looked at them. He put on his hat and asked, "Where may I find my sick wife?"

The short man in the corner remarked, "Sir, you will find her in the guest house of the pastor just one mile south of town off the main road, the two-story white house."

The men knew the pox was incurable and that his wife would not last but a couple more weeks or at most a month. They watched as George quietly walked out the door, and the room remained silent for a while due to all the men feeling somewhat sorry for George.

George got on his horse and headed to the pastor's farmhouse.

Once he found the place, it was late afternoon. He would need a place to spend the night, but his first concern was Phoebe. He knocked on the door. A tall, thin proper man opened the door and asked, "May I help you?" and his voice was sullen and sad as if he was distressed.

"Sir, I hate to intrude but my wife, Phoebe, has been staying with you and I received a note from her that she is sick, dire sick."

The pastor said, "Good evening, sir, yes, please

come in, we need to talk about things." George slowly walked into the comfortable farmhouse, and he could see that the pastor had a family as he led George to a study where they could talk.

The pastor introduced himself and said, "Sir, we did not know that Phoebe was married."

George said, "I have been informed and that is not my concern right now. My only concern right now is my wife's health. Could you tell me where Phoebe is?"

"She is sick, sir; it looks like she has the pox. Such a young and beautiful woman, it is surprising she has the disease and how she made contact with anyone with it. The last ship that came into port with cases of the pox was four weeks ago, but all forty-five men of the crew are in quarantine."

The pastor escorted George to Phoebe's isolated room and opened the door to his ill wife sleeping in the bed. George walked into the room quietly, observing that Phoebe had marks on her skin from the pox and that he had to keep a distance. She looked calm and restful. George whispered, "Sir, please leave us alone for a while. I would appreciate to be by her bedside when she awakens."

The pastor quickly agreed and said, "Sir, take as long as you want. She has not had many visitors the last week. I assume she will be happy to see you."

George moved quietly to sit on a chair next to her bed to wait until she awoke. He loved her deeply and was going to ignore the facts about her not informing the town that she was married right now, because her health was a priority. It took a lot for him to convince himself to get married so late in his adventurous life, but she had a way to convince him and to believe in her dreams, and he truly loved her. He could not bear to think of her deceitfulness with her death so near at hand. He wanted to remember her passion and her hopeful love toward him.

He sat in the chair and watched her sleep for at least a couple hours in solitude. As he watched her awaken, he could see her smile that would always weaken him in the knees and put a fire in his heart. No, he could not think about her betrayal to their marriage right now.

As her eyes opened, she smiled at him and said, "George my love, I knew you would come for my rescue, I so love you."

He replied, "My dear Phoebe, I love you too and I got here as soon as I could."

"My beloved, I did a horrible thing. I have been mischievous. I have not been fully honest here, but, my dear, I so missed you but you were not here with me, and I so wanted any attention but you were not giving me any the last couple of months since you were gone. I have done some things I am not proud of here, and I am so sorry. I just wanted attention, I so needed attention. I am so sorry. Could you ever forgive me?"

"Let's not worry about what you have done; let's worry about your health and getting you home." He could see in her exposed skin that the pox was in an advanced stage of exposure, and the prospect of her recovering was slim, so the most important thing he could do for his sanity, love, and compassion was to make her comfortable and think positive.

He went up from his chair and got her a glass of water to drink because she looked thirsty and he brought it to her. She took both hands to hold it and he could tell how weak she had become. George asked kindly, "Love, tell me about your stay here in this town."

Phoebe looked up and asked, "Did you come straight from the line? Have you talked to anyone?"

He just said, "I talked with the pastor when I showed up today, that was all."

She then looked relaxed as if her stress was gone, and she smiled and said, "Well, darling, I had such a great and wonderful time here before I got sick. I was so social, more social than I have been in a very long time, and it was nice to have fun again with girls and so many nice boys. Six months was such a long time to be lonely at our home, that was why I wanted to get away. Go somewhere where I wasn't drowning in loneliness and reminders of you gone everywhere about me. I was the center of attention for a while until one of my friends betrayed me."

He sat back in his wooden chair and smiled and said, "Please tell me more, tell me all about your fun. Let's not worry about the other things. It does not matter right now."

She continued, "Well, I got to go shopping and spend time with women my own age and I have gotten to go to dances and dance for fun again, and it was so much fun and I received so much attention from so many nice boys. There were so many nice boys who taught me new dances, it was so much." She was moving her hands as she was describing the events, and she noticed she was not wearing her wedding ring and felt embarrassed and said, "My dear, can you hand me my purse over there? Since I have been sick, I took off my wedding ring for safekeeping."

He leaned over to the dresser and picked up her purse and handed it to her and she dug in it and found her wedding ring and put it on her finger and said, "Dear, see it is back on my finger where it belongs."

He smiled back trying to hide in his face that he knew she had not worn the ring in weeks; he tried to keep it together and not show his sadness at her words. Her husband was here with her now, and she needed to act like a proper wife. She looked at the ring and smiled back at him and said, "It is the most beautiful ring, and I am so proud to be your wife." Then she coughed really hard and the pain in her neck muscles showed and there was a small drip of blood on her hand from her mouth as she coughed and she felt so embarrassed. George gave his handkerchief to her to wipe the blood from her hand and then he took the cloth back and gently wiped a small portion of blood from the edge of her mouth.

She looked up at him like last year when they fell in love, and his heart warmed and instantly forgave, knowing the disease had gotten into her lungs and her weeks or maybe days were numbered. She said, "Dear, my beloved, could you let me sleep some? I am so very tired and not feeling so well. I am so very tired."

George smiled and got up. "My dear, please sleep and get your rest and we will talk later this evening or tomorrow. I apologize for you to exert so much energy in our discussion. I love you and will be staying in a hotel in town."

She pulled up the covers and rolled over. "George, thank you, you are wonderful and I do not deserve you. Thank you for letting me rest. I do not deserve such a wonderful and faithful man to be my husband. I so do not deserve someone so kind as you. I am sorry for everything that I am putting you through. I am so tired right now; I need to sleep."

George said softly, "I love you, never forget that. Phoebe, I love you more than anyone no matter what you have done. Please do not worry about such petty things." He got up and watched her quietly smile back at him and looked into his eyes and he quietly closed the door as he exited her room.

His step was solemn as he made his way through the hallway into the kitchen. George walked up to the pastor sitting at the dining room table. "Sir, I want to thank you for taking care of Phoebe in my absence. I have been on the British front lines for the last six months. May I compensate you for any expenses you might have incurred while caring for my wife?"

The pastor quietly said, "Sir, would you like some coffee? We have to talk about your wife."

"Sure, some coffee would be nice after such a long

day."

The pastor got up and pulled out two cups and set them on the table and pulled off the coffee kettle from the stove. He poured warm coffee into both cups and sat back down at the table. The kitchen was quiet and it seemed the rest of the house was empty.

"Sir, your wife, Phoebe ... your wife has caused some major concerns in our small town. She has caused some trouble with rumors and accusations of sorcery and other things."

George leaned into the table and said, "Please continue and tell me everything, sir. I need to know every detail of what my wife has said and done."

The pastor continued, "Sir, well, she has made claims that certain women are under a witchcraft spell, witches and sorcerers, and some of these women were her best friends just a few weeks ago. Now it has all changed. There seems to have been a falling out among her girlfriends. From what I could gather, there was intense arguing over several men's attention and then all of a sudden all of these witchcraft accusations that unfortunately are being believed by the townfolk. It's like a spark that lit an ember ready to catch, but eventually this will turn into a fire. Your wife has been fueling a fire of hysteria and panic among the townfolk, especially the young women. I can't prove it but my own children last week had a mysterious fit like a seizure, and she claimed it was a woman, her former friend, that put a curse on them, and these accusations are building and about to get serious. My children have never had these seizures in their lives."

George drank his coffee and listened attentively and said, "That is very troubling. I am worried about her safety and the safety of your children. How serious were the seizures? How long did they last? Please describe them."

The pastor said, "I was scared to death that a demon might have taken over my two daughters. I was so scared of losing them, and I prayed for their lives, but it only lasted a few minutes. I can't really explain the seizures. They were under some spell is what Phoebe claimed and quickly accused her former friend."

George knew many medicinal herb combinations from his travels in Africa, Asia, and the Caribbean, and he knew certain natural herbs and wheats could cause fits and in the voodoo tradition or ancient Asian religion there was a way certain herbs could open the mind to their spiritualty, which could cause something like speaking in tongues, but mostly it was a hallucination. He looked puzzled and knew that he had talked about, showed, and personally taught Phoebe about specific combination of herbs, and he was very concerned over this turn of events. He knew that a certain darkened rye could contain a fungus. The rye looks like wheat and could be put in flour for normal bread with none the wiser. The nickname of its effect was called Saint Anthony's fire because this rye could cause severe convulsions, muscle spasms, delusions, and sensations of crawling under the skin, and most important, hallucinations. He desperately wanted it to turn out that she would never do such a terrible thing. He asked, "Sir, I must immediately look through Phoebe's clothes trunks and all of her personal things," so that he could look through them for the poisoned rye kernels that might have caused the pastor's daughters' seizures.

The pastor said, "We brought all of her things out of the room a couple days ago once she looked like she could have the pox. We had to take precautions to save the rest of my family."

George said, "Could I look at them now? It is critically important that I look through them now and it might solve our problem. There are no guarantees, but it would put my heart at ease if I could look through her things."

The pastor got up from his chair and led George to a back room where Phoebe's personal belongings were and then stepped out of the room to give George privacy. As George opened up all the trunks and suitcases, he looked for some bag of rye seeds or other herbs. Within a minute, he found what he did not want to find. In the corner of her trunk lay a large linen bag, like a small pillowcase. His stomach dropped and churned with fear and dread. He stared at it, dreading what was inside. But he opened it up to confront the truth, and he saw the spoiled darkened black rye and then he smelled it to confirm that this was the poisonous rye that could cause convulsions and seizures. George was so saddened and his grief deepened. It was a hard blow to realize her betrayal of their marriage.

To think his love would so hurt others staggered him, wounded him to the core of who he was. There was one last hope that this wasn't incontrovertible evidence of her sin, so he had to ask one last question, "Sir, has Phoebe made bread for your family?"

The pastor said, "Yes, often. One time she made a special bread for my daughters, but something was peculiar and she insisted to not let the rest of the family eat from it. That was odd, but since she was a guest in our house, we agreed to her requests. It seemed strange but harmless that she'd make bread specifically for my daughters, so we didn't think much of it and complied."

George just looked down onto the floor in great sadness, his heart heavy with grief and disgust. He then had to think if he should disclose this key incriminating information about Phoebe, because it could cause more trouble for his beloved dying wife. He decided not to divulge any of it to the pastor, but to keep it all a deep dark secret; he thought this was the only option he had for his own personal situation and most important for his wife's last few days on earth. The girls were fine, and Phoebe could no longer harm anyone. "Sir, thank you, it was not what I thought it was, never mind, thank you, but could I take my wife's things with me to the room I am renting in town, so they are in safekeeping?"

The pastor said, "It is only right for you to take charge of your wife's things. My son will help you transport them to your room. The doctor has concluded your wife has the pox and we would recommend you dispose of her belongings."

George knew the protocol and knew the worries that the disease could be carried by clothes and personal items. George decided on staying here in this town while Phoebe lived her last days to make her comfortable. He would not divulge what he knew about the rye to the pastor or to anyone and he would never bring it up to Phoebe. He would let events happen the way they would, but knowing that Phoebe would be gone before any trouble manifested in this strange and gloomy town.

He spent the next day listening to Phoebe tell him her adventures during her travels and all the social events and all the people that she had met. She once accidently said she met a man from one of the local ships and they had a wonderful intellectual discussion but he never inquired any more than knowing that the man gave her the pox. He knew that they would have had to be physically close for her to have been infected, but he tried to keep her last days happy. She did admit that she was angry with one of her friends over the attention of several young men and that she did something she regretted but she did not say what it was. She said it did not matter in the end. Life was not fair that she got the pox and her friends did not but the look in her eyes showed she hoped they received worse.

His evening discussions with the pastor were more troubling as he found out more of what Phoebe had done while staying with them. She did make bread for his daughters, and the next day they had seizures and were not acting normal. She did flirt with multiple men in town and there were rumors she was seen with many non-Puritan men in her adventures at not so good establishments for a woman, let alone a married woman. There was rumors also that she told people that she knew who were witches and who were not in the town to a point people believed her. The pastor had even seen Phoebe in the woods alone acting ceremonial in her prayers to God, a non-orthodox way. The pastor was terribly sorry that Phoebe had come across the smallpox, but he was not all that sad in seeing bad things happen to her. He showed great sadness and remorse, but there was some due pain toward Phoebe for not living God's way. The pastor's intuition had been right about Phoebe the whole time. The pastor was glad George had arrived and now no strange men would dare visit Phoebe in his house.

Phoebe passed away three days after George arrived. He spent every day by her side. He buried her after a small and quiet funeral in an unmarked grave up on a hill looking over the town. It was a quiet place under a grove of trees. He also burned her belongings and all the darkened rye so there would never be a trace of what Phoebe did to several young women to make them have convulsions. George did keep her personal diary. He would read it later when he could emotionally be ready to acknowledge her true self.

George left the town before the small embers of societal fear grew into a panic of accusations, and he never divulged his wife's deceitful actions and how she fully started the first domino in the chain of horrible events of this future historic town.

George left the town alone after only a week but with enough pain to last a lifetime. His beloved wife had only been married to him for thirteen months before she died but he thanked her in spirit for his short happiness and he tried to make her last days as comfortable as possible in spite of all her deception. George believed everyone deserved a dignified death no matter what deceitful things they had done in their life. He rationalized that her actions were due to her youth and inexperience and hoped she was not deceitful in her pure nature.

George returned to the war and was later a regional British hero and had a farm with land and notoriety to last himself a lifetime. His guilt on what his wife had started in that small Essex County town stayed with him the rest of his life and his later years of alcoholism was his method of curing the pain.

A year after Phoebe's death, George finally did open up and read her diary. He read about how much she loved him and how he had changed her life for good but then he also read how she was working with stones, crystals, and herbs, and he read her chants and rituals to gods and goddesses. His concern and memories were recalled, when he read how she was pretending to be single again because she only married George for his money and his position in authority. His heart sank and saddened, and he continued to read how she fell in love with other men in the town and one handsome sailor who might have the pox. She also talked about how she loved another man but her friend won him which upset her greatly and her jealousy took her over so she purposively used the poison rye to make the young girls go into convulsions and then she sneakily told some political officials under confidence that her friend was a witch. She described the things in great detail. One of her last writings was how joyous she was when her friend was accused of witchcraft and was going to go to jail so that she could have the man she was pursuing all to herself. Her deceitful plan worked somewhat, but her last journal entry was: "Today, I feel sick and the doctors have isolated me in the pastor's house. I now realize that I have come down with the pox and that I need my beloved George. My George would protect me, if the county authorities would try to investigate my doings because they are becoming suspicious. If they try and search my belongings, they might find my rye. If George, my fool husband, would come here, the townfolk would not dare have the authorities or sheriff accuse me or investigate me, not with my fooled husband, a senior British officer, yes, George would save me, he was such a fool. I was so good in pretending that I loved him. I shall write him and he will drop everything to be here by my side. I will write the most saddened letter so he will be here so quickly. I know if he learns I was pretending not to be married he will be disappointed but he will quickly forgive me if I bat my brown eyes and act kind to him. So gullible! It is so good that he is wealthy or I would never would have married him. The pastor wants to talk again to me tonight, I think he is suspicious of me. I so hope

George comes to my aid soon before they find out about me."

George was so sad and depressed as he finished the pages of Phoebe's journal and realized how she really was in her heart. But she did marry him under God, and he had kept his honorable oath to be a devoted husband until death and he was by her side on her last days of life. He was an honorable man and maybe the greatest fool of all because he kept his promise of marriage as a husband. He kept the book as a valuable memory when he thought he could fall in love again and was always shy and quiet in regard to women. George remained a noble soldier and a kind churchgoer and philanthropist, even though he increasingly turned to drink to help him sleep and forget.

At the age of fifty, George's life was somewhat saved when he met a much younger woman named Samantha, who filled him with love, life, and passion again that he thought he had lost forever. She was nineteen years younger, only just turned thirty, but had a love for life and was so adorable that it made him happy just to be in her presence. She was not into money or status, and she didn't care what others thought about her. She was an independent artist at heart and full of love. They were friends first and he knew she cherished their friendship and talks and walks in nature. He married her after two years of courting and many years of friendship, and they made each other happy. This beauty of life had a way of seeing through George's walls and seeing the real him and she worked with him through all of the dark pain that Phoebe had caused him. George and Samantha lived together for the next twenty-five years on his small farm in Pennsylvania and he loved her the rest of his days.

Chapter 14
Two Days Later

Paul walked through the chilly, overcast evening into downtown. It had been two days since he had talked with Nera, and they were about to meet again in the quiet library room at Casaneta's. He purposely tried to arrive early, but she was already there, sitting on the couch with a glass of red wine. No fashion jeans with matching expensive blouse and no made-up hair or full makeup, she sat there in jeans and a t-shirt with no makeup, looking plain and disheveled. He could tell something was different in her expressions and her mood.

Paul walked over to Nera. "Hello, thank you again for meeting me tonight."

She merely smiled. "You are welcome, it has been a tough last twenty-four hours for me."

Paul sat down in the plush, faded easy chair next to

her couch. Nera looked up at him with saddened brown eyes. The skin around her eyes was reddened and swollen, as if she'd been crying for days. The depth and sincerity of hurt in her eyes as they made eye contact sent Paul into thoughts on why she would have been so upset, because she had somewhat been in control of all the visits they had had so far since they met less than a week ago. Nera was now vulnerable at this moment—or seemed to present it that way—something had internally shaken her.

"Nera, you promised that you would tell me about the athame. I need to know why you gave it to me and why you had it. I don't have strangers every day give me an antique dagger that has Thebian and Celtic inscriptions on it."

She looked at him gently like, releasing some type of stress and curious on how he would know so much. Half grinning, she said, "You have certainly done your homework again. I guess I underestimated your ability to do research on artifacts and witchcraft. Just give me a few moments to collect myself. I'm not quite ready to jump into it. Can we talk simple stuff for a while and then I will tell you the rest of the story about the athame and why I gave it to you? Would that be ok? We might be here a while."

Paul merely said, "That would be perfect. Let's warm up the brain cells with red wine so we are more open to metaphysical and spiritual thoughts." He said that to counter her mysterious statements that had bothered him for the last two days and to challenge her with the rest of the story because he had done his homework, and even had another session with Lena to somewhat prepare himself for this next couple of hours of conversation with Nera. Over two glasses of wine each, they talked about the town, the university, their careers. The conversation was light, but there was no laughter.

Finally, Nera set her empty wineglass down with a sense of deliberate purpose. "Did you bring it with you?"

He replied, "No, it is wrapped up in my office, very safe."

"Well, you are right that it is an athame, a ceremonial witchcraft knife, a special knife, a magical knife, possibly a cursed knife. You seem to already know what the inscriptions are, so let me tell you where I got it and why I had to give it to you. Paul, I am a practicing witch. I am not a bad witch, not like anything you've seen in the movies, not Glinda or Ursula. The women in my family have been Italian gypsy witches since at least the 1500s. I do not know who my father was because my mom was a hippy in California and got around a lot. One day she was pregnant and none of the countless men raised their hand that she had slept with; so, she just raised me as a single parent. My mom later married a guy who would become my stepfather. Growing up in California, my mother was always into herbs and into cats and we always had people visiting the house and doing socials outside with campfires. When I went to bed, they would still be outside singing, drinking, and smoking until late at night. They would always say 'blessed be' and other sayings that I took as normal but were not. I thought all families were like mine, especially in California."

Nera continued to explain, "We always had Tarot cards and Oracle cards out, and crystals and stones were all over the house, especially on the tables and the windowsills. I just thought everyone had these items. As I grew into my late teens, I would find journals and notebooks and pieces of paper with spells and Celtic runes and witch artwork in them and lots of sage, so much sage, in the house. Then one day after high school graduation my mother told me she was a practicing witch, and it was time for my initiation. I was destined to be a witch, but I wasn't ready and I ran off to a local college and was confused for the next two years. But being confused and on my own helped me sort some stuff out. I started my witchcraft classes when I was twenty, the real witchcraft classes. After a year and a day of classes, I was initiated into witchcraft in the family coven. I became an official and real witch."

Paul just sat there a little confused but not afraid. With everything else going on, he was not surprised at the information though he allowed some surprise to show on his face, but really, he was not. He politely asked, "What about the athame?"

Nera collected her thoughts and reengaged. "One night while I was giving a psychic reading to a customer, a stranger came in and waited in the next room for my current client to be done. She was dressed in fine clothes and had a scarf over her head and asked to sit down.

"This strange woman asked, 'May I have a past life reading?' and I said yes and then the strange woman gripped my arm, closed her eyes, and started chanting. I was a little afraid and did not know if she was acting, but then she looked at me and said, 'Young woman, you are the reason I am here. I know who you are, who you really are in your past lives. You are evil and dark. You pretend to be white but you are black and evil. You are more dark than white, you can't hide from your evilness, your true darkness, your deceitfulness.'

"I started to try and get out of her hold on my arm, but the woman continued, 'You are the one who tried to kill my love, you are the one who sent innocent women to the stake, you are the one who lied to the church authorities. You are the darkest one, you spend your current life hiding from facing and owning your past.

"'This magical artifact you took in a past life without permission, this now belongs to you with the curse that is carried with it.' Then she pulled out the white wrapped linen and laid it onto the table. And she said quietly, 'Now you, Nera, must find the one that you stole it from in a past life or you will continue to be cursed.' And she got up, wrapped her scarf around her head, and left the place leaving me completely drained."

Nera looked at Paul with saddened brown eyes, almost heartbroken. She sat up in her chair and collected her thoughts as she looked around the room and a soft tear slowly ran down her cheek.

Paul drank some of his wine and let her collect

herself and control her emotions then asked, "What did the woman mean when she said you were dark?"

"Paul, I am a witch and I have been a witch in many past lives as a white and dark witch, and I have been going to many psychic readers to pull out those past lives, the white and the dark, but I can't recollect them. The psychic readers have had many difficulties because I am emotionally and psychologically blocked for some reason. There are past lives that are blocked, memories that have not been opened. I feel like the victim here. I did not decide to do any of this. I swear I am not dark. I am a white good witch."

Paul asked, "So how did I get involved? Why me?"

Then she looked up into his eyes and softly stared at him almost seductively and said, "I had a dream about someone whose father died, who had past lives with me. The dream reoccurred many nights, and when I saw the obituary of your father in the paper, I knew that it must be you.

"When I contacted you, over e-mail, I thought it might spark a past life emotion, but it did not, and then when I shook your hand at your father's funeral, I thought when our hands touched it might reconnect if we had a past life together, but I guess it didn't. My intuition insisted I bring the athame to you, so I came by your office that evening. I never meant to make you feel like I was stalking you. The dreams started a week ago, my head is spinning. It all makes me feel crazy inside ... I feel like I am losing my mind and losing control of my thoughts."

Paul somewhat relaxed at realizing they were both equally overwhelmed at the events of the past week. The way you feel when all of a sudden you are thrown into a raging river, and you have a life vest on but you can't reach the shore, no matter how hard you kick. You can either exhaust yourself trying, or relax, stay above water, and wait for the river to carry you to calmer waters.

Nera started to softly cry in her chair, the soft very deep cries of a person who wants to give up on life and the stressors around them are overwhelming. Paul reached over and touched her shoulder to console her, and there was a small shock of static electricity, which he thought was odd because there wasn't any carpet or fabrics in the room that would have caused that. As he kept his hand on her shoulder, thoughts and images started to flow into his head, random images and situations, like watching a fast-forward movie, but going too fast to comprehend.

Nera slowly looked at him with eyes full of tears. "I believe we have both been thrown into this crazy situation together by the cosmos and I think we can help each other out of this frightening situation. Could we work together to find the solution so this craziness will go away?"

She sat next to him on the couch in the room and reached out and held his hand. She said, "I feel alone, and I have no one I can trust. I need your help."

Paul touched her other hand and looked at her and agreed to help her because he thought he really had no other choice in the current situation. He consoled her on the couch and was in a whirl of emotion. It was automatic for him to do the simple, honorable thing and console a woman in need. He understood better now how Nera was involved but the question of the athame was not fully resolved. He needed to know who the woman was that gave Nera the athame and why.

They sat there, leaning into the simple comfort of touch, and decided a third glass of wine was a good idea, either to help the situation or to help forget the situation. The third glass of wine lowered their inhibitions and Nera became more open and extremely flirty in her mannerisms as the conversation turned to a more intellectual discussion of witchcraft. Nera asked if they could go on a walk, that after three glasses of wine it was time to go home. She said she lived just three blocks from Casaneta's. As they paid the bill, Paul held out his elbow and they entwined arms to help each other from looking intoxicated walking through downtown. She kept rubbing against him and stumbling a little where he assisted in getting her to walk more vertical and not look so drunk. They arrived at her townhouse and he was pulling out his phone to call a cab, when she said, "My husband is gone. Would you care for one more drink and I will tell you more what you seek?"

Paul watched as she fumbled with the keys to her townhouse door and opened the door and he hesitated to walk in, debating if it was a good idea. He knew she knew more about the mysteries that were storming in his life but that she was not fully divulging. Yet Lena's words about staying away from her echoed in his mind. Whether it was the alcohol talking or the curiosity of the moment, he followed her.

As they walked into the townhouse, Nera stumbled again, leaning fully on Paul to rescue her but they both fell on the floor, she on top of him, in an awkward moment, she just sat on him. He looked up at her, and then she rolled off of him, and decided to take off her shoes and walked to the bar for another glass of wine. Paul shook his head, wanting to decline another glass but if it could help to get more information from her, he was going to walk into the drunken darkness tonight. They both slowly held up another glass of wine together when Nera came up with an idea. "We have to conduct a magick circle now, right now, to call the Goddess Diana, to seek the answers we are searching for. Paul, I want you to sit on the floor right there in the middle of the living room."

Nera went to her desk and pulled out some stones and some crystals and set them in a circle around Paul as he sat on the carpet. She seemed somber and a little bit regal as she told Paul to be silent and started to construct the sacred magical circle.

Paul thought about leaving, a sacred circle was an unknown to him, and he was very drunk, but that urge to discover the truth kept him still and silent on the floor. He intuitively knew she was withholding key information— his body just knew it.

Nera stood straight up and said, "Paul, we are calling this sacred circle to find the answers you seek." Standing facing the front door of the townhouse, she chanted in a low melodic intonation, no evidence of intoxication in her movement or speech, "I call the Guardian of the East and the element of Air to watch over this sacred circle," and she placed a stone on the ground, then she turned to her right and chanted, "I call the Guardian of the South and the element of Fire to watch over this sacred circle," then placed another stone. Facing the back wall of the house, she chanted, "I call the Guardian of the West and the element of Water to watch over this sacred circle" and then placed a third stone. Facing the final wall, she said, "I call the Guardian of the North and the element of Earth to watch over this sacred circle," and she placed the fourth stone. Sedately stepping into the middle of the circle, less than a foot from Paul, her voice deepening in intensity, she said, "I call upon the spirit of the universe to watch over this circle, fill it with love, peace, and divinity." She sank to the floor, gracefully arranging herself so that their knees touched, and she said, "Thank you, thank you, the circle is cast, blessed be."

They sat on the floor facing each other, crisscrossed legs, knees touching, and she grabbed both of Paul's hands and looked straight into his eyes. "Paul, I am going to call on the Goddess Diana for assistance for both of us, to seek the answers we need."

Paul had no idea what she was talking about, but the practiced grace of her calling the circle sparked his curiosity for this next part of a witchcraft ritual. He watched how she completely relaxed her body for a few breaths before becoming more alert like she'd received a message, tilting her head slightly to one side. Nera twitched and shook and held his hands strongly and then she said, "William, what do you seek?"

"My name is Paul, not William." The complete shift in the pitch and cadence of her voice threw him as much as the wrong name.

"What do you seek, William?"

Paul decided to let it go and get to what he wanted to know. "Why is the athame in my life now? Why did Nera give it to me?"

"I am Diana. Nera can't hear us now, this conversation is between you and me, love. The athame killed you once in a past life. The hand that held the blade was Nera in one of her past lives. The woman used it for evil and so Nera is cursed. The consequences are hers to bear. She has not told you the whole story. Do not trust her, because her heart is dark. Hear my words, do not trust her. She does not know what I am telling you now, you must not tell her."

Paul leaned in closer to Nera's face to hear the last words, hoping for more information than vague warnings, but as Paul leaned in, Nera opened her eyes. She looked a little dazed, but when she made eye contact with Paul, her eyes immediately sharpened. "What just happened?" She sounded eager and curious. Such an emotional shift would have been hard to fake. After just a few conversations with Nera, Paul felt confident that he had a good read on when she was lying. Decades worth of students and office politics had trained his intuition well. Still, it was a lot to take in, that just a moment before some spirit or something was telling Paul not to trust the very person who called the spirit into her body. All of this was new and hard to comprehend but deep inside it felt so familiar.

Paul sat there, trying to process all of this new information, when it hit him. This felt completely normal. Sitting here between four rocks, centering his mind and spirit with ritual words, reaching out to invisible forces for answers felt as natural as a day teaching or a weekend hiking or tooling around with one of his mechanical projects in the garage. The whole experience of the circle felt like any other activity he'd performed dozens upon dozens of times across his life.

Nera let go of Paul's hands, her demeanor returning a bit to how she looked at the beginning of the evening. Once again, she looked oddly vulnerable, her incredible sense of self-possession gone. Catching and holding eye contact with Paul, she asked, "What did I say? I felt like I was gone but I lost a sense of time. What happened … you must tell me."

Paul realized that he could not be honest and he had to lie to her because he was slightly afraid and actually trusted the message from the so-called Diana voice. He said, "Nera, you did not say anything to me, I promise. You just sat there dazed."

Nera looked at him and insisted, "You have to tell me the truth. Please, I am in turmoil and must know if Diana gave you a message!"

Paul gently said, "Nera, there was no message. You have had too much to drink, you did not say anything … I think you need to go to bed." Paul slowly started to uncurl his legs to stand up.

Nera grabbed his hand and pleaded, "There was no message?"

"No, there was no message."

Paul helped her up off the floor and assisted the drunken Nera to her bedroom where she collapsed on her bed. She seemed to fall asleep the second she laid down, her breathing slowing and deepening within a few breaths. He found a blanket near her bed and gently covered her up. She was going to have a terrible headache, having likely drunk two bottles of wine across the evening. As he turned around in the bedroom toward the door, Paul noticed some unusual items on her dresser. There were occult items, like figurines of witches in black pointed hats, figurines of a gingerbread house, odd crystals and stones. As he paused to absorb the array of items, he noticed an athame. It looked similar to the one at his house, only much older and more brittle. He thought about looking more, but decided to leave Nera's townhouse while she was still asleep. He slowly walked out of the bedroom, turned off the light, and walked out through the living room, locking her front door before walking out onto the dark street just a few blocks outside of downtown.

Paul had had about as much wine as Nera. He hadn't driven into town. Normally he would call a cab, but he felt that he could handle a twenty-minute walk. As he started toward home, he was sharply reminded of all the other times he'd stumbled home drunk in the middle of the night the years after his wife died. The pain of her death still hurt. She was so young. He had spent almost every night drinking for years after she died as a way to appease the pain of the loss. His best friend. Gone. The alcohol had been a friend, delaying the realization that she would never be by his side anymore. He hadn't been ready to face that until several years after her death. Somehow, the way the wind blew, or the way the houses looked on the streets reminded him of that first night of struggling to survive minute to minute after his best friend, daily companion, beloved wife passed. Paul had closed down the bar that night, drinking steadily in a corner of the room, afraid to be alone, but afraid to talk to anyone lest the hole in his heart rip open wider. His father was dead. His brothers and mother, dead. Of all his family, he was the last one left to live. The shock, the pain flooded Paul's body. He dropped to the curb, a block from his home. Sobs wracked his body. His whole body shuddered uncontrollably. At first, he tried to stay silent, but it was too much effort. Paul let the pain have its way with him.

The sky, dense with clouds, started letting loose freezing drops of rain. Paul felt comforted by the icy water, thinking that God was crying with him. He did not know why life was so painful to him. But he had inner toughness, he had survived so many funerals of friends and family. So many friends, dead in war. Family, lost to illness. The pain of years of death and sorrow avalanched through his being, unleashed from some hidden space inside him. Paul sat in the rain, huddled on a curb, crying out to God, asking questions he'd never dared to ask before, his heart shouting a pained and frantic defiance against the flood of grief and anguish: *why me, why should I have to suffer so much?* Why was so much pain living in his heart? Where were the joy and love, had they died forever, suffocating under ever-greater burdens of heartache?

Paul tipped over, curling up on the sidewalk, his body an empty puddle. Let the rain devour him. Maybe he would get hypothermia and die tonight, if the rain couldn't dissolve his body and flow down a storm sewer. His cheeks stung with the icy cold of the water. Years of loss. Weird mysteries and ancient knives and witches and Oracle readers speaking for his dead father. It was all too much. Paul longed to fall asleep, and stay asleep, never waking back up into this awful madness called living. As his head was on the concrete and the rain splashed on the sidewalk drenching him, he saw a man in a raincoat holding an umbrella walking toward him smoking a long pipe; it was like the character of Gandalf from *Lord of the Rings*. Or maybe he had too much to drink. It didn't matter. Paul closed his eyes. He heard a voice getting closer to him. Blearily, he realized the voice was calling his name.

"Paul? Where have you been?"

Paul didn't know. His body ached with loss and the cold.

Robert walked up to Paul. He poked his back with a toe. No response. Robert sighed in pity and exasperation before yelling, "Paul, I have solved the puzzle of the athame!!"

Paul continued to slumber on the sidewalk soaked wet to the bone, his hair wet on the concrete and so cold, but he heard the words "solved the puzzle" and his subconscious mind slowly woke him up and his mind became curious again of the present moment and he opened his eyes to Robert, "How did you solve the problem?"

Robert leaned over Paul, lowering his umbrella to dump rain into Paul's face to wake him up. "You will have to walk with me to my house and have a cup of tea before I will tell you. This is not the place to discuss such important events in a cold rain, drunk on the curb." Robert smiled and glanced around the street as if to say he had the answers but was not going to tell in this weather when a warm fire and cup of tea are just around the corner. Paul remembered how nice a cup of tea in Robert's comfy chairs by a crackling fire was. Paul exhaled the air he'd been holding in his lungs. He tried to sit up. Robert gripped his arm and pulled him to his feet. Wordlessly, Robert threw his arm around Paul's shoulder, holding the umbrella over their heads as they lurched down the street.

Paul felt a dull sense of gratitude well up in his misery-encrusted heart. Robert had somehow taken care of him again. Remembering Robert's patience and good cheer and gentle honesty in the years after his wife's passing, Paul started crying again. When you are drunk on a sidewalk wanting to end it all, friends like that are gold.

As the two friends walked on the sidewalk in the

cold rain, Paul realized Robert was walking him home to his own place so he could fall asleep in his bed. As they entered Paul's driveway, Paul, in a drunken stupor, said, "Robert, were you just messing with me to get me home and save my life or were you telling me the truth that you solved the problem?"

Robert gently opened the door to Paul's house and said, "Paul, my dear friend, not all who wander are lost. Just like a good professor would, to leave with a riddle, yes, Paul, I solved the problem of what you have and the rest of the story, but you are not in a condition to truly enjoy the revelation so I must delay until tomorrow when you are not so drunk. I will see you tomorrow. Sleep well, my friend."

Robert gently got Paul inside his house and on his couch and put a blanket on him, and Paul quickly passed out. Robert knew he would wake with anticipation of what he had found on the athame. Robert quietly left the house and locked the door behind and departed back to the bar where the bartender, Scott, had called him after Paul left the bar accompanied by Nera. Scott knew Paul and his other regulars very well regarding drinking, and knew the condition Paul was in, leaving the bar with a strange, equally drunk woman. The small community of friends for Paul had deep roots because of all the loss he had experienced over the last couple of years. Everyone looked after everyone in this small town. Scott did not trust Nera from his first impression of her interaction with Paul and that was the main reason he called Robert. Working in a bar for a couple decades had made Scott a quick and very accurate judge of character. He hadn't seen Paul that drunk since the year after his wife died. And it wasn't the kind of drunk of young love. It reminded Scott too much of that dark long year.

Robert returned to the bar after walking Paul home to thank Scott and to have a last drink for the night since he knew the bar would be full of good friends. Robert wanted Scott to tell him what had happened and discuss who this Nera person was that could mean trouble for their friend Paul.

Chapter 15
Chasing Ghosts

As Paul woke up with a terrible hangover and blurry images of sleeping in the rain, he realized he was on his couch with some damp clothes on and he could smell wine on his breath. He closed his eyes, trying to recollect the evening's events, but couldn't get his mind in gear. Maybe some coffee would help. Slowly opening his eyes again, he noticed that the sunlight was flooding the living room. He squinted at his watch. 11:15. Paul laid back down and closed his aching eyes. He hadn't slept in that late in at least twenty years. Definitely too much to drink last night.

His rule was to stop at two drinks in public, but in private he would stop at four drinks. He found his coffee maker and slowly tried to make coffee but his head was aching terribly and it took all his effort to pour the ground coffee into the filter for that essential cup of morning coffee to help make his headache go away. He had not felt this bad since his infamous tequila and darts all-nighter in the university dorms back when he was twenty years old, almost twenty-eight years ago. His last taste of tequila. This time he knew he just had too many glasses of wine. As the smell of coffee wafted into his nose, bits and pieces of the previous evening's conversations with Nera crept into his brain. The odd vulnerability. The idle pleasantries. The walk to her house. The magical circle, how familiar and comfortable that experience was. Realizing he was receiving a message from a goddess. That Nera hadn't heard it. Keeping the truth of the message from her.

He then recollected the walk out of the condo and the rain and then lying on the sidewalk and his good friend Robert finding him and getting him home. As his memory was coming back with the first sip of the coffee elixir, he noticed a big yellow note from Robert next to the coffee machine.

My dearest friend Paul,

When awake and sober,

> **And after 2 cups of coffee,**
>
> **A hot shower,**
>
> **call me when ready,**
>
> **I solved our problem!**
>
> **PS, you were a stupid drunk last night.**
>
> **You, so owe me!**

Robert, your dearest friend

PSS. We have to discuss the woman you were with.

Paul drank another sip of coffee and thanked God for the dear friends he had in his life. He plopped back onto the couch, still in damp clothes, just savoring the hot coffee and his good friends. His full recollection was coming onboard with every sip of coffee and the feeling of being alive was creeping back into his flesh.

After two cups of coffee Paul stripped off his damp clothes and threw them in the washer and walked naked across his house to shower. As the bathroom steamed up with the heat and Paul slowly cleaned and tended to his aching body, a familiar post-hangover ritual, he let his mind work over all the events and thoughts of the last few days, organizing all the clues and bits of information leading up to the magic circle with Nera last night. Some clues were coming together and others seemed more complicated but he knew now more about the athame and that it was actual a part of one of his past lives.

As he came out of the shower and started drying off, he went over to his desk to write a note on his sticky pad. The MacGregor invitation to Scotland lay on his keyboard. Paul picked it up. At this point it was only a week away. All of the rooms were probably full. But a part of him longed to get away, to rest and clear his mind. He put the invitation back on his computer keyboard to remind him to call once he got dressed. He had nothing to lose by at least calling. But, first thing first: he owed a good friend an apology. And maybe a nice bottle of Scotch, that was a cold rain last night.

He called Robert but got his answering machine. Robert used his thirty-year-old answering machine with the old mini tape deck with 1970s apologetic response on why he was not home that was in fashion only in the '70s. The message had not changed since 1988, and Paul left a message letting him know that he was available the rest of the day for consultation and that he greatly appreciated their friendship and thanked him again for helping him out of the so-called gutter last night. As usual, the beep was too early and so only half the message recorded but Robert would know what wasn't said.

Paul went back to his computer to check if any rooms were still available at the MacGregor reunion. There were, so he went ahead and reserved a room for himself and then scoped out airline tickets and found a discount code for an airline straight to Scotland with a reasonable price so he reserved a seat and then realized that he just booked a ticket and hotel to Scotland, leaving in less than a week. It was so spontaneous, so unlike him. He had the money to do it and he needed to get away. He needed the break. His ancestors were from Scotland and he always wanted to visit, and this invitation to the MacGregor reunion was almost the perfect excuse to jump and go to Scotland. As he thought about what he just did, he realized that he was being pulled to Scotland

and this trip might also connect the dots and continue to solve this spiritual journey he'd found himself on. He just needed to go to Scotland. That was that, it was done, he was going to Scotland.

As he sat at his desk reflecting on his intuition, his emotional needs, and this spontaneous decision to fly to Scotland, he felt good about taking a risk and making a decision to follow through on his intuition, which was telling him to go. He sat there proud of himself on following his inner wisdom to make the leap of faith. Then he was reminded about Robert's note and looked for his phone to try and call him again. He looked across his desk and found his cell phone and saw that Robert had texted him to meet him at the anthropology department storeroom annex where they kept artifacts that were waiting for a museum. He'd heard from faculty that it was one big storage room of museum trinkets and fun to explore. The annex was once a storage room built in the 1920s before WWII and rumored to have a nuclear safe storage area. The exterior still looked like a large carriage house from the 1920s. Paul, now in a great mood, picked up his keys, took a final drink of his cold coffee, and walked out the door.

Paul drove up to the anthropology annex behind the university museum and saw Robert sitting by his 1965 convertible Jaguar, a James Bond car from the Sean Connery period not the Roger Moore era. Robert was smiling and leaning against his sports car. Paul drove up, got out of his car, and said, "Robert, I did not know you were getting the classic car out for this special occasion."

Robert chuckled and said, "Well, the weather is beautiful and the car just wanted out of the garage one more time before winter arrives. Now, Paul, let's go inside. I have something to show you." Robert had a key code to get through the warehouse door and they walked into the darkened warehouse. There were few lights but boxes and crates were everywhere.

Paul just laughed. "Robert, how can you find anything in this building?"

Robert chuckled again too. "Well, we all know where all the important stuff is and the security is really good especially to where we are going and what I am about to show you." They continued to walk through a small aisle toward a steel swinging door that looked like a bank vault, but Paul could tell it was newly installed and fully modified even with its appearance of just an old vault. Robert walked to another access panel and when he pushed in the numbers two electronic devices opened up. He put his thumbprint on one and his eye on the other and a blue light scanned both at the same time. There was a green light with letters that said, "Confirmed identification. Welcome, Dr. Robert." The door creaked and slowly clicked multiple mechanisms before opening.

Paul was amazed about this secure device inside a university anthropology annex on a liberal college campus in the Midwest. He had no idea this existed.

They entered the corridor, which was lighting up as they walked in and down the hallway. A computer voice said, "Welcome, Robert. Hope you are having a good day."

Paul guessed it was an AI computer voice from a main frame. He kept thinking of HAL from *Space Odyssey*, where the computer would not let the astronauts back on board the spacecraft. The door closed behind them and Paul jumped a little, but they kept walking. As they walked, the lights came on just in front of them and then turned off once they were past, like walking with a flashlight.

"Alex, I am doing fine. Thank you for asking. I enjoy your new voice. I should only be here about thirty minutes. This is my friend Paul. Please do facial recognition on him for if he does return to your home in the future, I vouch for him and will escort him to Area 23."

The computer voice said, "Thank you for the compliment, Robert. It is always a pleasure to talk with you. I acknowledge. Mr. Paul's facial scan is now complete. Dr. Paul, welcome to the annex, codename OSCAR, my home."

"Robert, what the hell is this ... and, well, what the hell is this?" Strained nerves showed up in Paul's voice despite his best efforts.

Robert just laughed. "Well, Paul, while you teach education classes to students on the theory of education and psychology from famous authors like Brookfield, a few of us old guys got federal top-secret grants to work on classified anthropological and archaeological challenges that, well, the public is not quite ready for, because we are still working on what they are. We can't describe these artifacts quite yet, but we are getting closer."

He gestured mock-grandiosely at the room. "This is a classified government research lab that only a few people know about, and you will sign a document tonight that you will never say anything about this place or you will go to jail, lose your job and your pension, and never see daylight again." Robert smiled as he looked back at Paul and chuckled. "I am sure you thought so low of us desert dirt diggers, but we might just get more credit from you now. You can never tell anyone about this. Secrets are about 30 percent of my job performance evaluations now. These projects help me keep my tenure. The president of the university does not have access to this either. Kind of funny, I think. By the way, you are being rude to Alex. Please thank him for his welcome to you ... he can be temperamental. Common courtesy, Paul!" Robert waved at him to say something.

Paul said, "Alex, thank you, it is nice meeting you."

Alex's computer voice said, "Paul, thank you too, and your voice recognition is now complete too. You are now on the registry. By the way, Paul, you need to pay your unpaid parking ticket from 1996 in Denton, Texas."

Paul smiled at Robert and said, "Really?" and Robert just laughed.

Robert continued to Area 23, which was just a hallway and as they walked into the hallway, the lights automatically came on and there was another door, this time stainless steel and very modern. Robert simply put his hand and eye on the separate scanners and the door unlocked and he pulled it open. Robert led Paul into the small, well-lit room. Three walls had weapons under glass within individual cases, the room must have had twenty to thirty swords, knives, and daggers and a few other artifacts. Robert walked to the left wall, typed numbers into a key code, and a glass window slid open. He put on his gloves and pulled out a dagger from the case. "Paul, does this knife look like anything you have seen lately?"

Paul studied the knife. It was an older and longer version of what Nera had given him. The handle was thicker, but the writing on the blade also looked foreign. Celtic like the blade Nera gave him. It looked like a big brother of the knife now in his office.

Robert said, "Paul, the blade we have here was forged in iron ore metal from mines from Scotland between 100 BC and AD 50. The blade contains an unidentified metal, hence its residence in a classified vault and not a museum. The other important fact about this blade is that it has an unexplained power source. This blade generates heat. Theoretical physicists, nuclear engineers, and top metallurgists can't explain it. There are also stories about this blade that have been taken out of history to protect the blade from notoriety. This particular blade has killed over one thousand people if you believe folklore and myths. The inscription on the blade doesn't match with any known language on this planet. It has also been said to have a power to transfer to other worlds like a portal.

That is why it is in this vault.

"Twenty-five years ago, one of our university's brightest young anthropology professors began studying this knife. Understanding the blade became the man's main intellectual pursuit. After a few years, he began to claim it took him to other worlds and other dimensions, that this knife could give him contact with the gods themselves. Dr. Jim was a great and promising professor but once he started working on the blade, he sort of went mad, acting funny, claimed he had talks with gods. He's been in a psych ward for the last twenty-three years because he was about to tell the world about all of our artifacts so the government took over. Government doctors diagnosed him with schizophrenia and dementia and as being a danger to society so they locked him up in the special government-backed ward at the university medical behavioral clinic. The government pays all the bills for those that they psychologically imprison. Cleaner than a federal prison. He did not have a family so the process was tidy. Never threaten the government, Paul.

"He really is crazy now. We all make a point to visit him regularly. Pretty sure they're giving him drugs to fog his memory about the blade. Sometimes when we visit, he tells us the visions he had while holding the knife and the trips he took through the blade's portal. He would always say he was speaking with the divine when he worked with the blade. He even dipped into a little witchcraft toward the end. That was when the government took over."

Robert walked over to a computer on the table and

said, "Paul, I took some photos of your specific athame, but did not tell you, so I could look it up and do some classified research on it, for you of course but also for my curiosity. The knife that you have is old but not an antiquity type, and it was cited, or could be cited, in two situations in history not in public records. The research was written, but the government prevented the articles from being published and gave the professor double his pay. It's not the same as notoriety, but the professor has a nice house on the beach in Panama City during the winter, and a summer home in Boston near his classified research area. He is well rewarded for not publishing to the masses but to continue classified history research. The government always pays more than what a tenured professor would make. Creature comforts tip the balance toward the human penchant for conformity."

Robert pulled up a photo of Paul's athame and another image of a knife. Robert said, "Well, Paul, what do you think? Is it close?"

Paul looked at the computer screen image. "That almost looks exactly like it. Where did you find the photo? I scoured the internet and nothing came close."

Robert laughed and said, "Paul, we control what is on the internet and what is not and this particular blade is not for public use due to certain historical factors. Let me tell you the story of this knife. We can't prove that this painted canvas is drawn based off your blade. This type of knife in this painting was a 'witch pricker' knife, used in Scotland and England in the 1600s. Witch prickers were paid very handsomely to find the devil's mark, usually a birthmark or a scar, on accused witches. Back then, many people thought a birthmark was the sign of the devil. Today, many people believe birthmarks are evidence of wounds from past lives. Witch prickers during this period were mainly male, and the accused were mainly female, but this painting depicts Christian Caddell. She disguised herself as a man to accuse women she disliked in England, and that is what this painting shows." Paul studied the image of a knife pricking a mole and a feminine-looking male pointing at the judge.

Robert continued his lecture, "This knife could be that knife in the painting that she is using against that innocent woman's back. That knife in the painting was recorded as having sent over fifty women to death due to her proven antics as a so-called pricker. She was later found out as a woman and sent to prison, but she is rumored to have escaped a year later and no one went searching for her. Rumors and hearsay state that she found a simple British officer to marry and take her to America to escape persecution. That knife sent many innocent women to their death. Lots of death has followed that blade. If you believe in curses, this might be the biggest one we have ever seen."

Robert continued, "This legendary knife might also be depicted in this painting," which he pulled up on the computer screen. "This painting is from the Salem Witch Trials. Sarah Good was accused of witchcraft in February 1692 when two young girls were having seizures and strange fits, which they blamed Sarah for. A former slave Tituba threw Sarah under the bus to save her own skin. During the trial a young, unnamed brunette accuser claimed she was stabbed by Sarah and said the tip was broken inside her and she pulled out a tip of a blade. A so-called boyfriend stood up in the courtroom and informed the court that it was a lie and he had broken the tip, and produced the rest of the knife, a perfect fit with the tip the woman held, and said his so-called girlfriend was a fraud. The woman was escorted out of the courtroom and was later rumored to have died of smallpox.

"The knife we have does not have a chip in the point, but your knife does. If you look at it closely, there is a fine line of fracture; the smith who fixed it did an excellent job. Sarah was pregnant when she was convicted and they let her have her baby first, but the baby died soon after childbirth. Sarah was then hanged on Proctor's Ledge. The best part of the story is that when she was on the platform, she called out to the people and said she was not a witch, said that the witch was still among them waiting and if they kill her, God would kill them. The story ended twenty-five years later when the judge Reverend Noyes suffered a hemorrhage and died on his own blood just like Sarah predicted. If you have ever read Arthur Miller's 1953 play *The Crucible*, Sarah's character is in the play as a poor beggar who is looked down upon by Puritan society."

Paul said, "It would seem there is a curse or just some bad stuff surrounding the blade."

Robert said, "There is a curse on this blade we have here under study. My hypothesis is that your particular blade has a curse on it also, so please be careful with it and if you ever want to keep it here, we would secure it for you. You have seen our security system. We can craft a waiver so the government will not own it, but hold it secure for testing. We like to test with other blades and metals to look for inexplicable energy.

"Paul, with all of this going on about your athame, I believe we should go to Scotland to explore the area where your knife originated. What do you think?"

Paul smiled, thinking about the coincidence that he just booked his trip. "Well, Robert, I have my plane ticket booked already to go to a MacGregor Clan reunion next week. Why don't you join me?"

Robert said with a handshake, "That sounds like a lovely adventure. I'm in."

Chapter 16
Rebecca and Abdul

Abdul and Rebecca rode all night. Abdul gave a promise to the bishop who had saved his life during many battles that he would make sure this woman would get to safety in the northern country where his family, especially his younger brother, resided. Rebecca held on tight for hours on the first night like a scared little girl, not letting go of Abdul's waist until he commanded her to. At dawn, they entered a village for the first time in their hours of riding. Abdul got off his horse and walked it into the village looking for a place to rest for the day. After today, they wouldn't enter a village again—the risk of rumors catching up and identifying Rebecca as the one who attacked the most popular bishop in Italy was too great. They couldn't afford even a hint of suspicion landing on them, leaving a log of their movements for others to trace. Rebecca remained on the horse until they reached an inn, waiting outside while Abdul made arrangements for food and lodgings.

He helped her off the horse. The woman was fatigued and couldn't get down on her own. Her movements were stiff with exhaustion. He asked one of the boys to feed and groom the horse, as he felt he couldn't leave the woman alone in a crowd. Abdul had arranged food to be brought to them in the room. Within a few moments a steaming bowl of lamb meat stew and fresh bread with wine were brought up by a young girl. They ate wordlessly in their room, exhausted.

Rebecca devoured her food quickly. Setting her empty bowl back on the tray she spoke for the first time since they'd left. "Thank you, Abdul, for saving me."

"I owe allegiance to Xavier. He saved my life. I will protect you until we reach Xavier's estate. That is my duty to him and therefore to you."

Rebecca asked, "Where shall I sleep?"

Abdul quickly said, "I am a gentleman. The bed is yours, and I will sleep on the floor. I told the innkeeper we were married to cover our identity but that does not mean we have to share a bed."

Rebecca smiled. "That is nonsense, let's share the warmth of the bed and just sleep. Both of us need a good night's sleep. You need your rest, you're the one on high alert all day. No need to question honor. It's a practical matter. We both need our rest."

Abdul hesitated. Christian women of these northern lands cherished their feminine purity. "Are you sure? I do not want to question or challenge your honor."

"I am a witch, do not be afraid. I have honor in myself and care not what others think of me. I know what I am, I am proud of what I am. Tonight we are two companions and fugitives sharing a resting place."

Once Rebecca made herself comfortable facing the wall on her half of the bed, Abdul got in, careful to maintain distance, his back to hers. Eventually, they shared the blanket and their inner heat warmed each other in the cold and drafty inn and they both kept their promise and their boundaries and rested until midday, when they woke up to the sun coming through the window and the sounds of the dinner crowd downstairs.

They actually awoke in each other's arms, slightly innocent but also slightly intimate and quickly recognized the situation and moved to a more neutral location. Abdul got up first to put on his clothes and she noticed the scars on his back and asked politely, "Abdul, if you do not mind to tell me, where do the scars come from?"

"That is for an inner friend and those with the privilege of knowing me. Do not be offended. Only a few people know the story and I only tell those who are in my inner circle."

"I promise someday you will trust me and you will tell me the story." She grinned deeply at him, playfully acknowledging the challenge. They both got dressed, giving each other privacy, and went down into the tavern for food and drink.

A young woman attended their table and brought

them breakfast and drink, and they finally started to talk to each other. Abdul had the gold coins to pay for the food and the inn. He kept the money pouch inside his shirt next to his belt.

"Thank you again, Abdul, for accompanying me to safety. Where is safety located?"

Abdul quietly said, "We are going to Xavier's younger brother's estate in the Scottish Highlands where it will be safe for you. You will be one of the most-wanted women in the church and the region since you attacked Xavier the bishop. He is a national hero, and there will be no safe place for you unless you are protected by him and the church. The bishop is the only one with the money, power, and position to protect you."

Rebecca calmly said, "I do not remember what I did to Xavier that made him send me away; do you know?"

Abdul looked at her straight into her eyes and said, "Rebecca, you tried to kill him. You stabbed him with a knife. You almost killed him. How do you not remember?"

Rebecca started to tear up not knowing why she left in such a hurry and now realizing that she tried to kill her best friend, Xavier, her dearest friend. Her only friend, she admitted to herself. Deep in her inner heart, she wished she loved Xavier but she did not, he was a friend at least, a very close friend.

Abdul said, "You have already informed me that you are witch. Under some spell or mind control or a magic dark circle, you made an attempt to kill my master, my best friend, my only trusted friend, so I will never trust you, ever. But my master has asked me to take you to a refuge to be safe until he can return and I will risk my life for Xavier, my bishop, for he saved my life when he was my commander in war before he took the cloth of religion and priesthood. If you did not know, he was one of the most decorated officers in the church's army. He was an excellent battle commander and was always perfectly poised in the most heated of battles. He was a ruthless warrior. I owe him my life and I will protect you with what I owe to Xavier. But you are evil. I can smell the evil in you right now. I will not lower my defenses to your charm and seductive looks. I know what you are in your dark soul."

Rebecca was confused and calmly said, "I am a witch, a real witch, but I will do you no harm, I promise. That is the one promise I can honestly make you."

Abdul just laughed and said, "I do not trust your words because my intuition and heart tell me you will be evil when you need to be and twist words to get your way, and you will never be a good person in your core. I will never trust you."

Rebecca just smiled back. "I will change your opinion of me on our travels, I promise."

Abdul just laughed and they ate the rest of the meal in silence; both were starving from their prior night's traveling through the countryside. They both knew they needed all the food they could get for their travel that evening and the next days and weeks on the road.

As the afternoon was ending, they packed their

things and got on their horse and continued north toward France. Crossing the border near the Duchy of Savoy was the first real danger. Hopefully the papers that Abdul carried would give them a free pass through the kingdoms that they must travel through. That second day, early in their ride, Abdul said, "We will sleep outside from now on, to avoid the authorities and stay hidden. I apologize for the future discomfort but it will be safer. Especially if the rumors have continued and spread about what you tried to do to the bishop. We can't risk the chance of being connected in any way to such rumors."

They rode in silence for hours. Abdul expected Rebecca to complain but she did not say or complain a word on their travel that day through all the tough and barren terrain. As evening neared, they stopped and settled in a small copse of trees. Abdul set up camp and laid out the blankets on the ground and started a fire. The first night, Rebecca had done nothing but sit and stare into the fire. This time, however, she wordlessly helped set up camp and prepare the meal and their bedding as Abdul tended to the horse and scouted the perimeter. They did not talk much that night mainly due to the words that were already spoken in daylight at the inn. They slept on the ground near each other but not close, but during deep sleep, when the fire died down to embers, their bodies came into contact. They awoke in the morning to the warmth of each other and realized their closeness and then immediately separated to not cross any lines.

As their travel stretched from days into weeks, they

began to banter and trade compliments at each other's skillfulness in camping, cooking, and reading the land. Their daily routines became comfortable and relaxed, a communal letting go of the tension of sneaking across the country and avoiding being recognized as the starring characters in fearful rumors about the popular Italian bishop. They even began to share a blanket each night, a simple practicality to keep their health in the damp and chilly nights. They were becoming physically close without being intimate.

As they continued through Europe into the northern countries, they did not know that Xavier had left just three days behind them, trying to catch up. Neither had any idea he intended to travel to his brother's estates, let alone that he would try to catch up to them. Xavier had informed his church chain of command and they agreed to give him furlough to reflect on the tragedy and its implications. He had official sanction to take four months off to travel to his brother's land to heal and recover from the knife wound and spend time with his family, and if he needed more time, he could provide church services in the northern regions until ready to return to Italy.

Abdul and Rebecca continued to travel and continued to get closer to each other. They never kissed or were intimate but began to walk shoulder to shoulder, then hold hands, even laughed together and were happy just to enjoy each other's company. She flirted with him more and more as the weeks went on. But she never crossed the final boundary, merely began to be slightly bolder and playful in her talk and looks. They were getting closer to Scotland and only had a day or two left before making it to the bishop's family estate. They touched hands more, knowing that their time together was about to end. Abdul had told Rebecca that once he had brought her to the estate he would head back to serve the bishop and the church. Rebecca was put off, wanting him to stay with her and be entertained and she liked his attention. She was actually pouting.

Meanwhile, Xavier was catching up, traveling twice as fast as them every day, with an abundance of fresh horses and meals prepared for him and soft inn beds, sparing no expense to catch them before they made it to his estate. Xavier wanted to protect them once they got into the Highland estates, not knowing how fast the rumors about the incident had spread. Girolamo, the young priest-historian, was accompanying him, and they would ask village folks along the way but most had not seen Abdul or Rebecca so Xavier knew that Abdul was protecting their travel with secrecy and discretion of the highest caliber, as was his way.

Abdul and Rebecca made camp. It was their last night in the woods before they entered the bishop's Highland estate just a few miles away. They could see the large castle along the horizon toward the east. Abdul knew the best time to arrive was not in the darkness but in the morning, where suspicions of evading or running from something would not be in the equation. People who traveled during the morning and during the light were not afraid to be seen. Abdul and Rebecca started their routine as was now a comfortable habit. They each tended to their chores in companionable silence. Even though Abdul said he would never trust her, his boundaries and walls were eroding, and in his mind, he was thankful they only had one more night together because every evening they spent together his defenses got thinner to her charm and her smile. He did not know how much longer he could restrain from her attractiveness and charm and his yearning to be with her. They were sleeping every night together under the blankets for warmth and they had never crossed any line, nor even come close, but he could tell she wanted to.

As they set up their fire for the night and were eating their last dinner together, they were both quiet, knowing that this was the end of their journey. Finally, the last few bites of food were gone and they went under the blanket together for the last time. Rebecca gently rolled into his arm, her hand hovering, fingertips brushing his chest. "Abdul, may I feel your heartbeat tonight?" Without pausing for an answer, she swiveled her hips to where she was sitting on top of him. As he opened his mouth to answer, she kissed him on the lips and her hair dropped on his face. Her lips moved with passion that had been restrained for weeks and he succumbed to his desires. They embraced and kissed deeply under the blankets and their warmth between them was becoming quick heat as dress and shirt were removed to have access to shoulders and necks, and stomachs, backs, and breasts to touch. They were now too far gone; pure instinctive desire drove them. Rebecca lowered Abdul's pants and could see his excitement, and she pulled up her skirt and positioned herself to engulf him, which drove Abdul wild. Abdul opened up her blouse to expose her breasts and pulled her skirt over her head and they were deep in a rhythm of pure lust and sex. Their movements were synchronized and they were nearing their climax, when she looked at him and said, "Abdul, do you trust me now?"

In a delirium of intellectual conflict, Abdul said, "I finally trust you now, I love you."

She smiled and leaned back to take him fully inside and to expose her breasts and her left hand was searching for something in her dress that she had taken off and she found what she was looking for. She looked at him in his eyes and said, "Well, Abdul, you should never trust me. I am a witch."

As his eyes looked confused, she took the blade that was in hidden in her hand and sliced hard at Abdul's throat. Blood poured out as he put both hands on his throat to save himself. She started to laugh at him, and the blood was now on her naked body as she remained on top of him, preventing him finding something to stop the bleeding. As Rebecca continued to sit on Abdul, the blood continued to pour and squirt on her naked body and she sat up and started chanting and raising the blade up in the air, worshiping other deities and Gods.

At that moment Xavier was riding up to their camp and saw what was happening and immediately jumped off his horse to try and save Abdul from Rebecca. He ran to them and threw her off his body and tried to stop the bleeding with his shirt, but he could see the look in Abdul's eyes and knew he was not going to make it, that he couldn't save his dear friend and servant. Abdul was gagging on his blood, through the bubbles through the open wound on his neck. He was trying to say something to Xavier. Xavier grabbed his hand to offer absolution, thinking that was Abdul's dying request, but Abdul's last words were, "Watch out for Rebecca." And with his last air in his bloody lungs his eyes rolled in the back of his head and air bubbles came out with the blood through the slice on his neck.

Xavier sat there, stunned, trying to make sense of his last words when Rebecca stabbed him in the back. This time she had forced the blade sideways between the ribs to go into the heart because the last time the blade was vertical and the ribcage had protected Xavier's heart. She pushed the blade deeper into his back with all her weight, through his ribcage and through his heart and the end of the blade punctured though the skin right below the sternum. She knew she had landed a fatal blow to Xavier. She was on his back and leaped on top of him and kissed him on his ear as she heard his last gasps of life. Rebecca pushed the blade even deeper, watching the last pain in Xavier's eyes because she knew that he loved her, they both fell in love with her. She whispered in his ear, "My beloved, you should never trust me, but I so love you both."

Then there was a cry next to her, "What have you

done?"

Rebecca looked to the left and received a huge tree limb to the side of her face from Girolamo. Girolamo had paused to tie up the horses and had come up late to the scene, but saw Rebecca run her blade deep into his bishop. Inside himself, he found the courage to find a strong oak limb and try to hit her as hard as he could on the head to try and protect Xavier if at all possible. His insides were afraid but his courage rose to the occasion and he hit her so hard that she fell over several feet and was immediately unconscious.

He tried to save Xavier, but it was too late. Girolamo's sadness became direct visceral anger toward this woman, lying naked and unconscious a few feet from the bodies of the two men she had callously murdered in their vulnerability. There was nothing he could do for Abdul and Xavier except give them an honorable funeral but this woman, he would make sure she was punished to the full extent of church law and even more if he could.

He tied her up as if his life depended on it before strapping her into the saddle on Xavier's horse. He rode with his prisoner to the Highland estate to secure and jail this woman and to get help to retrieve the bodies.

The Highland estate woke up upon his arrival and everyone was there to assist Girolamo on securing this evil woman. A dozen men went with him to gather the bodies, all there had loved Xavier deeply. Naked and bloody, Rebecca looked as evil as she was. The men left her tied up in the courtyard, dreading touching her.

The women peeked out at the scene, but let well enough alone. Xavier's blood drenched her body. The constable arrived, covered her up, and put her in custody and the rest of the men who'd been standing watch over her went to the site where she had murdered their liege and his faithful servant. The men who accompanied Girolamo would give their testimonial in Rebecca's murder trial at the magistrate's office. The men found Xavier and Abdul and wrapped them properly and brought their bodies back to the estate in a cart for a proper and honorable funeral.

Girolamo soon took charge of the case against Rebecca and as an eyewitness gave the most damning testimony against her. In the trial proceedings, he was calm and collected, the voice of reason. None saw the way that anger now shaped him. His calmness earned him his coveted spot in the inquisition proceedings in testing Rebecca for heresy.

The inquisition was entirely unsatisfying in its uselessness. Guidelines for inquisition were few and vague. Those in charge were content to let the matter drop and merely hang Rebecca for murder. Girolamo made it his personal mission once he returned to Italy was to work on a guide and handbook to help the authorities prove heresy and evilness.

The funeral for the bishop and his servant Abdul was done with full honors. They were made papal heroes and received the highest honors from the pope and the people of Xavier's congregation. No inquiry was made into why they were in Scotland with Rebecca, other than to record they were doing the Lord's work.

Girolamo watched Rebecca hang and promised himself to vindicate his teacher and master, Xavier. Xavier was like a big brother to him, and Abdul was a loyal servant. He would never forget the sight of that naked witch shivering in ecstasy at the touch of Xavier's blood.

Girolamo would return to Italy to fiercely strive to fulfill his new holy mission and his writings would later inspire other priests to continue to pursue the persecution of women that could be witches. He would never forget what Rebecca had done to Xavier and Abdul. In 1484, he helped his colleague Heinrich to receive a papal bull, and also assisted in him being an inquisitor for the church. These events would help contribute to the final writing of the *Malleus*, which would then bring justice to the deaths of Xavier and Abdul all because of Rebecca's betrayal.

There were always rumors in the country by the simple folk that Rebecca survived the hanging, or that local witches had summoned her from the dead and took care of her and hid her safely. Rumors continued for decades that she continued to live and became dark, one of the darkest witches, but her charming and deceitful ways got her way with men and their fortunes. The Italian witches claimed her story as one of their own and continued to spread tales that she married men throughout the lands and took them for their wealth to share with her covens. There are other stories that she was eventually caught again and they burned her for witchcraft and adultery to make sure she could not be summoned again from the grave. They also say Girolamo was the one who caught her the second time, but there are no records of it, just folklore and stories.

Chapter 17
Scotland

Paul and Robert sat, staving off yawns in the dingy waiting room, awaiting their flight to Scotland. A few minutes before boarding was scheduled to begin, Robert said, "Thank you for inviting me to go with you. You know you need a security force to protect you."

Paul's yawn got interrupted by a snort of amusement. "You are like twenty-five years older than me, and on partial retirement. How much help can you give me, old man?"

Robert only laughed as he stood up to board the airplane. "Well, you don't seem to need me to hold your hand, but let's see what Scotland has in store for us."

Standing in the row of the ten-odd people waiting to board first class, Robert and Paul were each deeply absorbed in their own reflections and musings about the trip ahead. They paid no attention to anyone else in line with them as they made their way to their seats. The young blonde woman, elegantly clad in high-end European fashion, standing behind them, would normally have been the type to catch their eye: poised, beautiful, and clearly not from around here.

Once Paul and Robert were settled into their seats and waiting for the rest of the passengers to get settled in for departure, Robert asked, "Why are we going to Scotland, my dear friend?"

Paul grinned. "Well, I guess today it's my turn to give the lecture and the tour. Clan MacGregor is a Highland Scottish clan, whose laird was executed, even though they won the war and were greatly outnumbered. They warred with King James's Clan Colquhoun, whom the MacGregors had been feuding with for generations. They were outlawed for almost two hundred years, and they lost their lands. To be a MacGregor was a death sentence. The MacGregors were one of the first clans, originated in Scotland in the 800s during the war of Scottish Independence. Clan MacGregor fought at the Battle of Bannockburn under Malcolm MacGregor. When the name was outlawed, many chose different names, such as my ancestors, who changed their name to MacGehee and came to America in the early 1700s to find a new homeland. So that is how I came to be and why we are going to Scotland."

Robert was slightly impressed. "What about Rob Roy and the MacGregors?"

"And how is Rob Roy linked to all this, oh wise, slightly elderly professor?"

Robert smiled and said, "Well, Paul, that is why you need a historian on your trip to keep you straight."

They continued to laugh about each other and argue about Scottish history like a duel and eventually the flight was well on its way. The young blonde in the seat behind them was fast asleep, quietly awaiting their landing.

Eventually the two friends had completed their duel of knowledge and the one glass of wine had its effect at 35,000 feet and they both dozed off in the long flight over the ocean. Their ten-hour flight was due to arrive the next morning into Edinburgh where they would start their next adventure by ground. They were going to travel to the land of Paul's MacGregor ancestors, "The Children of the Mists."

The sun had just started to peek over the horizon in Edinburgh when they both tiredly got off the plane and headed to baggage pickup. As they slowly made their way off the plane, Paul noticed a woman still asleep in her seat in first class, but he was too tired to investigate further.

They both made it to the baggage claim. As they were loading their bags onto a cart a young man approached them and asked if they were here for the MacGregor gathering, and Paul casually said, "Yes, I am and I dragged my friend along."

Robert waved his hand. "Yep, I am the friend."

The stranger said, "Well, sir, I did not mean to listen to your conversation, but I did hear that you were discussing the MacGregor clan. I'm also heading to the clan gathering. Hope to see you there and have a discussion with you over some whisky."

Robert said, "Deal. We will see you there."

The three men shook hands and the stranger introduced himself as Frank, who was a farmer from a little town in Arkansas with Scottish roots who also had finally agreed to attend the clan gathering.

The strange, beautiful woman from first class kept her distance from Paul and Robert but watched their conversation intently. She did not have a rental but had her own chauffeured car waiting for her at the airport. She quietly heard what she needed to hear and quickly departed without being noticed by either man.

After an hour of driving and getting lost only twice, Robert found the Loch Awe Hotel. The hotel overlooked beautiful Loch Awe and beneath the towering slopes of Ben Cruachan and along the shore of Kilchurn Castle. Paul read the history plaques of the hotel, finding that it was built in 1881 and founded by Duncan Fraser and built in the Scottish-Baronial style. He also read how part of *To Catch Me a Spy,* starring Kirk Douglas, was filmed in the hotel. They made it to the front desk and checked in with no issues except the weary weight of jetlag on their bodies and minds.

Robert and Paul agreed to take a nap and meet up for a late lunch. Paul found his room and hit a wall of physical exhaustion. On autopilot, he set down his baggage, took off his jacket, shoes, and socks, and set his alarm for one hour from now. He wasn't sure if he'd be able to wake up, but it didn't matter, he needed to fall asleep. He laid down on the comfortable bed, pulled up a blanket, and quickly fell deep asleep.

He dreamt he was standing in a quiet field with heavy dew on the ground. The field was on the lea side of a low mountain, one that matched some of the scenery from the drive to the hotel. Paul could hear men around him breathing hard, he could hear the horses shake off the dew and the slow sounds of bagpipes warming up in the distance. The fight was about to start. The flags of the clans were flying in the small, playful wind. The air was thick with moisture and his boots were already wet and his feet were cold. Paul looked down at his thighs and saw a heraldry kilt; his legs and groin were warm and free to maneuver. He stood there, not knowing what to do and somewhat frozen. It was like he was standing in a first-person shooter game, all of the details felt so vivid. The bagpipes shifted from their gentle warm-up to a higher intensity. The men to his left and right were moving forward and the banging of shields with swords and axes began, immediately followed by yells echoing back and forth across the fields. He knew instinctively that he needed to move with the men and so Paul started walking forward to stay in the column with the men around him. The bagpipes reached a crescendo, the yells became wild in their ferocity. The men started to run and he could see the opposing men he was running toward with their swords in hand, movements and shouts as full of the blood-boiling wrath of battle as the men around him. The momentum was building, and the gap was closing quickly. Everyone raised their swords and the huge clash of swords reverberated with carnage and blood and thirst entwined in the mangle of bodies fighting to the death; there must have been over two hundred men swinging swords and axes and cutting flesh and causing blood to spurt.

Paul tried to swing but did not know how to maneuver the heavy metal blade; he'd never held one in his life. But if he didn't learn, he was going to die, so he swung with all his might and then he wounded his first enemy and then another fight of two men bumped into him and he slashed at another enemy, and then instinct overtook him and he started to swing with more precision, his mind and senses in overdrive with the singing of survival in his veins. Without warning, he felt a blow and the driving of metal into his back by a sword or a spear. He tried to twist away from the blade, but the weight of the unseen foe drove deep into his back and into his heart. He could not breath. He could feel the numbness, the blood started to fill his mouth, and his legs gave out on him and he could not stand anymore. The person who drove the blade deep into his back was still pushing hard, sending the weapon deeper as he twisted the blade to destroy the life of what was left in him. The pain dizzied and overwhelmed Paul. He collapsed and blacked out. There was darkness and quiet and only the slow beats of blood dripping out on his body. Death was approaching quickly. In those last moments, he heard a woman's voice but could not understand what she was saying.

Paul woke up in a sweat and raised himself up out of bed. He did not know where he was. As he got to his feet, he recognized a hotel room and then he realized that he was on a trip and his clouded mind cleared and he remembered that he was in Scotland. His alarm was going off and that woke him up. Then he realized he was only taking a nap and he was supposed to meet Robert for lunch. He had only about fifteen minutes left until they were to meet back in the lobby, so he went to take a quick shower to wake himself up. As the water hit his naked body, Paul calmed down from the dream. Now that he had time to process, he was not afraid of the event and welcomed the dream and now wanted to try and see if it was connected. He jumped out, dried off, and made it in time for lunch. He did not want to share his dream with Robert today, maybe another time. He was hungry and eager to learn more about Scotland.

As they all made it downstairs to the lobby to start their Scotland exploring, Robert asked, "Are you feeling ok?"

Paul smiled and said, "I am just tired from the jet lag, but I will be fine."

Robert said, "You look pale as if you saw a ghost."

Paul shrugged it off and replied, "Robert, ok, I had a bad dream that I died here in battle, are you happy?"

Robert said, "Dear friend, the truth will set you free, and yes, that is a much better answer, so now let's see where you died. Come, my friend."

Once again Paul felt like he was the student and Robert was the teacher as they departed the lobby.

see where you died. Come, my friend."
Once again Paul felt like he was the student and
Robert was the teacher as they departed the lobby.

Chapter 18
Glen Fruin

Robert had been grinning madly for the past hour drive through the Scottish countryside in their small car. The grin only grew at any signs of restlessness or agitation from Paul. Robert loved his mysteries and jokes, and it was a golden opportunity, not telling Paul where they were going and sitting with him in the dark the entire drive. He hinted it was one of the famous battlefield victories of the MacGregors. Paul knew Robert well enough not to ask more than once. He occasionally came up with a subtle effort to pierce the mystery, but mostly focused on enjoying and observing the ride. About forty minutes into the ride, Paul noticed that the street signs to Glen Fruin Road were the constant theme in the drive route and soon they came upon another turn into a valley. Robert smiled and said, "Almost there! You are on the high road of the Highlanders or in Scottish Gaelic *Rathad Mor nan Gaidheal*." The drive was downhill now through a beautiful green valley.

They drove to the bottom of the valley and stopped at an intersection where there was a rock monument by the road with a field next to it. They stopped along the road in a gravel lot big enough for three to four cars to park.

There was another car parked there, an old 1970s red Volkswagen bug, and a woman stood next to the car. She was short and thin, with curly slightly unkept brown hair always falling into her eyes that she kept moving away with fingers as she waved to Robert gleefully.

"Robert, what have you done?"

"It is all about the process of learning, Paul. Thank me later."

They got out of the car and Robert went over to the woman and gave her a hug like a lost friend that you have not seen in years, and they both smiled and kissed each other on the cheek and hugged again. Paul stood there slightly awkward just watching.

Robert held his hand up and said, "Paul, excuse my rudeness. Let me formally introduce you. Dr. Brynn MacGregor, a dear friend through mainly e-mail correspondence. Your kinswoman is a famous professor at the local university." Robert looked at Brynn and said politely, "My dear Brynn, this is Paul, the one I have been e-mailing you about."

Brynn looked at Paul with eyes that were so

comforting that he felt everything slow down as he stared into her eyes while she extended her hand for a handshake. As their hands touched, flashes of images burst into his mind like an old slide projector; they felt so familiar, but he could not place them and as he was trying to comprehend them but could not yet, his heart longed to rediscover their meaning. She took her hand back and the images disappeared instantly like a switch turned off.

Paul said, "I assume you two already know each other and I am at a disadvantage somehow."

Brynn tilted her head, an impish grin playing across her lips. "It is so nice to finally meet you, Paul. And, yes, Robert and I are professor friends and writing partners with a mutual interest in archaeology and other special artifacts. I think I can help you—well, I hope I can help you—to find what you're looking for. You will have to trust me, cousin."

Brynn took Paul's arm. "May I give you a history lesson of this land?"

Robert smiled, "Paul, she would like to share with you your special family history, which we both think you will find enlightening and help you on your path toward some answers."

Paul again felt like he was a student and now had two professors leading him through the lessons, but Brynn was so adorable and charming that he did not mind the additional professor teaching him more about Scotland. Brynn's Scottish lilt to her velvety rich voice was just breathtaking, almost hypnotic. She had this energy about her that instantly made Paul smile.

They all walked up to a rock historical marker which read:

Near this spot
The
Battle of Glen Fruin
Was fought
Between
Clan Colquhouns
And
Clan Gregor
On 7 February
1603

"Glen Fruin, as you can see, is adjacent to Loch Lomond over there. The Battle of Glen Fruin was fought between the MacGregors, or Gregors, on foot, and their rivals, the Colquhoun. The three hundred MacGregors emerged victorious over the five to eight hundred Colquhoun, who also had over three hundred men on horseback."

Brynn continued walking around the nearby wet field showing the terrain as she kept talking. "Before the battle there was a rumor that a seer—a person who see visions and the future—encouraged Clan MacGregors that they would win if they fought on that specific day. Though the MacGregors were on foot in the wet ground, and the opposing force had over three hundred soldiers on horseback, it was the terrain that made the critical decision of victory. The muddy battlefield disadvantaged the horses and by the end of the battle, the MacGregors routed the other clans. They were truly the underdogs. The rest of the story after the battle, was the fall of the Gregors. Oral histories have been told of the MacGregors and other clans, that indicate the tale of this mysterious seer has been passed down for several generations, but while the oral histories are well researched, they amount to little more than rumor, and don't help us learn more about who this man was and what happened to him or his immediate family."

As Paul walked along the wet field listening, he was getting chills. There were goose bumps along his neck; he felt some pain in his shoulder; and his heart was beating faster. He bent down and touched the ground with his hand. He felt the wet land and the tall grass; he felt like he had been there before. The memory itched in the back of his mind. He just could not place it.

Brynn touched his arm, "No worries, the message will come when it is time. Your Gregor family fought here, and your ancestors had one of their last clan battles here before they lost their name and were virtually banished from Scotland." She smiled at him with a smile that made him smile back. "We need to go to another site before we head to the gathering this evening. You must know that in a past life, you died on this battlefield among your clansmen and your friends."

Paul gaped at her. He was still grappling with the strange feelings he was getting, walking through this glen. He'd only just met this woman, and Robert had only corresponded electronically. Paul wondered how many people of his circle had this psychic power that he did not know about.

As Paul walked back to the car, his mind traveled back to Lena's words about him dying on the battlefield, and he thought of his dream that morning. He paused with his hand on the passenger door, then turned around to look out at the field before getting in the car. He just could not put his finger on it. They followed Brynn in her Volkswagen back onto the road, heading further away from the hotel. She liked to drive fast and Robert was swearing and tense trying to keep up with her. Paul laughed at how the professor was so out of his comfort zone and kept driving on the wrong side of the road because in Scotland everyone drives on the left and not the right side. Paul felt as light-hearted as a child as he laughed and enjoyed the silliness of the moment. All they could do was watch the back of her bug and see her curly red-brown hair blowing around. She was driving with the window down and she must have been listening to some music because she was waving her hands and appeared to be singing along.

Since Paul also had his window open to feel the cool air in his hair, he could almost hear some Tom Petty and the Heartbreakers music or something of that era from her car when they got closer during traffic intersections. With the fun of her driving and the frustrating driving skills of

Robert, Paul had a wonderful time watching life and not knowing where they were going as the gorgeous green landscape rolled by.

Paul felt the relaxation of the drive permeate through his psyche as his thoughts wandered over the strange events showing up in his life. He was not afraid anymore of the unknown. The thoughts of his inner temple and meeting Mercury and the others and knowing those spirits or gods were looking after him in this lifetime and other lifetimes gave him a sense of security. He felt like he had been in this country and this land and terrain before—on these specific lands—and the smell of wet grass and the cold air were comforting to him like an old sweatshirt that he had owned for years. It felt like home.

They drove to the Killing Stones. Brynn took Paul's hand and said, "These stones have been here for at least three thousand years. Many speculate the stones are an astronomical calendar, used in agricultural rituals of some sort. The true story of such circles is lost in time. Unless some miraculous archaeological find happens, we will never know their purpose. Most still believe it is part of the Druid history, but the only ones who really know are those whose past lives lived here." She squeezed his hand while she said this like she was giving him a hint.

Paul looked at the stones standing in front of him. He touched the stones and let the emotion of the experience well up inside, and he quieted his mind to listen to them. He felt his mind touch each standing stone one at a time as if he knew them. Brynn and Robert watched in amazement at Paul as he almost embraced each of the stones and laid his hands on them as if he were communicating with them. Paul knew where he was but did not know why; he had been there, he had touched these stones before, he knew them. Paul touched one of the last standing stones and fell to his knees, crying uncontrollably; he was emotionally attached to the stones.

Paul started to speak in Gaelic for no known reason as he communed with the stones, one by one. Robert and Brynn were concerned but let the experience happen. Paul touched the last of the standing stones and sat down, leaning his back to the stones feeling fully exhausted, and said lightly, "I am done with this site and I can't take any more of these standing stones. I have been here before, but do not know when. I have fought here before but do not know why, but this is my home, I do know that. This was a holy place to me once and my people."

He sat on the ground, blinking blearily at Robert and Brynn. "Would you help me up?"

Robert and Brynn helped him to his feet, and he said to both of them, "I think I am ready to depart this place. Thank you for bringing me here. I now know where it all began."

They started their journey back to the car and back to the hotel, heading toward the event that had pulled Paul to Scotland in the first place. Paul was different now; they could tell he was trying to comprehend too much at the moment but neither Robert nor Brynn knew what to do to comfort him. So, they all got in the cars to continue their journey in companionable silence.

During the drive, Paul was quiet and Robert could tell that he was still trying to comprehend all the experiences he had just encountered. Robert knew the need for the silence when one is thinking deeply. They continued to drive and follow Brynn in her Volkswagen, still driving fast and sporadically.

They finally made it to the annual Gregor gathering and Brynn let Paul and Robert check into their conference event and the events of the evening. She went over to Paul and gave him a long hug and whispered into his ear, "I will meet you after the night's events and take you where you need to go to find what you are looking for. I'll be at the bar across the street from your hotel tonight after 11 p.m. Meet me there tonight to find what you seek." Brynn kissed him gently on his cheek as they finished their hug. Brynn then hugged Robert like a friend and said something to him that Paul didn't catch. She pivoted gracefully, hopped back into her Volkswagen bug, and sped off into the night. Paul smiled at how much energy she had and how her hugs made him feel familiar and safe and he knew he must meet her tonight. Then he saw her car driving back into the parking lot. Paul and Robert looked puzzled and she jumped out of her car and rummaged in the back seat. "Gentlemen, I have something for you, so now both of you take off your pants."

Paul and Robert both said, "Excuse me?"

Brynn pulled out two red and black tartan kilts for them to wear for the gathering. Then they both smiled at each other and agreed and walked to the back of the car and took off their shoes and slacks. Brynn reacted like a professional tailor by moving her hands around both of their waists and putting on their kilts, explaining it would just delay the event, and she ran her hands up Paul's legs to make sure the cloth looked right. She tightened the belts quickly on both of them and then tucked in their shirts. Her casual boldness surprised them. She stepped back and twisted each of the kilts about two inches to the right and smiled at both men. She grabbed their discarded pants and said, "I am taking your pants so you both have to wear your kilts the rest of the night. Meet me at the tavern in town when you are done socializing. I will be there with your pants. Maybe, if I feel like it." And she hopped into her car and drove away. Paul and Robert grinned at each other and inspected each other's kilts with approval.

The two men walked toward the castle where the gathering was going to be held. They both knew how to socialize from years of campus events. Since they were from America, their unique English accents would bring them the full touristy attention all night, so they just laughed at each other as they walked up the steps and entered the fully occupied event of people in kilts and a room filled with bagpipes. Paul knew he must endure the evening for the next four hours so that he could focus on meeting Brynn later. He wanted to meet his kin, but in his heart, he knew he was really here on a spiritual journey of discovery, and nothing of that sort would happen in mingling and small talk, however much he learned about family history. He and Robert entered the room, and the door closed behind them like a cell door in jail.

In another car in the parking lot, a woman was waiting in her black Audi coupe looking at everyone walking to the gathering while pretending to read something on her phone. She followed Brynn out of the parking lot, keeping a safe distance not to be noticed by Brynn as she followed her to her next destination. The brunette in the Audi was crying and physically upset as she drove away.

Brynn turned into the parking lot of the local pub where she was going to meet Paul and Robert later, but instead of walking into the pub, she walked behind the pub to a set of stairs that led to an apartment above the pub. The lights were turned on as the brunette that had followed Brynn stepped out of her Audi and looked up at the apartment. She stood next to her car, hesitating. She lit up a cigarette, questioning herself what she should do next as she smoked. The woman dropped her cigarette and crushed it out on the pavement and decided to walk into the pub instead and to patiently wait.

Brynn went into her living room, dimmed the lights, and poured a drink. Her black cat jumped on the kitchen counter to get some attention and purred loudly. Brynn gave a gentle pet on the cat and picked her up and lit a couple of candles and incense on her table. She grabbed her drink and went to the center of her living room and sat on the floor. She crossed her legs and put her drink on the floor next to her and pulled out some small objects hidden under her couch. She carefully placed the crystals and other objects in a circle in front of her. She pulled out her necklace from under her shirt, letting the large blue amulet swing freely on the front of her blouse. She put her hands together like in a prayer, closed her eyes, and started to chant in Celtic. As she started chanting, the amulet brightened and glowed, and the runic inscriptions seemed to dance.

Chapter 19

The Druid Ceremony

Robert looked at his watch and nudged Paul. They excused themselves from the conversation with a Scottish MacGregor and headed toward the exit, still wearing their kilts that Brynn had given them. She had taken their pants, teasingly promising to give them back only if they met her at the pub. The hours of comradery, discussion of clan history, folklore, and rumors were thoroughly enjoyable, but both had had their fill. Paul loved how everyone had fully accepted and welcomed him into the clan, though wasn't sure about their idea of him forming a chapter in Kansas City and starting a membership drive in his area. They hoped that Brynn was still waiting for them, getting their pants back would be nice, but they really wanted to hear Brynn finish describing her side of the story. She was so charming and full of a certain vivacious energy about her that made Paul feel safe and just enjoy being around her.

Robert and Paul found the pub after a short walk. They didn't see her, so sat down at an empty table in their kilts. They had several pints during the party earlier in the evening so they were happy to have another pint as they waited.

As they finished their first round in the Scottish pub, Brynn walked up to their table and asked, "Do you mind if I join you?" as if there were any doubt.

Robert said, "My dear, we are here only to await your company. Please join us."

Brynn sat down with Paul and Robert and ordered a pint. Soon they were laughing and giving three-pint toasts, together among friends and talking about Scotland, the Highlanders, their unique fellowship, folklores, and then the discussion of past lives and the metaphysical. Brynn disclosed that she was a Scottish daughter, she had trained to be an energy healer and herbal practitioner, and that she had an herbal shop downtown just a few buildings from the pub. The shop was a good side income in addition to being a poor university professor. Brynn also disclosed that she lived in an apartment above the bar and could walk on the roof all the way to her herbal shop.

Around 1:00, the energy of the evening together shifted. Without speaking, they knew it was time to head their separate ways for the night. Just as the pause was about to drag on too long, Brynn said, "Paul, before you leave Scotland you must let me do a Scottish energy healing on you. I think you'll find it a memorable and meaningful experience." Realizing that Paul didn't quite know how to respond, she shifted gears, "Gentlemen, I have so adored our evening together that I did bring your pants back, but you both look so handsome in your kilts that I recommend you keep them on to your hotel. Oh, and I have a predawn Druid ceremony to attend with my fellow Druids at some nearby standing stones. My colleagues and I celebrate Yule, the longest night of the year at the same place our ancestors celebrated the rebirth of the Oak King, the Sun King, the Giver of Life that warmed the Earth. Paul and Robert, if you would like to join me, I will pick you up at 3:30 in the morning, just a couple hours from now. Perhaps, Paul, participating in a centuries-old family tradition will shed some light on your path to finding what you are seeking." Brynn said this as if knowing exactly what he was truly seeking.

Paul and Robert both smiled and Paul said, "We would be honored to accompany you to a Druid ceremony. I guess we should all depart now so that we can sleep a mere two hours before the ceremony."

They all started to get up from the table and pay individually but Robert dropped his credit card down first to pay their entire bill. "Well, my dear friends, since I am the oldest professor of our special group, I shall pay tonight and acknowledge that the next time we all three meet that Paul pays, Brynn after that, etc. etc., whenever that will be in the future."

Brynn and Paul both looked at each other and said,

"Sure, we agree to your terms."

Robert then looked at his watch and said, "Well, it is late, why don't we just hop in Brynn's car and go to the site of the ceremony and sleep in her car until the ceremony then we will not be late to the event, because if we go back to our hotel and get to bed our likelihood of waking up and meeting you to take us there is highly against the odds. How about we just go there now and sleep a few hours in the small car?"

Brynn said, "Gentlemen, that sounds actually like a very common-sense idea. I am in."

So they all made their way out of the pub and crammed inside Brynn's small VW and since she knew the way to the standing stones by heart and it was in the middle of the night, they were in the parking lot at 2:30 in the morning with about two hours to doze off before folks started showing up to prepare for the morning ritual at the standing stones. The car was just too small for Paul to get any rest so he got out and walked up to the standing stones to stretch his legs. There were six standing stones, each about eight to ten feet tall in an unevenly distributed circle. Well, positioned in relation to one another in a way that seemed uneven and strange to the modern eye. He could see them in the moonlight since the sun had not started rising yet and he walked up to each, resting his palm on each one for a few seconds. He'd looked up standing stones in Scotland after their trip to the Killin Stones, and these didn't show up on any internet search. They were on private land, and so stayed out of the tourist network and public discussion. A little private sanctuary for locals. The owner of the land participated in the ceremonies and had added a gravel driveway for those in town who couldn't make their way there by bike or foot.

Paul was so tired and a little—or maybe a lot—intoxicated that his imagination was running wild with thoughts. The cold air and dew on the ground brought back memories, not of this time, but familiar. He was soaking in thoughts as if they were in the air waiting for him to catch them with a butterfly net; there were so many memories that it was overwhelming to his consciousness. Paul sat down next the largest standing stone with his back to the stone looking at the circle of stones. A woman in a black cloak walked from behind a stone, slowing as she approached. Paul thought it was a dream because as she walked, she did not make any sound and her face was hidden behind a black cloak. The moon was full. Paul could not decipher if it was a dream or real. She walked in front of him and stood and looked down at him and pulled her hood off her head.

It was Nera. Paul was totally confused on how she was in Scotland at this time at this particular moment and place. Paul thought he was losing it, that his mind was playing tricks on him as she stood before him. Her face was cold and serene and her dark hair was flowing out of her hood. She stared at Paul with severe determination and purpose. Paul felt like evil had approached him in this serene, beautiful place. Nera had an aura of darkness, sending goose bumps racing down the back of his neck and fear into his heart. How she was here? Why? He quickly deducted that she must have followed him to Scotland and was watching their moves as they traveled the last thirty-six hours and decided that this place and time was her best opportunity to do something harmful to him. What authorities, what person, would think to check flights for her name and connect it to his? If she even flew under her own name. Paul instinctively stood up to face his aggressor and convey with his body that whatever she was planning didn't stand a chance. He said, "Nera, how on earth are you here now in front of me, what brought you to follow me?"

Nera stood there, her lips curled into a beautiful smile, with frigid cold in her heart. "Oh, Paul, don't you remember our last little visit in this location? I was flattered by your handsomeness and your status as a Knight Templar. You took your work so seriously, it was quite endearing. But you then mocked me and called me spoiled. I was quite devastated. Cried long hours into the night and all that. You've been a bit lazy with all your past life regressions. Remember Anna? No? Well, she was a common woman, a simple herbalist and some would call a forest or green witch but you loved her over me. Really pissed me off. I loved you. I thought I loved you. I just was wild to spend my life with you, and you should have loved me but you didn't. Every other young man at court fell for me. Every man in the region wanted to love me and I knew it and I loved the attention but you, damn you, you loved another and *mocked* me. A royal! Born to lead and be admired. And then you had the king take away my royal status. The hatred I had for you has lasted many lifetimes. I did get even with you in that past life. I always fight back."

Paul stood in disbelief at this torrent of words. Her words matched his memories and Lena's visions. Finally, his analytical mind snapped into the hypothesis of past lives being validated. It was a visceral feeling, having his analytical mind suddenly sync up with his intuition and subconscious. Or maybe it was that Nera was walking closer, with one hand hidden in her cloak.

"Do you have a pain in your left shoulder? I know you do. I know you have a scar there too; I have seen it in my vision. May I see it? After all, I put it there in another past life." Paul started to back away. Nera continued, "If you let me see it, I'll depart before people start to show up for your little Druid jerk-off circle of goody-goodyness. I need to prove to myself that I gave the athame to the right person and my curse might be closer to be lifted. It's not about you, you self-absorbed man. I'm really quite distraught, and you haven't been very helpful at all."

Paul had thoughts about his scar and realized he needed to trust his gut and his intuition, he needed to trust the voices in his head and show her the scar on his shoulder. "All right, I will show you my scar and then you will leave." Paul slowly unbuttoned his shirt and slowly pulled off his shirt and turned around so Nera could see it.

Nera took a sharp breath, almost not believing what she was seeing. She exhaled slowly and walked to

Paul's back to touch the scar with her fingers, which sent chills and goose bumps on his back and neck. She ran her fingers up and down the scar tissue with two fingers. Paul thought it sounded like she was crying but he could not see her face. Nera ran her other hand along his entire spine like she was feeling for something, something else that could have happened to his back. Paul abruptly said, "Well, you have examined my scar, you can go now." He pulled away from her and turned toward her and could see her beautiful green eyes full of tears. She was crying. This cold-hearted person was crying at the sight of his scar. Paul felt compelled to ask her, "May I ask why you wanted to see my scar?"

Nera looked down at the ground for a second and then looked up with her sad eyes. "Paul, in another lifetime, in many lifetimes, my past lives made horrible mistakes, and my past lives carry curses to my current lifetime. I live with an unbearable agony in my heart every day. In one of my past lives, I created that scar during one of your past life incarnations. I tried to accuse your common woman of witchcraft and wanted to hurt her, because you denied me, but then you showed up to save her and instead of her getting whipped and burnt at the stake, you, in your damn honor, took the lashings for her to protect her. I tried to kill her with an athame but you dove to protect her and I drove the knife deep into your back, exactly in that spot where you have that scar. So that is a piece of that story of my curse. The other time, you gave me two chances and I was successful on the second one, dreadfully accurate. That should solve some of what you are looking for, for now."

Nera looked up, her sincere green eyes looking for any sign of compassion or forgiveness. Paul was confused, intrigued, but knew it was true, all of it was true. His inner voice was agreeing with her story and told him to show compassion even though logic said not to.

Nera did not allow Paul to comment before she started to walk away from the standing stones. She stopped before exiting the circle, turned around, and walked back to Paul, right up to his face, put both of her hands on his cheeks and kissed him on the lips, full passion and the intensity of their entwined past lives. She grabbed him passionately and he slowly wrapped his arms around her also, and they were lost in time for a few seconds on something that was never meant to be. She pulled away from him, biting his lower lip, and said, "I will tell you everything that I know when you return home under different circumstances. I'm told by my visions that you have to experience this predawn ritual and that some kind of energy healing with your new friend Brynn is also important. But you already knew that, right? Bye, Paul." She walked away into the night and never turned back as she made her way down the hill away from the standing stones.

Paul stood there, trying to comprehend everything that had happened in the last thirty minutes.

Within minutes, cars with their headlights on in the moonlight were pulling into the small parking area at the bottom of the hill from the standing stones. Brynn and Robert were walking up with women dressed in white robes carrying torches up the hill and they saw Paul.

Robert's curiosity was piqued. "There you are. We have been looking for you but could not find or see you. Where have you been?"

Paul said, "I have been here the entire time. What are you talking about?"

Brynn replied, "Paul, we looked up here first and did not see you here, so, where were you?"

Paul smirked and said, "I have been here the entire time almost thirty minutes, standing here talking to Nera."

Brynn touched his arm and quietly said, "You have been missing for ninety minutes. We will talk later, whoever this Nera is, she must be important to your journey. We have been down the hill the entire time and did not see anyone walking up here for the past two hours."

Robert said, "Paul, I swear to God, we did not see anyone walk up or down the hill. When did you meet Nera and why on earth would she be here in Scotland? Is she stalking you from Kansas? My dear friend, how many pints of beer did you have?"

Paul suddenly doubted the whole discussion he had just had with Nera with his mind grasping for facts to prove it happened. He was doubting himself because he was just so assured the whole past life was so correct and the kiss with Nera was so real. Paul could not comprehend it all right there in the moment as the women in robes with torches walked by him. He had too much to think about right now. He shelved it all away for later. The predawn ceremony was about to happen and he wanted to savor the experience. Not that he really had a choice about shelving it, the shock of the experience, the scar, the kiss, his disappearance, it was too much.

There were about twenty women all dressed in white robes carrying torches inside the circle of standing stones. Paul walked next to Brynn and Robert to get out of the way and to follow suit as an observer and not a participant. The women all stood in a circle inside the circle of stones and Paul, Brynn, and Robert were inside the standing stones but outside the human circle of the women. The only sounds were of the hiss of the burning torches. Simultaneously, all the women put their hoods over their heads and held hands between torches to form a human circle.

The women started to move to the left and to the right in a circle and then started to spin and the only sounds were of their feet on the ground and of torches moving quickly back and forth between the dancing of the women. Paul was looking at the unison of the women and then caught the eye of one of the women and was in shock. One of the women looked just like Lilith. He did a double take but could only see her face as she came closer to him and she looked at him and winked.

Paul questioned reality for at least the fourth time that night. This woman that he had dreamed about in his inner temple under his tree of life was actually dancing in a robe in a circle of standing stones. How could someone he dreamt about possibly be physically right here in his present time? Then he looked to his left and across the circle he saw a man in a black robe with a hood and he was looking straight at Paul. Merc. There were two people from his dream, from his inner temple, people he imagined, who were right here in front of him in physical form in Scotland in this circle of standing stones. Paul was dizzy from too many thoughts in his head in conflict all at the same time. The dancing was more active, and the women now sang in unison and the moving of the torches in unison was hypnotic and Paul's mind was overwhelmed. His mind was spilling over with too many concurrent thoughts. Paul fell down. Overanalysis, too much alcohol, challenges with reality, and the climax of the dawn peering from the eastern horizon and Paul passed out along the standing stone with his vision tunneling and his knees giving out on him and Robert and Brynn asking if he was ok as his mind faded fast into darkness.

Paul fell into a dream state and in complete darkness heard Lena's voice from his first meeting with her. Lena's voice was saying, "Paul, do you have a scar on your left shoulder?" Lena continued, "A knife will drive into your left shoulder, and it was in the 1200s on a field in Scotland, and the dagger killed you on the battlefield." Then in this darkness, Paul heard Nera's voice when she said, "I need to give this to you … and I am sorry for everything." And Paul visualized the athame in his hands but he could not see it but only feel it in the darkness in his mind. Another voice came into his mind, and it was Lena, saying, "Paul, what does the word Hermes or Mercury mean to you?" In Paul's mind of utter darkness there was only silence now. Nothing but silence.

Chapter 20
The Healing Session

Paul was slowly waking up in a darkened room with candles and incense and soft music of the ocean playing on one of those white noise machines to help people go to sleep. There was someone in the room with him, walking around like preparing for something. Paul's vision was slowly coming back, and he could see Brynn next to him. He asked, "Where am I?"

Brynn said, "Well, Paul, you are in my shop in my energy room and I am about to give you an energy session—are you feeling all right? You looked pale as a ghost as you came in here."

Paul asked slurring, "What happened at the standing stones, when I passed out?"

Brynn giggled. "What standing stones, there are no standing stones within fifty kilometers. You came to my shop about fifteen minutes ago because you had a cab bring you from the hotel and you used the address I gave you on the back of my business card to give the taxi driver to get here this morning. Are you feeling ok? It was like you were in a sleep or trance when you walked into my shop this morning."

Paul's vision was becoming clearer as he looked around the room. The healing room looked more like a library, but then the figurines of fairies and deities made it also look like a mystical shop. He laid back on the massage table, fully exhausted and totally confused on what reality was really upon him now. The unending cascade of events left him feeling bereft of the energy to keep treading water, let alone find any answers, closure, or sense of peace.

Brynn put on some music and lit more candles, and Paul fully gave in to the experience. He felt the black and white yoga blanket underneath him, scratchy but comforting and warm at the same time and provided warmth at the same time. It looked like a Native American blanket. Paul realized his shoes and socks were already off and his bare feet were exposed to Brynn's healing session. He released himself to her to work on him so he could find his center.

Brynn asked if he was comfortable and then started at his feet working the energy healing on him. In Kansas, he never would have gone in for an energy healing; it was too much of a stretch for his logical mind. But here he was, in Scotland, seeking adventure and the unknown and he had nothing to lose. His feet became warm by her touch and he could feel the warmth from her hands like nothing he had felt before. Inwardly, it felt like his blood capillaries were healing as she moved her hands. She knew certain pressure points to fully relax him and he was almost at a paralyzed situation where the energy level was so high that he could not move.

Within minutes that passed, and Paul was physically exhausted but mentally calm. Then Brynn at the end of the session asked Paul if it would be ok to embrace so their heart chakras could touch for a few minutes and Paul sluggishly and shyly agreed, not knowing exactly what she meant and he sat up and over the side of the table with his legs dangling and she climbed up on him and wrapped her legs around him. She held him tightly and asked him to just breathe so they could synchronize their hearts on the same breath together. Their hearts were within inches of each other. Paul could feel her heartbeat and he was aligning his rate with hers, and as they held each other, their breathing melded together and they both could feel each other's heart and the beat of their hearts became one.

Paul started to slip away. He felt like he was projecting himself, and he was back at the tree of life. This time he knew the way though the tree root through the tunnel to his inner circle and his inner sanctuary. Paul walked out to the back porch again to the patio that faced the lake. His inner temple. Some of the same people were there but with an extra two people, one woman and one young girl. He slowly walked on the back porch and Merc immediately recognized him and then Diana and Lilith and his grandfather. They all looked up at Paul, and Merc said, "About time you meet our Brynn; she has been looking for you for years but you never seemed to make it to Scotland. She is the key to you visiting us more often. She is linked to you through multiple lifetimes."

Paul smiled and walked over to Lilith, who was sitting on a chaise lounge, and asked, "Could I have a better drink this time?"

Lilith just smiled. "Of course and I will not tease you like last time."

As she handed him a glass of wine, he smiled and said, "And how old is this?"

Lilith touched his arm seductively and said, "It's three hundred and eighteen years old but it is from a nice region in France that I used to visit a long time ago and the owner of the land is very noble. Do not worry. It is exceptional wine like he was."

Paul thanked her with a genuine flirting smile and sat down next to her in a chair as the fire pit roared with the circle of chairs on the back patio. He put his arm around her and sat close, knowing she would be flirting this session and she was the oldest and knew the most secrets throughout time.

Merc took the other chair next to him and everyone seemed to be comfortable to sit down again after Paul's arrival.

Merc started, "So Nera's past life has had meaningful histories throughout time. You can already figure that one out. She has murdered you twice in your past lives. That's why we are all interested in how she came back into your life and who gave the athame to her.

"There are many cosmic forces in movement. We are watching from afar but like you, we are interested in finding the key information you also seek so we will assist in this session. That is why you needed to meet Brynn; she is a supreme energy healer. That wonderful powerful spirit has had many past lives with you so we knew you would trust her instantly. She is your personal portal to us for this session, and she knows it, which means she will keep you in this status longer than usual because she knows and can hear what we all are saying right now. As she holds you with her hands between your temples, you will stay in this metaphysical state."

Merc hesitated and added, "Lilith, do you want to continue the conversation?"

Lilith acknowledged, "Well, ok, I will start this process of thinking. The blade that Nera gave you is significant to cosmic history. It has had some notorious horrifying events regarding witches, demons, and other entities, but the most important fact you must know is that the metal in that athame came from another more historic blade, the Holy Lance, also known as the Lance of Longinus. It is more famously called the Spear of Destiny. It is the holy spear legendary for piercing the side of Jesus Christ as he hung on the cross. Now this spear was rediscovered in AD 1098 during the first Crusades at Antioch and was used as a relic. The recovery of the relic inspired the Crusaders to take the offensive against the Muslims, routing them in the battle and securing Christian possession of Antioch. The artifact had disputes of holy authenticity like every other holy artifact. Peter Bartholomew, the discoverer, was eventually discredited by historians. Peter had said he had a vision from Saint Andrew to where the blade was, he informed the church and leaders of the first crusade. Bishop Adhemar of Le Puy was skeptical of the authenticity; Count Raymond of Toulouse was impressed. The blade was discovered in the cathedral of Saint Peter in Antioch, and during the digging he jumped in one of the holes and came out with a form of iron that was assumed to be the relic. Most of the believers accepted that it was the famous blade and it inspired them to win. Eventually the people began to doubt the blade, and the authenticity of the blade, and back in the day, people thought relics of Jesus and God could save them or grant supernatural powers. Peter promised the relic would save him during his ordeal by fire but the flames fatally burned him and the blade lost its power to awe. As the blade went into obscurity, we all know that the so-called blade was melted and made into several notorious blades. The Vatican is always looking for the rest of them, so let's not tell them about this one or the one your friend Robert has in a secret government secure area.

"Being forged of the metal that killed Jesus, the blade carries a curse. Paul, this blade has another special history on how it came to be on the Roman soldier's spear because it was charged by a witch in AD 33, which is another story."

Lilith continued after finishing her drink, her every gesture elegant and refined. "As we go farther back into time, Nera has had many current past lives readings in which the readers and psychics have told her she could have been the beloved Mary Magdalene. She was a Mary, 'the other Mary,' during the time of Jesus but not the Holy Mary. That Mary was evil and deceitful. They looked like sisters, they resembled each other. After the crucifixion, Nera—rather Mary—claimed to be a devotee of Christ. Many of the gospels merged the two Marys into one, by rumor alone. The Mary that Jesus cast seven devils and demons out of was Nera in a past life but then her true heart showed up and she seduced the Roman guard who was going to be guarding Jesus for the crucifixion and she put a death spell on his spear, which is against the witch rede. That spear became the 'spear of destiny,' which caused a curse, killed Jesus, and has followed Nera throughout the last two thousand years, because of the evilness she cast back in AD 33. With the repetitive remembered acts of evil, she would be cursed to her next several lifetimes.

"The blade must be secured in a safe place to protect it from other people and from Nera. She has spent lifetimes separating herself from the blade, but somehow the blade has returned to her to remind herself of the evilness she did over two thousand years ago. This blade is only partially formed from the iron of the blade of destiny. There are other blades that have the rest of the iron of the spear of destiny that exist, and you have seen where they are located."

Merc interjected, "To keep this simple because you look lost, the blade that has killed you twice by the hands of Nera's past lives was forged out of the blade that killed Jesus in AD 33, so the metal carries some fucking dark horrific energy, hatred, despair, and total death in the metal."

Lilith sniffed. "He may be a man, but I don't think he needs it that oversimplified, Merc. Now, if I may continue ..."

Paul kept the laughter out of his face, contriving to only show his genuine curiosity as he nodded.

Lilith began again, "There is also rumor that the blade of destiny was cursed by a dark woman or witch that assured that the blade would kill and curse Jesus. It is all rumor and fable and not written in the Bible. I almost forgot, Hitler was obsessed with all the spears of destiny out there and collected them during the war. There is rumor that the spears possessed him to carry out the war, but that's just another tale."

Lilith showed a mischievous smile with a little evil. Paul felt there was more information that she was withholding, but he was still trying to process what she had told him so far.

Lilith continued, "The challenge we all have is what spirit is behind the actions of Nera. What entity has been inside Nera each of the times she has killed you, other more important people, and why? We among your spiritual protection circle are also trying to work it out and identify the spirit or being or intergalactic force that is behind this. Given how long this metal's been around and cursed, it has to be something really ancient."

All of a sudden everyone looked at a figure walking from the lake shore toward the back porch. It was a large black man in Middle Eastern attire wearing a tunic and tan robe to his feet. He walked up to the front porch and everyone welcomed him to the back porch. The strange man walked up to Paul, who stood up from his chair. The man said, "You may not remember me, but you tried to save my life from an evil woman." The man stood proud with full empathy and said, "In one moment of weakness, that evil bitch killed me with a blade, but in my last breaths of life you covered my body with your own as she killed you too. I have been traveling for centuries in the spirit world for this moment to personally thank you for your honor." The large black man hugged Paul with the intensity of the brotherhood of war and a respectful thankfulness, then kissed him on both sides of his cheeks. "I can now depart to the other upper world. I have been waiting for this moment for a long time to thank you. I thank you, Brynn, for your skills allowing Paul to travel to his inner circle today, I now have freedom of honor and spirit and soul to depart from this world."

Paul was stunned. As they embraced, he felt a wash of familiarity, a feeling of love and regard for this stranger. Paul watched in silence as the man walked off the porch and back near the lake and eventually disappeared behind the trees.

Merc asked, "Do you remember who that was from your past life?"

Paul quietly said, "I feel that I know him like a brother, but no thoughts are coming to me yet as to where it was from."

Merc said, "His name was Abdul. You once saved him in multiple battles, and he was indebted to your services. One night when you were a bishop in Italy, you had a friend who happened to be a witch, and also happened to be another one of Nera's past lives, and she tried to kill you and you saved her and had Abdul take her to Scotland to your family. As they traveled Abdul fell victim to her beauty and charm. The night before they were to reach your lands in Scotland, she cut his throat as they were making love. You tried to save his life but then you were killed, in that damn left shoulder of yours. Here's the kicker—the same woman stabbed you in the same spot twice but the second time the angle was deeper, and you died a painful death. Abdul has been waiting to thank you in this spectral plane, to see you and to thank you, and so he could go in peace from this plane."

Paul believed the story because it felt right and aligned with everything else that was happening to him. He sat there, exhausted from processing, and drank some of the exceptional vintage wine that Lilith poured him. Lilith smiled and said, "I told you the wine was good." She leaned her head on his shoulder and put her arms around him.

Paul just sat there contemplating it all, the back patio

with all these beings, the lake in the background and the beautiful mountain scenery and he knew this must be his true inner temple where his conscious and subconscious challenged each other. Paul asked, "I would also assume that Nera has been trying to kill or hurt me multiple times throughout the centuries that Brynn has been trying to save me?"

Merc smiled and said, "Paul, my dear friend, that is correct. Brynn has been in multiple past lives with you. She has saved you, loved you, and taught you throughout the ages, and you both have saved each other through timelines. We were grateful that you took the trip to Scotland and that she would meet you. We also might have interfered a little, but it was for the right reasons."

Paul grinned. "Well, you interfered, huh! I do not mind, the point was that I am back here with the help of Brynn, and to all of you I am very grateful to meet everyone and receive guidance and spiritual direction."

Paul asked one last question because he knew his time here was about to end. "So for all of you, why does Nera keep hurting people and keep hurting me?"

They all looked at one another as if they each knew the answer, but no one wanted to say it to him and then they all looked at Merc to say something. Merc took a long drink from his cup and said, "I guess I will take the lead on this one and tell you simply it is all about love and hate."

Merc slowly said, "If I get the story wrong, please assist me as I recall it, but I think I know the story as well as anyone." But as Merc was starting to explain, Paul he was being physically pulled from the patio and inner circle back though the tree of life and back to reality. Brynn had held him in his inner temple as long as she physically could and his time was up. Merc yelled out, "Next time, my friend, when you come, I will tell the final chapter that you seek and the why, first thing."

As Paul was being pulled through the tree of life and back into reality, he felt Brynn's hands on his head and her body still sitting on his on the table, but he could feel that she was totally exhausted.

When he fully came back, they just held each other in silence. Paul could feel Brynn's ragged breathing and increased heart rate. They held each other in comfort and full trust for almost ten minutes before looking at each other and smiling softly. Paul said, "I guess we have had many past lives together."

Brynn just looked at him with a puzzled look. "You think?"

They started to unlock from each other, and she moved to the other side of the room, asking, "Would you like some tea?"

Paul said, "Yes, that would be delightful."

"We can talk while I brew a pot. It looks like we have had many lives together, but it looks like we have always cared about each other too. How about we just take this moment and experience one day at a time, ok?"

"That is some of the best advice I have been given the last ten days."

They both laughed like learning about an entire novel in which they were the main characters but not really knowing all the details yet. Brynn touched his hand and said, "We will do this together, somehow. It was meant to be that way."

Brynn heard the whistle of the tea and readied the cups and started to pour. She handed Paul his tea, and they both sat down at a small table in the corner of the room.

Paul said, "Thank you for the healing session and thank you for being my portal to my inner temple." He assumed she heard the entire conversation and just wanted to be fully forward with everything.

She smiled and said, "Well, Paul, you are welcome, and it is my pleasure that my skills and spiritual abilities allow you to travel to your inner temple as we conduct a healing session."

That ended the awkwardness, and they acted like two old friends over tea, the conversation friendly and comforting. They continued to talk and enjoy each other's company until there was a knock on the store door. They looked at the front door, and there stood Robert. He was anxious to have the door opened for him.

Brynn walked over and opened the door. Robert cheerfully walked into the shop and said, "Good morning to you both, my friends. Brynn, did you get Paul to his inner temple?"

Brynn smiled and said, "Robert, of course I did, and he is comprehending it all right over tea that you are interrupting, but since you're here, would you like some tea?"

Robert pulled up a third chair to their small table and asked them, "So what answers do we need to know about?"

Paul just smiled and guessed he was sort of the last one to the party and that Brynn and Robert were much more along than he was in the process of past lives and of the blade.

Robert smiled and said, "Paul, why does Nera keep killing you?"

"Merc was about to tell me when I got pulled out of the inner temple to come back to current time."

"Well, Merc needs to speed something up and stop making everything so dramatic with Lilith and company."

Paul looked puzzled and said, "Robert, how do you know about Mercury and Lilith in my inner temple?"

"Paul, the three of us, you, Brynn, and I are all connected throughout the ages. All of our inner temples are interconnected. Don't look so surprised."

Paul said, "I am not surprised anymore."

"Paul, have you ever of heard of synchronicity?"

"You mean the Police album in 1985 that Sting was the lead singer for?"

Robert shook his head and then commented, "No, but that was a great album back in 1983 not 1985, and I still have it in my office with the tricolored album cover, oh yeah, those songs especially 'Every Breath You Take,' 'Wrapped around your Finger,' and 'King of Pain.'"

Brynn said, "Please stop, we were not talking

about an album—it was a great album—we were talking about synchronicity. Focus, please! Are you sure I am the youngest one here?"

Robert played repentant. "Brynn, you are right." He adopted his most pontificating professorial tone, but there was a twinkle in his eye as he talked. "Synchronicity is the driving force behind coincidence. There's a lot of white noise, and the mind can over or under attribute significance, but they are like universal nods, that you are meant to be on the right road, for best direction. They are like whispers and get louder when they need your attention. These types of messages are historic in the Bible.

"I know you know of Carl Jung, the analytical psychologist. Jung called this phenomenon the 'acausal connecting principle' and 'acausal parallelism' and he believed events are connected by causality and may also be connected by meaning. He's famous for arguing the existence of the paranormal, and how the paranormal could affect synchronicity, archetypes, and the collective unconscious. From the religious perspective, it's understood as the intervention of grace. Jung also discusses how synchronicity serves a role in our dreams. People, including myself, believe angels, gods, and goddesses cause synchronicity."

Paul finished the tea and said, "So, Robert, what you and Brynn are saying is all these events are divinely lined up by gods, the psychic world, and the paranormal?"

Robert and Brynn both looked up at Paul with a

smile and together said, "Yes!"

Paul smiled back. "So we need to see this through to the end?"

Robert looked at Brynn with sarcasm and said, "My dear Brynn, I think our student finally understands the lesson." Everyone was cheerful that Paul was putting all the pieces together and they chatted the rest of the hour over more tea.

Chapter 21
William and Anna

William's protection and courage had rung through the crowd with every snap of the lash. There was no joy in the shedding of this blood. Starting to hate themselves for their earlier viciousness, the crowd's mood was turning restive and ugly. They were looking for an outlet. The judge didn't care about the mood of the crowd. Appalled by the stabbing, he wanted the situation to get closed down, but felt helpless. The crowd shouted insults at everyone on stage, except William. Scuffles broke out among hotheads. Margaret ripped the knife out of William's left shoulder, causing a new shower of blood to exit William's body along with the knife. Margaret stomped over to Anna, bound and helpless at the edge of the platform, grabbing her hair from behind and raising the knife up high. The judge, calculating madly, drew a breath to order the guard to stop her when everything changed.

A group of horses galloped, steaming and exhausted, into the square, scattering the peasants. Armored knights maintained formation as they slowed and moved toward the platform. The knights wore the king's colors and crest. Even Margaret froze in place with the bloodied knife in her hand, still gripping Anna's hair. Everyone stopped moving as the king entered the square, flanked by knights. Almost frozen in place, everyone waited to see what would happen next.

The horses fully encircled the square and King James VI rode up to the platform, jumping off the horse and walking over to his niece. "Margaret, you stupid woman, I order you to stop this immediately! You are such a spoiled bitch!" The king grabbed the knife from her hand and slapped her across the face with the back of his hand for the crowd to see who was in charge. He turned his back on her, directing two of his knights to take custody of Margaret for acts against the king. The king looked at Anna. Everyone in the crowd could see his compassion for the helpless, bound woman. The king ordered, in a stern voice for all to hear, "Knights, if anyone tries to hurt this innocent young woman today or in the future, you kill them and cut off their head." All the knights pulled out their swords in unison before bowing to the king in acknowledgment.

The king looked at Margaret, whimpering between two men. His mouth curled in disgust as he turned away again and walked over to William, lying face down, blood dripping from his wounds. "William, I can see you have everything under control," with a small smile for his friend. The king then proclaimed, "Who is the judge in this town?" and the judge cautiously said, "I am."

The king thundered, "Who told you to conduct a witch inquiry about an innocent woman?"

The judge bowed and said, "Margaret said it was the king's authority."

The king looked at Margaret again. Making a quick assessment of the situation, he asked, "Did this noble knight take punishment for this accused, innocent woman?"

"Yes, all twenty lashings," the judge answered.

The king said, "I declare that the matter is final." He turned to the crowd, "The woman is innocent and protected under the king. Do you all understand?"

The judge spoke for his town, "I fully understand."

The king continued, "Please tell every town in the countryside that if my niece ever comes into a town and says she is speaking for me, whip her twenty times for lying." Margaret screamed at the king and knights quickly picked her up and took her away. The king gently touched the judge. "Please tell everyone to go home and swear that you will never let my niece influence you again. If you ever let her do this again to your town, I will personally whip you myself for being disloyal to the crown."

The judge grinned. Having now personally witnessed his king for the first time, though he knew the threat was serious, he saw that the king was kind and just and felt no fear. He did as the king said and addressed the crowd, "Ladies and gentlemen, please go home."

The crowd started to dissipate. The king went over to William and asked if he needed a surgeon and William said he needed Anna, that she knew how to heal him. So, the king made sure that William and Anna returned to her house and the king's flag was placed in front of it with a proclamation of protection. The town had heard from the king that Anna was not a witch, which was good enough for them.

The king left gold for William and Anna, knowing they would be doing little else for several weeks beyond healing each other. He left a guard detail outside Anna's house for a couple of days to give teeth to the rumors spreading along the countryside of his message not to listen to Margaret and to leave Anna alone. Anna was publicly protected by the king.

The flayed and open tangle of flesh the lashings had left took weeks to heal but Anna was there to heal William one day at a time. She knew all the healing methods, sewed the open wounds, and made poultices to soothe the pain and assist the healing process. They loved each other dearly and healed each other day by day. The knife wound was the hardest to heal because Margaret had sent it deep into his shoulder and had almost killed him but the stroke had hit bone and stopped before there was any serious organ damage. The scars would heal and the wounds would be just other character spots in a long career. William and Anna ended up spending a couple months together convalescing. William was a good patient under Anna's care and she gave him ointments every evening to work into the cuts on his back and then she would use her energy healing to heal him on the inside. They took daily walks in the woods.

William was getting his strength up and knew he needed to go back to his headquarters and continue his important work as a Knight Templar. One morning in early fall, he packed up his possessions. As he was tying his bag shut, Anna came up to him and gave him a mala of purple stones to wear and to carry for protection. He hadn't said he was leaving that day. He hadn't needed to.

"The mala is from the Buddhist tradition from the Far East," Anna explained. "I added some extra power to it for your protection." They embraced fiercely. William knew if he asked her to come to the capital she would not go and leave her warm home and her forest and he knew he could not stay there because his duty was to the church. As they walked outside, he checked one last time that the king's flag was still present. There was little more he could do; the flag was a strong, respected symbol of royal decree. He could relax. They embraced one last time and he said he would come back in a year and she rolled her beautiful green eyes and said, "I love you; I will see you when you return." They had never kissed, but this time they kissed to remind themselves how much they loved each other, to remind themselves how deep their hearts were for each other, and to set a seed to remember and never to forget each other for lifetimes.

William got on his horse and checked all his weapons, his sword, his shield, his axe; he reached for his dagger in his boot and realized it was missing. That was the dagger Margaret had taken from him and stabbed him in the back with. He guessed someone picked it up in the courtyard or it was now a souvenir for someone in the village. He would just have another one made.

As he turned his horse to ride away, he gave one more wave to Anna and hoped he would see her again. He yelled out, "I love you."

She only said, "I have known that for years, thank you." She waved to him. "I will always love you throughout time."

He rode away, slightly confused by her last statement, but he was in a good mental and physical place to return back to his knight career and his intention was to return as soon as he could. His thoughts turned away from Anna and toward his work as he rode out.

CHAPTER 22
WILLIAM'S RETURN

After a year, William was able to take leave from the Knights Templars to return to Anna. He rode across Europe in anticipation of seeing her beautiful smile, her curly hair that was always in her eyes, and her gentleness. Since most of his men knew how important Anna was to him, they rode with him most of the journey to assure no delay.

William's men had heard all the stories of the last time he visited Anna and of the whipping he received. They saw the scars of it every day, just as he saw the scars of their battle wounds. They also remembered the story of how the king arrived just in time to assist him after he was stabbed in the shoulder by the king's niece Margaret.

The king could not completely disown Margaret. It went against the laws of his land, and the consequences of breaking the law were not worth the price. Instead, he sent her to the most distanced castle in the most desolate area for her to live her life alone with no noble advantages and a reputation of hatred. He told the court the story of her cruelty and wickedness. His men knew that Margaret would never forgive William for what he did to her. The king publicly rewarded and honored him for his bravery and compassion, taking the lashings to protect an innocent.

William's men escorted him to the village. They took lodging in town while he visited Anna alone. Knowing how much in love William was with Anna, they let him ride the last couple of miles by himself.

Riding through the dark forests, William was fast approaching Anna's homeplace but something was so different. Where was beauty in the forests? There was only darkness and sadness. The road to Anna's cottage looked abandoned and unkept for a long time. William stopped his horse on the pathway and got off to walk the rest of the way. It did not feel right. He started to worry.

William found Anna's house on the road, but it did not look alive, it looked abandoned. William went into alert mode looking for someone to jump out of the trees; his gut knew something was terribly wrong. The gardens were overgrown with weeds. No one had looked after the place for months. He screamed, "Anna, where are you!" but there was only silence.

He was trembling as he touched the front door. Opening it, he could see no one had lived there for a while. His only concern was Anna. Was she safe? Where could she be? He felt on full alert and pulled out his sword and started to walk around Anna's house toward the back of the yard and then his heart stopped and he dropped to his knees and started crying with total despair as if his heart had been ripped out. Behind Anna's house was a makeshift burning post and he could tell that wood had been gathered and that there was a burning. A fully decomposed body was still at the post. William collapsed on the ground and knew it was Anna. He cried with heartbroken abandon. It felt as if a spear had ripped through his heart. He was on his knees and crying out to God why did this happen to Anna, the most beautiful soul he had ever met.

He shouted at the heavens, "Who could burn innocent Anna after everything and what evil person would do such a thing to a gracious soul?" and then he looked up from his agony, afraid to look at the burnt body anymore. He only knew of one person ... Margaret.

Emotionally shaken, William knew he needed to provide the proper burial to his beloved Anna, whose bones were still tied to the burning stake and left for nature to go through like savages. Anna deserved a proper burial and he would seek vengeance for the one person who did this. He found a burlap bag and went to the burning stake and while crying with grief, took the bones from the burning stakes and gently put them in the burlap sack with full respect guiding his every movement. He gently picked up her skull, his touch full of reverence and care. As he was moving her skull, he noticed a necklace she had been wearing that had somehow survived the burning. He picked it up and cleaned the necklace made of blue stones with runes imprinted on each and put it in his pocket.

He continued to remove each of the bones with respect and care from the burning stake when he heard a rush of horses coming up the path to Anna's house. He pulled out his sword to defend Anna's honor in death as he stood at the front of her house, expecting pillagers and expecting to kill them all. He was calmed when he saw his own men arrive in mass at Anna's house.

The lead officer said, "Sir, we just heard what happened as we were moving into the nightly quarters, when the magistrate gave us this letter to give to you."

William said, "A letter?"

His senior officer said the magistrate had given it to him to only give to William who defended Anna a year ago.

William was in no mood to read a letter now. He instructed his men to help him respect Anna, who had been burned behind her house. He wanted every bone collected and there would be a proper ceremony to bury her remains. William insisted on his men giving the fullest respect to this woman who was innocent and protected by the king and was murdered.

His men gave the highest respect to collecting all the bones and remains of Anna and to assist William in giving her a proper burial. They collected everything from the burning stake where Anna had been burned, and they put all the remains in a burlap sack as directed by William.

A woman that William had loved had been burned to the stake and left for dead and they were a part of William's Army of the Knights Templar to bring justice to those who did this to Anna. One of William's highest officers said, "Sir, we still have this letter for you to read."

His officer said as soon as they checked into the local inn with witness of Sir William they had gone to the constable for directions. William's officer went to the high constable, who gave the officer a letter from Margaret, the niece of the king, to give to William.

William took the letter and read the following:

Dear William, my love,

As you know me, I could not just let it lie. You embarrassed me in front of the King which took months to mend, but you knew I could not let Anna just live a peaceful life. That is not my style. I was banished by the King to the most desolate state to be a figure head. Such a state was not going to work under my timetable. So, I hired some criminals who would help me revenge myself and we assaulted Anna's cottage and those nasty vile men raped her repeatedly. And then we did our own unlawful court hearing because she was a witch. We found her guilty. You know she did not defend herself. She stayed truthful to you until her end. We burned her good and watched her scream in agony. She died in burnt skin *without you to save her this time. This letter was given to the magistrate to give to you and make sure the scene was not disturbed until you arrived. I warned the magistrate not to touch anything until you arrived or the King would not be happy with the village.*

William, I know you are upset that I murdered your beloved Anna, so I challenge you to come and find me. I enjoyed watching her burn while so in love with you.

Too bad I was never yours,
Lady Margaret

William looked up from the letter in full sadness, anger, and disgust. He challenged his men to remember how they found the innocent woman named Anna behind her peaceful house and to use that anger once they found Margaret, wherever she was.

William's men all committed to finding Margaret and to bring her to justice or to just hang her or burn her. All of William's men were fully committed. The next day, William and his men conducted a proper Christian burial in full uniforms and full regalia for Anna in a proper cemetery for her fullest honor and respect. Many people from the town and all the magistrates also attended the funeral ceremony knowing the huge injustice and cruelty that ended Anna's life.

William first had to tell his men that this dangerous

journey would not be sanctioned by the knights, but they would all have to be volunteers. This action against Margaret would not be sponsored by the church; it would be pure vengeance to the vile Margaret. It was his oath to make sure she was put to justice and not just for vengeance. William and his men all discussed that due to their return, Margaret could have months head start on them and where would she go? William decided they must visit the king first and tell him their intent before they went on their quest. The king knew them all personally and would understand and might assist in pinpointing her location.

The next morning, they found that Anna had left the house and land to William because she had no family and he was her closest friend. William did not know how to react because he felt like he had failed her; how could she leave her house to him? As William was confused, he asked the magistrate, "Did Anna have any friends in the village whom she trusted?"

The magistrate said, "There was one poor girl, Lisa, I think is her name, who works as a housekeeper for one of the established families in town, but she has no husband and is already twenty-three years old. A simple girl, a good person, she spent lots of time with Anna at her house. She works just down the block at Mr. Smith's estate."

William thanked the magistrate and headed down the block to find this Lisa, who might give him a new solution to Anna's house. He walked up to the estate and the owner was on the front porch and greeted William.

William asked, "May I speak to Lisa? Does she still work for you?"

The gentleman said, "Why, yes, she is in the garden behind the house. You need to catch her now before she departs. We are having to let her go next week and she is looking to move soon."

William smiled and said, "Thank you, sir, I might have another opportunity for her, if she is willing."

William walked behind the house and found a full-figured young brunette who was finishing up picking the latest vegetables from the garden to prepare for dinner. William walked up to her and said, "Is your name Lisa and were you friends with Anna?"

The young girl stood up and said, "Yes, my name is Lisa. Anna was very dear to me, and I am ashamed and saddened by what happened to her and what happened to you. There are too many bad memories here of the last year for me to stay any longer."

William said, "Lisa, I have a proposal for you. Anna had no family and left her land and cottage to me to take care of. I was wondering if you would live there and take care of her house for me and I would pay you for upkeep?"

Lisa adjusted the vegetables resting on her hips and smiled and giggled. "You want me to live in the cottage and take over the place and you will pay me for it? Really?"

William looked at her. "Yes, that sums it up. I want to keep the place, but I do not live here. I want it to be taken care like Anna would want but I only would trust the cottage with someone Anna would trust. I would only want someone who Anna trusted to stay there and keep it up."

Lisa smiled and said, "I would love to return the place to the way Anna had it and make her proud of it. Would you mind if I did a cleansing spell to ward off evil spirits from the place? I don't think you would mind. Could I have a monthly salary to keep up the place?"

William extended his hand and said, "If we shake on it and you give me your word? I agree to all your terms and will write a letter to the judge before I leave that you will reside on the property indefinitely."

Lisa shook his hand with tears in her eyes. "Sir, you gave me a second chance in life. How can I thank you?"

William said, "Take care of Anna's property and return it to the respect of nature that it used to be, that is the best way to remember and respect Anna. My duty is to go find the woman who had her killed, so I think you have the easier part. One more thing—if I do not return and fall in battle, the property will be deeded to you."

With that last comment Lisa dropped her vegetable basket and hugged William, full of tears as if the past few minutes lifted the burden of a year of stress and direction she had lost and with just a simple act her life was changed.

William thanked her again and headed to the magistrate. He and his men needed to start their quest.

Chapter 23
Back in Kansas

As their delightful morning together in Brynn's shop was coming to a close over tea, they all knew that Paul and Robert needed to catch their flight that evening and start their trip back to America. Brynn asked, "So what else do you two need to do before you depart?"

Robert and Paul had not thought that far ahead. They exchanged a puzzled glance, saddened because they realized they had to leave and could not stay any longer. Their flight was at 8 p.m. and it was now 10 a.m. so they had about six hours remaining to explore Scotland. They both looked at Brynn and asked, "So what is a must-see in our last six hours here?"

She smiled, a mischievous sparkle dancing in her eyes.

They went to the tailor shop instead of sightseeing

and got custom-made kilts and tartans and shirts, and most important, a nice wool hat with a feather broach on the front. Brynn explained the feather gave good luck to the wearer. They were like kids trying on new clothes to see which ones looked best in the mirrors. In Scotland, custom tailor shops offer complimentary whisky and so they enjoyed a few glasses together. Brynn naturally ended up being the final inspector and approval of the clothes they chose or did not choose. She had the most fun watching them come out of the dressing expecting approval and quickly being returned to try something else.

As they paid for the pieces they finally decided on, Brynn offered to take the two men and their belongings to the airport. Robert said, "We already expected that since you got us drunk and we spent quite a bit of money buying authentic approved Scottish attire and helped improve the local economy."

Brynn just smiled knowing she orchestrated the mischievous delight of the afternoon with these two gentlemen. She crammed the slightly drunk professors into her car and drove them to the airport as they sang Tom Petty songs from her playlist. Brynn was going to miss them.

At the airport and before security, Brynn said her good-byes and expressed hope to someday visit America and get a tour of Kansas. Both men looked puzzled and smiled.

Paul said, "When you want to visit us, just let me know and I will support your efforts to come to Kansas."

She kissed Robert on the cheek and hugged him like an old friend.

She also kissed Paul on both cheeks and a quick kiss on the mouth and gave him a long hug.

Both men waved, sad of their departure, but they knew they had done what they came there to do.

As they boarded their plane, they decided to have another glass of whisky to start their flight, knowing they would be asleep soon to enjoy the thirteen-hour red-eye flight back to the States.

They arrived in Kansas City and drove together in exhausted silence in Robert's car back to the campus where Paul had left his car.

As Paul put his luggage into his car, he could see his building light was on and so was his office light. He was sure he turned off his lights, so he told Robert he was going to check his office and then head home. Paul trudged up to his building in the cold predawn and entered the dim hallway and walked up to his door. It was open and the light was on, and he could hear someone moving papers and books around.

He walked in and was surprised to see Nera digging in his office, looking through his drawers. Paul suspected she was looking for the athame.

Paul yelled, "What the hell are you doing?! This *is* stalking now, and I am calling campus security." Paul pulled out his cell phone and was about to dial 911.

Nera looked up, surprised to see Paul, and said, "Stop, don't do that. I will explain everything. Let's settle this, tonight. I know you want answers."

Paul said, "Ok, what are you looking for? Are you looking for the athame? Well, it's not here."

Nera said, "I need the athame back to end my curse and you will tell me where it is." As she said this, Nera pulled out a 9 mm gun from her purse and pointed it toward Paul. "We will go to your house and retrieve the athame, do you fucking understand me now?"

Paul silently raised his hands in the sign of peace and said, "Nera, it is at my house. I will take you there. Please do not hurt me ... again."

As they departed Paul's office and started to leave the building together Nera put the pistol back in her purse and they walked next to each other together down the block toward his house. Paul asked, "Did you follow me to Scotland?"

Nera smiled, "Yes, I followed you to Scotland. I watched you and Dr. Robert travel to key past lives locations and I watched you meet Brynn. I watched how you were kind and sweet to her like you knew her your whole life. I was watching as Robert arrived shortly after your healing session. What did her healing session show you, Paul? Did you go to your inner circle? Did you talk to your gods and goddesses about me?" She waved the gun, her voice and gesture full of menace and mockery.

Paul was walking next to an armed woman whom he felt was highly violent. She seemed very willing to kill him earlier, and now she wanted to know about a personal metaphysical trip he had to his inner temple. Why and how did she know so much about his gods and deities in his inner temple? Nera held his hand as they walked to his house through the neighborhood. Paul was merely walking to his house with her, hoping there would be no violence.

Paul saw that Robert's car was already there and there were other cars parked out front, and all the lights were on in his house, which gave him comfort but also told him he was not in control of the events that were about to happen.

Nera asked, "What's going on, Paul? Why are all these cars here?"

Paul replied, "I don't know. I just got off the plane and came straight to my office because my office light was on."

As Nera and Paul came closer to the door, Robert opened the door suddenly and said, "Well, it is about time you showed up, and I can see you brought Nera with you. My dear, it is such a pleasure to finally meet you." Robert put out his hand to shake hers, but she did not respond. Robert said, "My dear, what do you have in your pocket, a gun?"

Nera looked puzzled. Things were not turning out as she expected and there were too many variables in the equation right now. Nera pulled out her gun and pointed it toward Robert and said, "Why, yes, I do have a gun. Where is the athame?"

Robert laughed. "Well, you have a gun, but that will not help you get the athame. Plus we have too many gods and goddesses out in the backyard to allow you to hurt anyone." A steely glint entered his eye, though his voice remained calm and charming. "You do remember the witches' rede, don't you? 'You shall do no harm.' Now, my dear, this is where you keep that gun in your purse and you walk into the backyard and act proper."

Nera was flustered and impatient. "Listen, old man, give me the goddamn athame right fucking now."

Robert touched her arm strongly and firmly, looking right into her eyes and said, "Margaret, you are a stupid woman. I order you to stop immediately! You are such a spoiled bitch."

Nera was taken aback and instantly remembered a past life and was suddenly frightened. She said, "It can't … be you?"

Robert said gently, "It has been a long time since we met in a past life but now we must go into the backyard. We have important people waiting on us and important things to do in this current moment and this current life." Robert gently took her other hand and led her to the backyard while Paul followed them. There were six men gathered around a small bonfire. Paul didn't recognize any of them. Robert led Nera and Paul next to the fire and the rest of the men created a circle around them and held hands. Robert placed Paul and Nera next to each other before pulling the athame out of his pocket. He pulled it out and took off the cloth to expose it to the fire.

Nera started to pull her gun out of her pocket and two men from the circle grabbed her and took the gun before placing her back next to Paul, not allowing her to change the sequence of events.

Robert took the knife and smiled and moved it across the fire and then the rune letters glowed. Paul realized there were additional markings on the athame that were now exposed since the heat was applied to it. Those new markings were not like the others and looked much older.

Robert then walked over to a table which looked like an altar from a church with a chalice, several candles, which he lit, and other items, which Paul could not fully identify. Robert also put on a white robe and a white tunic over his head. Robert then took the blade up above his head and faced north and chanted, then faced east and chanted, then faced west and chanted.

Nera yelled at him while two men held her arms, "Old man, this is not going to work, you are going to fail, you do not want this to happen. You will lose again like last time."

Robert smiled at Nera and faced south and did a final chant. As the final chant wound down, a green mist came out of the athame and circled around the men and then covered over all of them, a green shield around them all. There was something else happening. Each of the men started to change into other men with much different older clothes like tunics and knight's attire from the Middle Ages. Paul started to look at his hands and clothes and the green mist was changing his appearance and his clothes. He was wearing a robe with tunic and on the front of his robe was a large red cross. Each of the strangers also wore robes with the red cross emblazed on their chests. Paul noticed that they all now had swords and there were horses outside their circle and there were trees all around them. They were not in his backyard in Kansas. His mind was racing and he tried to say something but the voice he had was not his own. He was someone else right now. Paul looked at Nera and she had also changed clothes and characteristics. She had longer, lighter brown hair and was wearing a purple royal dress with jewelry on her wrist. Each of the men looked at Paul with an acknowledgment of his authority.

Nera tried to pull away from the knights who held her arms, and one of the knights said, "Sir William, we have found Lady Margaret, the one who brutally killed Anna. What do you want us to do with her?"

Paul looked at his arms with their heavy gloves. He was finally realizing that he was William in the current moment or whatever moment this is right now, his dream was more alive than he had ever expected. He could feel in his bones that this was not a dream.

Robert and Paul looked at each other. Robert had changed to look like an older royal king. Robert walked over to Paul and said, "Paul, look at me, you are now Sir William, a noble Knight Templar. This Nera is now Lady Margaret, who viciously murdered sweet and innocent Anna. You are not in a dream. We are in parallel times, the events, both events are happening at the same time. We are here in Dark Forest in Germania where your men finally found and captured Nera, I mean Margaret, and we are also standing in your backyard in Kansas. You see the time portals are tied to this event right now and we have to conclude this sequence of present moments so that the follow-on moments can happen in both times. You see this needs to be decided so parallel time can untie. We have congestion in all the connected lives. Everyone needs you to decide on what should happen next."

Paul looked at Robert, who was now a king. He looked around at these strange men, who were now like brothers to him as fellow knights. And he looked at Nera, who was now a vengeful Margaret. His memories were rushing through his head, the men taking Anna from her house, finding her in a dark prison cell, he taking the lashings for her, then the sharp excruciating pain on his back reoccurred and then the horrifying sight of Anna's burnt body. Paul's breath was heaving, his blood was boiling, and he walked over to Robert and took the knife from his hand and approached Nera. Nera just smiled and yelled, "Do it, put me to death! Make my pain leave me! You know you want to do it, you know you want revenge, you know I don't deserve to be free! Go ahead!" Nera spat in Paul's face.

Paul took his left hand and grabbed her by the throat and raised the athame over his head. The athame was now glowing and markings were clearly visible. He raised it higher and then a voice from outside the circle said, "William, don't!"

Paul looked for the female voice and did not see

where it was coming from. A petite woman wearing a white robe walked through the green mist of the circle. Paul looked at her and said, "Anna, is that you?"

Anna smiled at him with such a charming smile that calmed his blood and lowered his heart rate and he lowered the athame. Anna touched Paul's shoulder where the scar was, and Paul felt more memories come into his head. Anna looked up at Paul's eyes and said, "My dear, you are a pure heart. You are full of love, a love throughout time to share and give and receive, love and hate are the yin and yang and the battle between the conscious and unconscious. Even though you want to hurt Margaret, even though your pain is too great to bear when you think what she did to me, you are better than hurting her. You want revenge and an 'eye for an eye' but you also must remember you must 'love your enemies.' Luke said to us together in a past life, 'You have heard that it is said, eye for an eye and tooth for a tooth but I tell you not to resist an evil person, if someone slaps you on the right cheek, turn to him the other side also, bless those who curse you, pray for those who mistreat you.'"

Anna looked at Nera. "Paul, she wants you to hurt her so that she can take the coward's way out from her cursed life. I can read it in her eyes, she will speak evil and say anything to manipulate your love and pain toward her own death. Do not give her that satisfaction. Do not hurt her at all. She broke the rede, she broke the witch's law. Let that be enough."

Anna touched Paul's arm and took his hand and put

it on her cheek as she looked up at him. She came up to his cheek and kissed it and then whispered in his ear, "Paul, you must hide the athame so no one will find it in future lives because all it brings is destruction and madness. You must hide it where no one will look for it." Anna started to move away from Paul and said, "I have to go now, but look for me in someone from your current present time. I am again in your life if you can see me." She looked back at Paul and then walked through the circle and disappeared in the darkness.

Nera looked at Paul and said, "You can't listen to her. You need to hurt me, you need your anger put on me with the athame, right now, tonight. Don't be a wilting lily. Listen to the fire in your heart. Take your revenge!"

Paul put the athame back in the white cloth and wrapped it again and said, "Men, let her go. Your honor is kept to your promise to me. She will do us no harm tonight, and it is done. Time can now move forward in all the dimensions. Thank you for all your honor."

The knights all became normal men, Paul lost all of his armor, Robert lost all of the king's identity and became a professor again. Nera also changed back into the modern woman she was. All of the men looked at each other and shook hands again, their souls felt freer from now knowing why they were called to this small Kansas town. Paul walked over to each of the men individually and shook their hands and hugged them, his heart singing with the memories of their bonds in their past lives together. Robert took advantage of the situation and said,

"Shall we all go inside and have some fellowship over whisky?" The men all agreed and started to move toward Paul's house.

Paul looked around and said to Robert, "Where is Nera? Where did she go?"

Robert patted Paul on the shoulder while Paul twitched with the contact of Robert's hand on his left shoulder and said, "Paul, let her go. There is no more for her or you to do tonight. It is done." Robert smiled with a nod of confirmation and put his arm around Paul. "Now let's go inside with these fine men who have traveled all over the world to be called to your home tonight for this event. I promise it will be fine."

They both walked slowly from the backyard into Paul's house and started to talk to the men who were strangers when he first met them but now the bond of brotherhood formed from facing death together sang in their shared words and gestures. Robert started by finding the whisky and several glasses and pouring everyone a drink. "Gentlemen, I will also call you knights, please each of you get a glass of whisky and we will have a toast." All the men raised their glasses into the air as Robert continued, "Knights, I would like to make a toast to our fellowship, our loyalty, our duty, and to Sir William and his knights."

All the men and Paul and Robert gave a full toast and touched each other's glasses, and each downed their shot in salute to their spiritual kinship. The men continued to drink and to have full comradery.

Nera had escaped and walked to her car down the street to the university parking lot where she had left it to break into Paul's office. She sat crying in her car, knowing that she would continue to be cursed for this lifetime for her actions of her past lives. Her cowardice flared into anger toward Paul. She muttered under her breath, trying to halt the sobs wracking her body. "Paul would not hurt me to release me from this curse, what else can I do? I do not know what to do next. Please help."

A middle-aged man was sitting in Nera's car with her. He touched her on her head and face wiping away her tears. The man consoled Nera and provided sympathy for her. He said, "It's not over. Do not worry about tonight. The fight tonight was uneven and against the odds for you, but you will have your day in this lifetime, you just have to trust yourself and use a little magic and use your special skills that I have taught you. You have to trust me."

Nera looked up at the man and said, "Thank you so much. I do not know what I would do without your guidance. Thank you so much, Samael."

Samael just smiled and continued to console Nera. "You will have your curse broken and released from you in this lifetime, you just have to follow my guidance and do exactly what I tell you. Robert did not play fair tonight and we will soon have another ally to assist our efforts."

Nera said, "I will do anything you say."

Samael just slowly smiled and said, "Yes, you will, my dear. Yes, you will."

CHAPTER 24
GREEN MAN'S FINAL ASCENT

The Green Man awoke in a puddle of damp sweat. Five nights running now of ominous dreams. He kept dreaming that someone was using dark powers against his teacher. Time to search her out on the mainland, the dreams were only increasing in urgency. That morning he informed his village what he must do. His village honored Chira as the one who taught the one who took care of the village and brought honor to their clan across the mountain. He himself had trained two other healers to assist him. They would be able to care for the village while he journeyed. He understood the dreams to be future messages of events that were about to darken his teacher's life. He departed on a full moon and the entire village wished him luck and he promised he would return and he always kept his promises.

He departed alone with his sword, his bow and

arrows, his hammer, and his special blade that his teacher had engraved with marks that she never explained and left as a mystery for him to decipher. His teacher had only said the blade had come from the heavens and held power from the gods. The Green Man made his way across the land mass by foot and then sailed onward to other farther lands. Every night he stared into the fire, carefully pondering every clue, hint, and mystery she had imparted during his training. He tries to contact her from his dreams. He receives only messages and clues and confirmation she is in need. He follows his messages from his mind and his messages and clues start coming true once he reaches the vast and forbidden mountain range that stood at the gateway of the dreamworld every night since he began his journey. Villages dot the mountainous countryside. The blue-tipped white mountains own the skyline for miles. The air of the entire country holds a tinge of the sharp clear cold tang of the rarified air of the peaks. The people of the mountain all accept him into their villages when he tells why he is traveling through their lands. The people give him guidance and direction that go with his dreams and messages.

One night, months into traveling, he came to Tollarqwin, a village at the base of the tallest mountain and famous for being a gateway to that sacred mountain for those who seek inner divining guidance. He stayed at a house that took him in and he told his story of his teacher who needs his help. The father of the house, Karnow, knew Chira. He was a former student and out of his sense of duty to his former teacher he gave his youngest son, Kino, to guide the Green Man up the mountain to the cave where she lived.

The Green Man and his new young companion, Kino, a fierce, black-eyed boy hungry to prove himself, started up the mountain the following day. The Kallup Trail had been used for centuries by traders to travel through the mountain pass. The two had packed well for it would take several days to reach the peak. They were steady in their hearts as they started their trek up the mountain and the trail.

Just after midday, they came upon a group huddled scared and shivering in a grove of spindly trees. As the Green Man approached the men, he noticed that two were blind and the third, a younger boy, seemed to be taking care of them. Their hushed murmur sounded frantic. Something had startled them and they were afraid to move forward along the trail.

The Green Man asked, "Men, why do you look afraid?"

The older man said, "We have had visions of the evil spirit on the mountain. Death lives up there and death shall come to those who seek the mountain. Beware if you continue. She is holding someone up there but she can't break their spirit. Death herself is upset and sending her wrath upon us who travel in our visions. The man who seeks his teacher must travel through perils and challenges to find her. Be afraid, be afraid."

The Green Man smiled and sat next to the blind

men and patted them on the back and said, "You wise men, thank you for sharing your vision. I also see a vision of me finding my teacher and sending the evil one back to where she came from. I am not afraid because I have been through the worst and best and walk proud to my death if required. I ask one thing. Would you go with me up the trail? My visions show me I will travel with five people to meet my enemy and I already have a travel partner, but you see I need three more men."

The old blind man said, "Why would you want to take blind men to accompany you to face your death? We are of no use to you."

"Your visions I cannot see, so you can assist me in encountering danger with your insight. I also know you were brave before you were blind, and you will know what you need to do when you need it."

The old man said, "Your inner spirit is strong; I can feel your strength in your voice, and my heart believes you, so we will join you. This young boy who accompanies us, his name is Sky, he is small, but is well trained. He has power over the air and could be useful."

The five travelers started up the trail with Kino leading the way, the Green Man next, and the two blind men followed by Sky. What was once an individual trek to find a teacher was now a group of men walking up the trail to an unknown enemy to save a teacher. This had slowly become a quest.

As the afternoon faded away, Kino informed everyone, "We need to find a place to camp on the mountain because it would be too dangerous to finish the trip in the dark due to the abundance of evil spirits at night with darkness protecting them. It would not be wise."

The Green Man agreed, and they found a grove of trees on the mountain to shelter in and soon had a fire going. The men gathered around the fire to get warm as the temperature was dropping quickly.

The old blind man with long gray hair sat and warmed at the fire and asked the Green Man, "My new companion, may I ask why you seek to face this dangerous unknown evil?"

The Green Man said, "You are now my friend since you joined my quest. I have a teacher who trained me since I was a child, I owe her my life, and I have had visions that she is in danger by evil. If there is a chance, I must make every effort to save my teacher who saved me so long ago."

"That is honorable," the old man said. "We gain in honor to be associated with such a mission. My name is Masho and my companion is Trexor. We were warriors once until we lost our sight but now our fighting skills are limited, due to being unable to see our enemies."

The Green Man said, "My friend, I need you to sense the enemy. Because we might not be able to see the evil through our own eyes, your abilities are critical. Our enemy may only be felt by your special abilities. So, yes, you are essential for our quest, you and Trexor." At that last statement, Trexor smiled and then turned over and fell asleep.

As the men fell asleep on the ground and their fire went out, the wind had increased and the moon was full and there was an entity looking at them from afar. The etheric consciousness started to move toward the Green Man. As the entity was about to touch the Green Man, all of the men got up and held hands and encircled the entity, and Masho said a spell while Trexor threw sandalwood dust over the entity to trap it inside the circle. The entity fiercely threw itself against the binding. It did not know such magic existed to trap it and was upset and almost frightened. The Green Man declared, "Who are you and what do you want, before we cast thee to nothingness with the last three words of the spell? Tell me now or your spirit will cease to exist."

As the dust was thrown on the immobilized entity, it became the shape of a woman, a small woman. The entity cried out in heart-wrenching desperation, "I am sent from the evil one up on the mountain that is holding your teacher. She sent me to scare you and warn you not to go any farther or she will kill your teacher."

The Green Man said, "I believe you but you are leaving something out of your information and my friend Kino will help me get it out of you."

The spirit did not know which one was Kino until the young man pulled out a blue crystal necklace, with a pearly glow emanating from it. He closed his eyes and gripped his hands together for a breath before pushing both palms apart and sending a blue light from his palms to the entity. The entity fell to the ground and glowed blue with mist that pulsed along a direct line from Kino's palms. The entity transformed into human flesh inside the mist. When Kino was done, this young woman fell onto the ground naked. Kino put his palms together and bowed his head and touched his blue glowing crystal with reverence before returning it inside his shirt. The young woman looked at herself now in full human form again and her face crumpled in shock at realizing a miracle had happened.

The Green Man walked up to the woman and touched her with comfort and gave her a hug. She burst into deep sobs of release and shock, years of suffering pouring forth. He asked, "What was the other part of the message?"

The woman looked up at the Green Man and said, "I have been a prisoner for the evil one for over three hundred years. She killed me and kept my spirit in her prison. Her oracle has predicted that a man of green skin will be immune to her powers and will destroy her to save his teacher and that he will have the help of others in his quest."

The Green Man smiled and continued to comfort the woman in her new form and quietly said, "My dear, would you accompany us to save my teacher now that you are back in human form?"

The woman looked up to the Green Man with her blue eyes and blonde hair and said, "I would be honored to join your group to put an end to the evil one. My name is Bakuri. First, I must thank the young man who changed me back from spirit to human." She walked over to Kino and gave him a long hug and kissed him on the mouth and both sides of his cheeks and whispered in his ear something that made him blush and then held his hand. Kino blushed and held her hand back as if his life depended on it.

As they all finished calming down from the recent experience, Kino said, still holding Bakuri's hand, "The sun is rising, we should start our movement to the crest of the mountain so we can make it to the evil one's cave during the day when it is the safest."

They all agreed and slowly started packing their things. Bakuri was now helping Kino with assisting the blinded Trexor and Masho in packing their items for the next part of their quest today. Bakuri kept looking at her skin in disbelief, or closing her eyes to feel the wind in her hair, and smell nature, things that she had not been able to experience in centuries.

The Green Man had packed his things into his shoulder bag and looked about and everyone else was ready to ascend up the mountain to their final destination of the evil one's cave. He did not know who had taken his teacher but knowing the prophecy that a man with green skin would be immune to the evil one's power gave him confidence as they started in line up the trail to the peak of the mountain.

They walked silently for hours. As the morning passed, clouds gathered in the sky above them. Late morning, they could see a gaping, ominous hole in the distance up the peak. As they neared the cave the clouds darkened and thunder and lightning presaged rain pounding on the group of travelers. The closer they got to the cave, the harder the wind blew to test them as they continued to come up the mountain.

Trexor then shouted up to the Green Man from his place in the line, "We are close to the entrance to the cave where your teacher is being held, the evil one is still there—are you ready to face her?" Everyone stopped in line as this was said and they all stopped and looked at the Green Man.

The Green Man stood tall as the rain pounded on his face. He quietly looked up toward the cave and then looked back at everyone and said, "My beloved and sacred teacher is up there, and I will do all I can as I still have air in my lungs to save my teacher for she has made me who I am today."

Everyone looked at the Green Man and contemplated his words in the rain and made their own choice to risk the unknown for this quest. Eternity as an imprisoned spirit was a fate worse than death. All followed the Green Man as he made the last movement to the cave entrance. The thunder and lightning increased as they got closer to the entrance, and despite the warning, they all continued.

The entrance was tall and dark, but they could all see the light from torches deep into the cave waiting for them to walk in and meet the evil one.

The Green Man looked back at his group of old men and boys and said, "We shall go into the cave together and we shall all come out of the cave together, I give you my promise."

All of them agreed and slowly walked into the cave, alert to every vibration, not knowing what awaited them inside.

The Green Man took one of the torches and walked up front to show the way to the others. The tunnel quickly opened up into a large cavern containing a lake. A boat lay on the shore near the tunnel. He could see a large island in the middle of the lake illuminated by some torches.

Blind Trexor said, "My friend, my brother and I are not supposed to go any further with you into the lake but we will protect you from the shore with our magic. Your teacher awaits you and told us you must only take Kino. There is a message from your teacher to Kino that he must hear. Leave us on the shore but we will set up a large fire so you will know the way back. Our magic is old and we are blind, but do not doubt the ability of a blind man. Now go, your teacher awaits."

The Green Man touched Trexor on the shoulder and said, "Thank you, my friend, please be safe on the shore and make a large fire so that I may find you again."

The Green Man and Kino got into the boat and started rowing toward the cave island, using the torches as a guide. The water was calm and deadly quiet. The sound of rowing echoed throughout the cavern. Soon they could not see the shore or the torches where their companions waited by the tunnel. All they kept doing was rowing toward the cavern island where there was a bonfire blazing along with dozens of torches. As they got

closer, they could see figures' shadows along the stones
on the island. Given the uncertain lighting, they had no
idea how many waited, or how they were armed. Soon,
the sound of several voices yelling reached them. Just
before they landed, a large explosion blasted their senses,
followed by a scream from his teacher. The Green Man
jumped from the boat onto the island. He ran up to the
area of the small island that was lit up by the bonfire and
could see his teacher chained to a stone. He ran to her and
could see she was hurt, not a wound or broken bone, but
rather blue streaks on her skin like she was suffering from
a poison or curse.

The Green Man tried to console her as he freed her
from the chains.

Kino spoke, "Sir, the evil one is escaping off the
island."

The Green Man looked at his teacher who was
suffering and was about to depart when the teacher in her
weakness grabbed his arm and said, "Let her go."

The Green Man was confused and looked at Chira.
Her elaborate map of tattoos seemed to be dissipating in
her poisoned state. She looked at him weakly and said,
"My student, let her go, I must tell you the code before I
pass away."

The Green Man was confused. "Why are you
dying? I do not see any wounds on you, only a reaction to
something."

Chira said, "My amulet has protected me for weeks
as she was trying to poison me, but I made a deal for her

to let me die in the arms of my student and I would stop you from trying to find her."

The Green Man looked frustrated and confused and thirsted to revenge his anger on the evil one. "Why would you say that?"

"She allowed me to live so that I may complete your training before I die," the teacher said. "Death is welcomed. It is my time, so you will let her live and not pursue her. We made a pact so you must promise not to pursue her." The Green Man shook his head yes because of his loyalty to his teacher.

"I have something for you that you must wear for protection. It is my most powerful relic that has kept me alive while the evil one continued to try to turn me. This amulet is now for you." She pulled an amulet from her neck where it lay beneath her garments. A blue deep dark crystal in a copper setting glowed in her hands. The Green Man saw writing amid the glow. She held the crystal in one hand as she used the other to take it off her neck to hand to the Green Man. She said, "Once I hand you this amulet, the protection will be broken from the poison and I will die, but it is time for me to pass this power onto my student to now be the teacher and the master. You are ready to be the master."

The Green Man looked at his teacher, who was now giving him her last protection to stay alive. She was willingly letting death welcome her, knowing that the Green Man would make her proud as a master and a teacher. He allowed his teacher to set the crystal on his trembling hand. They held hands for a long moment with the amulet between their palms, looking into each other's eyes. He said, "Thank you."

She smiled. "No, I thank you. Now be the master and teacher that I know you can be. It is now time to say good-bye."

She pulled her hand away and then the poison took full effect on her and her skin quickly faded into a light gray and her tattoos started to disappear. Her tattoos were part of her protection. The tattoos were being drawn on his skin as they were disappearing from hers. As all of her tattoos vanished, the Green Man's skin was now filled with tattoos that were identical to what his master once wore. She closed her eyes with a deep sense of peace and died in his arms. Her last complete action was to transfer her protection to include her sacred tattoos to the Green Man to finish his final lesson. The Green Man cried loudly and told her, "I give you my word that I will not pursue the evil one. I thank you for your final lesson, and I will make you proud of me." He held her lifeless body in his big arms. He looked up at Kino and said, "Let's get out of this evil place." He tenderly carried her to the boat. Kino rowed the boat away from the cavern island. As the oars moved the water, the sound of rippling water repeated in echoes in the cavern. They could see the blazing fire of their awaiting friends. Those on the shore were quiet, and they knew that the teacher was dead.

Trexor asked, "My teacher, what are we to do next?"

The Green Man said, "We shall give my teacher a

sacred ceremonial funeral, but we must do it from the top of this mountain and not here at the cave where she was tortured. We shall go up to the crest and build her an altar and give her a sacred burning so that she can pass to her next life and start anew in a new kingdom in a different world."

They walked up to the crest and built an altar where the Green Man prayed to the gods to watch over his teacher. As he was lighting the altar, the amulet glowed on his chest all through the sacred pyre transmuting his teacher's body via flame, opening the way for her spirit to pass to the next world. As the fire took hold and was in full force, the blue amulet glowed even brighter, then something happened to Trexor and Masho. They both started to cry and the Green Man said, "Why are you crying, old men?"

Trexor and Masho both said together, "My master, we are crying because we can see now."

The Green Man came over to them and looked at them and their eyes and confirmed that they both could now see. The Green Man hugged them cheerfully and realized that one of his teacher's last acts was to give sight to these two loyal friends. The three men hugged, smiling and appreciative of the teacher.

Trexor said, "You are now our master, we will now serve you in your vision. It is our duty and respect for both of us receiving our sight after it was taken away years ago."

The Green Man smiled and said, "My friends, a

vision I received while you were receiving your sight was that I should open up and form a sacred temple to pass my teacher's lessons to future students. I guess I am now the designated master. We shall go back to my homeland and build a temple and we shall all work there to assure my teacher's lessons are continued to be passed on and you will all be masters there."

All of the men got up with agreeance and loyalty after all they had been through the last couple of days. The Green Man had now fully become the master.

The group of friends traveled back to the Green Man's village where they slowly met the village elders and started to build a training school. All of them became important key people in the village, contributing in their own special ways to give back to the community. The students slowly came the first couple of years and became disciples of the Green Man's teachings, and then more and more students came throughout the years to learn the ways of the Green Man. The years continued to pass through and eventually the Green Man established a lineage of teachers and a reputation that drew students from across the islands and great continent. One day the Green Man filled his pack and departed to spend time in nature and never came back. There were rumors and legends that he became a part of the mountains that he loved and there were other rumors that he started another school across the world and other rumors that he found the evil one and confronted her, but the only fact was that the Green Man never returned to his home.

CHAPTER 25
THE INNER TEMPLE AGAIN

Robert and Paul were the last ones in Paul's house as the sky began to lighten to a predawn gray. Paul had connected with each of these strangers who in past lives were his loyal knights and tonight had become his close brothers again. He collected all their information so they could meet again. Each of the strangers had been called to this moment to be a part of Paul's decision on the ache of pain and grief in his heart born of a woman's cruelty and selfishness.

Robert suggested they sit on the back porch and watch the sunrise since they drank throughout the night and were sobering up as the morning hours started.

Paul said, "Robert, I have not drank and talked throughout the night in about thirty years, but what a night tonight was."

Robert agreed, "Yes, my dear friend, many things happened to unlock time and past lives."

Paul looked over to Robert, sitting in the Adirondack chair next to him, and said, "How did this all happen?"

Robert smiled. "Well, Paul, things do not just happen. There are synchronizations; nothing in this life just happens. There are forces in the universe and the spectral realms that are working toward certain events, and, well, you have to include the gods and goddesses and all the spirits in the equation and it soon gets complex and confusing, but I will say that the events tonight were meant to be in the grand scheme. Fate, if you will. Tonight good, honor, and forgiveness happened, and it was an honor to be a part of it."

Paul got up from the chair and said, "The sun is about to rise. Shall we have a drink to celebrate life for one last toast to honor?"

Robert smiled. "I thought you wouldn't offer, I think it is going to be a beautiful day today. Besides, who knows what any day will bring?"

As Paul sat down on the chair next to Robert and poured another round of whisky to celebrate the sunrise, he said, "Thank you, my friend, for being my friend in this lifetime and my past lives. I believe I owe you my life."

Robert smiled and said, "Paul, I saved your life in past lives three times, but who is counting? It seems to be what I do as our lives continue to entwine together. Yes, you are welcome. Certain adventures continue to follow you, and I end up pulling you out of the gutter." He toasted glasses with Paul with full sarcasm.

They both sat in their chairs in silence and slowly watched the colors of the sky change from black to gray to streaks of yellow and red and blue. Even with all the miracles and joy and mystery of the previous weeks, they were humbled at the majesty of the rising sun.

They heard the back door open and someone step out onto the deck. Paul said, "Did some drunk fellow forget something?"

A female's voice replied, "I guess I did not get here early enough. There seems to be no one at the party anymore except for two wannabe Scottish Highlanders. May this lady have a drink?"

Paul looked around and saw it was Brynn. "What the hell ... what are you doing here?"

Brynn smiled and sat on the chair with Paul and grabbed the bottle of whisky and poured herself a drink. She leaned back on Paul and said, "My dear friends, I had a vision after you left that you two were getting in trouble, and that I needed to follow you here, so I got on the very next flight to America and this state you call Kansas and came right here with the help of Robert, who gave me your address. So, what did I miss?"

Robert and Paul just laughed and as usual, Paul let Robert tell the story as the sunrise continued to unfold in all its glory. Brynn sat next to Paul, resting and soaking in the story and enjoying the sunrise.

As dawn transitioned into full morning, they all realized they needed some sleep. Paul offered all of them to stay at his place for a couple hours of sleep and to assure no drunk driving on Robert's part. They all meandered inside. Paul looked at the entryway and saw Brynn's suitcase and said, "Brynn, you must stay with me. I have an extra room and my house is your house."

Brynn smiled and said, "I was going to couch surf on your couch anyway. It's just the way I travel."

Robert crashed in the extra bedroom, and Brynn found a blanket and went on the couch, so Paul went to his bedroom and started to undress and get into his comfortable bed. He was starting to doze off when he felt someone coming into bed with him. Brynn climbed into bed and said, "The couch is too cold and I need a warm body to snuggle with. I hope you don't mind?"

She snuggled on his side with her head on his chest and before he could object, she was fast asleep on top of him and he did not have the heart to move her. She was so delicate and strong at the same time. He went ahead and put both of his arms around her and they shared the warmth together under the comforter. He was soon fast asleep.

Paul realized he was standing by a river in a dream-state. He could smell the scent of the moisture and the wet grass, and he heard the sound of the soft river flowing. He could see his tree of life in the distance. It was not too far and he knew the route. He took off his shoes and walked barefoot in the wet grass to fully immerse himself in the landscape. As he walked, opening his mind and heart to the land around him, he saw a woman by the river looking toward the tree. In all of his dream experiences he had never had people outside the tree only on the back porch of his inner temple. He walked up behind the woman and said, "Hello."

She turned around and it was Brynn. "I have been waiting for you here so we can go into your temple together this time."

He said, "Why didn't you tell me that when you crawled into bed?"

She said, "My dear, if I would have said that then you would still be awake overthinking it. Because I just crawled into bed and fell quickly asleep, you did not worry or distract yourself from being open to this. We are supposed to go into your temple together right now in the dream to get the final answers you seek so we can keep moving forward onto the other things we need to do."

Paul was slightly confused. "Ok, I trust you, thank you."

There was now music coming from afar and the more he listened he noticed it was an old 1960s rock song philosophizing the difference between wants and needs. It sounded like there was a large group of people inside the tree and he felt anxious and nervous. Brynn held his hand and said, "We'll go there together; there is nothing to be afraid or nervous about it. Trust me, it is a good thing." They held hands tightly and started to walk toward the tree entrance. The last time Brynn held him on the massage table as he walked into the inner temple but this time, she was with him and he assumed it was because she was asleep also, in proximity to him. He so enjoyed the company this time as he held her hand and they arrived at the tree and started to walk into the tunnel underneath it. As they walked the music got louder, and as they came out of the tunnel and onto the back patio of the lodge on the lake, there were over a hundred people all having drinks. The mood was distinctly celebratory. As Paul and Brynn walked onto the porch, there was a huge cheer for them and Paul felt confused and Brynn whispered in his ear, "Everything will be fine," and held his hand tighter.

Merc and Lilith took the attention of the social gathering by hitting their glasses. Both were smiling ear to ear. Merc shouted, "Friends, my dear friends, I would like everyone to give a toast, and please, Lilith, could you get them a good drink? I would like to catch everyone up on how we are all meeting tonight here and the why and how Paul and Brynn released most of you from your prisons. The current actions of one evil and troubled person throughout time had spiritually trapped the souls of all of you. One particular woman trapped your souls, and she was a part of your innocent deaths, one particular witch throughout time coming back over and over to continue to raise her debt of pain for her future lives and continuing to cause death. Well, today, Paul with the help of Brynn, and if you did not know these two have been entwined in history throughout time but that is another story ... Paul and Brynn—with the opportunity to physically hurt or kill Nera tonight in reprisal for her cruelty—forgave her. This act of love, this act of not hurting another person, did another great deed. This love and forgiveness released you all from her spiritual prison. You were all bound in Nera's web of pain from her part in condemning you to death. You are all here because Paul and Brynn broke the chain of events."

Merc was getting too emotional, so Lilith took over the speech.

Lilith said, "There are over three hundred free spirits among us tonight. You are free! So, everyone, please raise your glass up high and let's all toast to our dear and gracious friends." Everyone raised their glasses. Lilith continued, "To Paul and Brynn, thank you for your love and forgiveness." Everyone raised their glasses in homage, laughing and happy, with all the strangers surrounding them. Paul and Brynn had their drinks and toasted with new strangers and old friends. Then Lilith said, "Now, let's have a wonderful spiritual party." There were cheers and celebrations from people on the patio, in the house, and in the lake.

Paul had no idea his act of forgiveness would have second- and third-order effects in the realms of spirit. As the toasts and laughter died back down, Lilith told everyone to be quiet. "All friends and family, I would like to propose a toast to Paul and Brynn for forgiveness. By not killing or hurting Nera when the opportunity was available, he let his angry and vengeful feelings transform to instead find love in the worlds. Love is the key. Love connects all the worlds and all the metaphysical. Love is the answer. Love is all we need and a little war once in a while."

Everyone laughed and Paul assumed it was an inside joke.

Merc came to Paul and Brynn, and he clasped Paul in a bear hug and said, "Well done, my friend, well done!" The women and men who were on the patio were all familiar in some way but he could not place them, yet it all felt so right for everyone to be here. Paul felt like all the confusing, traumatic, and spiritual events had a purpose for this one moment in time, this love through forgiveness. It was a freedom in his heart, and he started to tear up.

Paul and Brynn were swarmed by people from all over time; they were hugged and kissed and thanked repeatedly for their simple and honorable actions. Paul was amazed how many women had been killed and trapped by Nera. None of the women who were there were guilty of what they had been accused and convicted of.

Everyone seemed to want to give gratitude for their kindness, and Paul felt overwhelmed and quite anxious. When his body started to tense, Brynn would touch his hand or arm and he would instantly calm down and feel assured, and when he looked into her eyes, he would send a thank-you note through his eyes to her and then she quickly would wink at him with a charming smile that left him weak in his knees.

The rest of the evening ended up being a quiet social and sips of wine between conversations. Paul never left Brynn's side as the people said their thank-you's and slowly departed into the woods, the lake, and house. After several hours, there were only a few people left. Then Paul noticed a woman in a cape with her head slightly hidden. He was intrigued by the woman. Why had he not noticed her all evening when she looked so different from everyone else? She was standing alone on the patio looking out onto the crystal lake and the mountains.

Paul moved away from Brynn, who was deep in conversation with a man from Denmark, and walked over to the woman and asked her, "May I help you?"

The woman turned toward Paul and he noticed green tattoos on her face. She looked at Paul and said, "I am not one that you saved in the past, but one that was saved in the far future, in the future of one of your future lives, but I wanted to meet you. Everyone knows you now for your honor of today that affected the past and the present at the same time. It has also started chains of events in the future. If you think of time as the past, present, and future all happening at the same time, then it will make more sense. Time is energy is the best way to say it, and energy is everything and everywhere. We are all just energy subatomic particles in the end."

She was so familiar, her eyes were so comforting, yet also painful and somewhat troubled. She walked up to him and gave him a long hug that was friendly and comfortable. As Paul was hugging her, Brynn touched his shoulder and all of a sudden he was in a desert alone in the sand. He felt scared and all alone and did not know how he moved from his sacred place at the lake house to this new desolate place. There was a strange figure covered by a black robe racing toward him on a black stallion, gripping a large curved sword with menace. Paul had no way to run away in the desert so he decided to face the riding horseman. As the horse came closer and the blade was raised high by the rider, he was suddenly back on the porch deck, at the mountain lake, talking with the tattooed woman with Brynn touching his hand, saying that it was time to leave.

Paul did not know what just happened with this desolate vision of the desert and a figure racing toward him, but he knew he was in his sacred place. He didn't know he could go to another place while traveling here, but he did not have the capacity to think about it right now.

Brynn said, "Paul, we have to go now, it's time. We are about to wake up. Please say good-bye to Merc and Lilith."

Brynn let go of his hand. The woman he was talking to had completely disappeared.

He went over to Merc and Lilith and said, "Thank you so much, I owe you so much."

He hugged them both and Lilith kissed him on his cheek long and whispered in his ear that she put something in his coat pocket for him to discover once he returned to his house. She looked at him with sincere love and said, "We will always be here for you when you want to make the journey." She put her arm around Merc and he waved back, while Brynn took Paul's hand and started walking him off the patio and back into the tunnel under the tree. As soon as he came out of the tree, the sun was shining on him and Brynn in his bed as she was also waking up. She had her head on his chest as they slept. They woke up simultaneously. They were intimately physically close and could almost kiss with little effort but Brynn mischievously smiled and said, "I need coffee." As she jumped out of bed, Paul noticed that she had one of his shirts on with nothing else underneath. His mind had a quick conversation about how he slept all night with a strange woman and had a spectacular dream together, but now he also agreed it was time for coffee. He got out of bed and realized he was naked but did not remember taking off his clothes. He just smiled and put on his robe and went out into the kitchen for coffee.

As Paul walked into the kitchen, Brynn was making them both a cup of a specialty coffee, it looked like a cappuccino or latte. She was pouring milk froth and made a beautiful flower on top of the coffee like a professional barista with a flourish and smile for Paul. He just smiled, amazed at what other talents Brynn had that he had no idea of. She picked up both coffees and said, "Dear, please open the back door and let's have coffee on your back patio." She looked at him and then the back door as if to say my hands are full, please do something.

Paul received the hint and opened the door quickly and Brynn took both coffees with her onto the back porch to enjoy the sunrise. As she gracefully slid into a chaise lounge chair, Paul noticed that she still only had on his shirt with nothing else. She was confident in her half-nakedness. "Please join me. The sunrise is beautiful."

Paul sat next to her and with two hands picked up his magnificent coffee, blew the steam off, and took a small sip. It was one of the best coffees that he had had in a long time. Between drinking the coffee and sitting next to Brynn and watching the sunrise, it was a perfect morning. They sat in silence just watching nature and being a part of nature with the colors of red and orange filling the sky. Paul sat there, not wanting to end the moment with any conversation, but he could not help himself.

He smiled at Brynn and said, "Well, thank you for accompanying me to my inner temple."

"You are welcome."

Paul then giggled. "Is that all we are going to say about that."

Brynn grinned fully. "Yes, for now, we will have more time to talk about it later." She got up and sat in front of Paul and leaned her back onto his chest and put her weight fully on him and they just enjoyed the sunrise together. As they sat there, their heartbeats unconsciously matched with exhaling and inhaling.

As they were synchronizing their moment, the phone rang. They both knew someone should get it, so Brynn gently got up and went to get the phone and handed it to Paul and said, "Well, it's Robert."

Paul took the phone and said, "Hello, Robert, you just interrupted a beautiful moment."

"Paul, listen to me carefully. Where is the athame?

Do you have it?"

Paul lost color in his face immediately and realized he had not seen it since the events of the previous night. He just assumed it was safe but he had not accounted for it since. Paul started to panic.

Robert said over the phone, "Paul, did you hear me?"

"Robert, I have not seen it since last night."

"Paul, please look for it. I had a dream that Nera had the athame and was going to try to use it against you soon, very soon."

Paul looked at Brynn and whispered, "Have you seen the athame? Robert had a dream that Nera was seeking it."

Brynn got up from the chair and went to her bag and pulled out the linen-wrapped package and brought it to Paul to show that it was secure.

Paul said, "Robert, Brynn had it secure, thank goodness. She is a wonderful woman. I do not know what I would do without her now."

Brynn whispered back, "You would be so lost without me," and she winked at him and walked into the bedroom and he noticed again that she was not wearing anything but his shirt, which instantly stumbled his conversation with Robert on the phone.

Robert said, "Paul, we need to secure it and I suggest my archives—you know the secure vault for safekeeping for the athame, plus I would like to put it next to the other artifacts and experiment with the energy."

"I agree, I think we need to secure it sooner than later. How about we meet in an hour in the parking lot by the secure door? I will bring Brynn and the athame."

Paul and Brynn got dressed, finished their coffee, and found a plain bagel to take with them because they were hungry. Brynn had no makeup, a pair of blue jeans, a t-shirt, and no bra and walked into the living room fully confident and said, "Let's go and secure this tool."

Paul and Brynn hopped into his truck and drove across town to meet Robert. Paul's mind was spinning on why Nera would still be seeking the athame out after having given it to him. He thought she wanted vengeance since he would not hurt her and let her escape the pain of her spiritual debt. He also was confused on why Robert had a dream about Nera and realized there might be a connection more than he thought between Nera, Brynn, and himself. He just did not know what it was yet. As he looked over at Brynn, who was enjoying the drive and wind in her hair, he felt a new sense of confidence that they would be able to come through the danger with success.

Robert was waiting for them in the parking lot and they walked into the secure facility. The voice in the sky identified and welcomed Dr. Brynn into the facility and she talked back to the computer as if they were old friends. Paul was confused on how the computer that secured this facility already knew Brynn, but he would ask Robert at a later time. Robert went into the final secure room where the top-secret knives were stored and as he was on the keypad to open up the glass, they all looked and noticed the other knives were missing. All of the other mystical artifacts were missing. Robert was stunned. He asked Oscar, "What happened to the artifacts and who has entered this room in the last forty-eight hours?"

OSCAR said, "Dr. Robert, I have a gap in the video but the only person that has been in this vault was Dr. Nera, who had the proper authority and clearance to enter."

Robert said, "Please put the video of her on the screen so I can see the event. My clearance number is 1643PB."

OSCAR provided the video and Robert, Paul, and Brynn watched as Nera entered the secure vault and took the artifacts out of the glass and put them in a briefcase. Nera looked up at the camera and smiled before waltzing out the door.

Robert looked over at Paul and Brynn. "I guess my dream was not about your athame but about my artifacts. I still do not know how she got in." He went over to the computer and typed some encrypted computer code and was asking the computer what access level Nera had to enter.

OSCAR replied, "Dr. Robert, the access level that Dr. Nera had was an original password, which only has been used once by the founder of the facility, who was Dr. Jane Lilith, in 1946. Her password bypassed all recent security protocols and was programmed by the original programmer of the security system."

Robert smiled and just laughed. "Well, Paul, it

seems not all things are what they seem. This facility has been compromised. You and Brynn must secure and hide the athame where no one will find it. You two must do it quickly and not tell anyone; do not write it down anywhere or e-mail its location. You must hide it. Please secure it and never go back and look for it because everyone is watching everything. That athame is one of the most powerful artifacts in this time and too many people want it."

Brynn grabbed Paul's hand and said, "We can go somewhere and hide it where no one will find it."

Paul and Robert both looked at Brynn and all agreed. They departed the government building and Paul and Brynn headed back to his house to pack and get ready to travel. They needed to leave as soon as possible. As they drove back in his truck, he had an urge to change their vehicle and asked if they could change their appearance since Nera would know his car and his looks.

Brynn chuckled. "I have always wanted to be a curly brunette. Would you color your hair with me, and maybe get a different car? What do you think?"

Paul just smiled and knew this was a part of the new adventure that he was about to embark on. They found a hair stylist who knew exactly what to do with Brynn's hair and another woman to change Paul's hair to a surprise color. Brynn whispered to the male hairdresser what she wanted and he just smiled and expressed his full approval. Paul just sat there and agreed to Brynn's guidance. In about an hour, they both came out of their hair coloring.

Brynn was now a messy brunette instead of a redhead, but she kept several red streaks, and Paul was now a blond with a short crew-cut and all of his gray gone. They both giggled, and having free drinks as they had their hair done only helped the process.

Paul and Brynn went out into the parking lot and Brynn said, "You know we should get a different car."

Paul smiled and said, "I have a car in storage. I need to drive it."

They went to his storage shed behind his house and Paul opened up the garage to a small car with a tarp on it. Brynn smiled with curiosity and Paul pulled the dusty tarp off the car and underneath it was a yellow Volkswagen convertible with the new style and the turbo charger. Brynn teased Paul, "A Volkswagen convertible, I would have never guessed."

"It was a car for another time. It's a relic of my traumatic past, but it is time for it to be free from storage and to let it drive again on the freeway."

Brynn smiled. They knew they needed to pack for wherever they were departing to for an unknown amount of time. Within forty-five minutes, they were both packed and Paul's house was locked and secure with a full security system and house cameras. Paul was in his sunglasses with his new blond hair and Brynn had her new dirty brunette curly hair that blew into her eyes and face as he drove to Robert's to say good-bye.

They pulled up into Robert's driveway and Robert instantly started laughing and was almost gleaming. He walked up to the convertible car and said, "My dear friends, you two be safe and go to Crestone, Colorado. There is a Buddhist monastery that is secure, and the monk is waiting for you. There you will find a place to bury the athame so no one can find it again for a long time. You two so amaze me in your new looks. Please be careful, and do not trust anyone. Now, do not say good-bye, just until we meet again. God speed and good luck, and now get going." He placed a business card into Paul's hand with the final directions to the sacred temple in the Rocky Mountains.

Paul shook Robert's hand, hoping it would not be the last time, and Brynn jumped onto Paul's lap so she could kiss Robert on his left and right cheek, and she spoke something softly in Robert's ear in Gaelic. Robert's smile held a new sense of peace and warmth and he winked back at Brynn. She hopped back into her passenger seat and put on her sunglasses and touched Paul's hand signaling to him it was time to go.

Chapter 26

Colorado

As Paul and Brynn drove the interstate across Kansas, Paul often looked over at Brynn and watched her with her big sunglasses and her brunette color hair blowing all over her face. He felt completely free spirited and alive, fully alive for the first time in many years, in decades.

They decided not to rush, and instead cruised the miles in the new convertible VW across Kansas. They stopped along the way to see all the unique tourist stops and to enjoy the land and scenery and the paintbrush of God on the land. They soaked in every mile as it came and as they came across the state line into Colorado, they took the typical tourist photo in front of the sign at the tourist center. As Paul was heading to the restroom, another visitor was telling someone how spiritual the Garden of the Gods was to visit. When Paul returned, he walked by the visitor pamphlet section and picked up a brochure of the Garden of the Gods in Colorado Springs. He thought of it as a sign to explore, so he followed his hunch. He went to the VW where Brynn was already in the convertible and said, "I know where we need to go first." He handed her the pamphlet to the park and she just smiled and said, "Sounds good, let's go." She knew they were just driving on intuition and hunches right now, not knowing where they were going but trusting spirit and intuition to guide them.

Within two hours, they were in Colorado Springs and pulled into a hotel to spend the night. They would tour the Garden of the Gods in the morning but needed to rest the evening. They found a small café that was almost thirty minutes from closing so they found a table and quickly ordered with the waitress. Their meals came out and the closing was in ten minutes, so Paul said to the waitress, "We will hurry up and eat so you can close on time."

The waitress was middle-aged and just smiled. "You two are just fine. Enjoy your dinner, and please do not rush. I own this restaurant, so I will just lock the front door and turn the close sign over. Would you mind sharing a bottle of wine with me tonight?"

Brynn and Paul looked at each other and smiled and simultaneously said, "Of course, yes. We have been traveling all day."

Jane introduced herself with a bow before she locked the door and flipped the sign and dimmed some of the lights but left the lights around our table section on. She had also turned off the lights outside. She walked to the back room and talked with the cook and server letting them close up and within minutes she came out with a nice bottle of merlot. She had the bottle already open and three empty glasses. Paul pulled a chair up to the table and she put the glasses on the table and served everyone. She said, "The bottle of wine is on the house, but we have to do a toast."

Paul and Brynn looked at each and smiled again, both wondering about their luck right now.

Jane raised her glass and said, "I bet you two are heading to the Garden of the Gods tomorrow. I could feel your energy when you came into my restaurant. I will explain later, but I need to make a toast tonight with you two. Please raise your glasses. I toast to my late husband, who died way too young, and I toast to the spirit of the mountain and all those who seek what they do not know, that they will be guided to where they need to go, blessed be."

Brynn, Paul, and Jane toasted their wineglasses with distinct sounds of crystal chiming and it all rang a sacred toast to the offerings. The sound of the three crystal glasses sent chills down Paul's neck. There was something unique with Jane.

Jane sat down and poured more wine in everyone's glasses and said, "You are going to the Garden of the Gods tomorrow, right?"

Brynn smiled and said, "Jane, yes, we are. How did

you know?"

"Well, your combined energy together when you came in my place was powerful and so positive, I am an empath and work with energy, and I am also a practicing witch. I knew you were different as soon as you walked in. You are seeking something at the Garden of the Gods."

Paul looked at Jane and said, "Well, you are right, we found this restaurant purely by convenience and chance, but we are being guided toward the Garden of the Gods, but that is not our final destination, which we do not know yet."

Jane slowly leaned back in her chair. "You must walk the path of the Garden of the Gods to seek your final destination to bury the athame, to keep it safe. You must go to the Shambhala in Crestone; only there will you find the final resting spot of what you both seek. The message will be given to you tomorrow."

Brynn looked at Jane. "How do you know about the athame?"

Jane said, "Well, it spoke to me, it is in your purse, right? It needs a secure resting place, and it must be safe from the evil one, the evil one who seeks it and will do anything to find it right now."

Paul looked worried. "Who is the evil one?"

Jane said, "Do not worry, I am a white witch and not a dark witch. I am for good. I only know what the athame in your purse communicates with me right now. I can feel its energy. It wants to be safe. Make sure you keep it from the one who seeks it."

"Do you want to see it?" Brynn asked.

"Please, if you do not mind," Jane replied. "It wants to connect with me. I want to help you both to find the person who will lead you to the place where no one will ever find it. Until it is time for it to be found again."

Paul looked at Brynn with a nod of approval and Brynn opened up her purse and pulled out the old linen cloth that wrapped the athame. Brynn put the wrapped object in front of Jane and nodded for Jane to open up the cloth.

Jane picked up her glass and took a large gulp and finished her wine, then set the empty glass down, took a deep breath, and slowly unwrapped the knot and opened up the cloth to expose the athame. Jane took a deep breath and exhaled at the sight of the blade. She became teary eyed as she continued to gaze at it. She slowly picked up the blade and closed her eyes. Paul and Brynn sat in silence and watched her absorb the energy of the blade. Both of them could tell she was communicating with the blade right now by the way she moved her facial expressions and her mouth was moving.

After a few moments, she opened up her eyes and put the blade back on the cloth and started to wrap it up and slowly tied it back as it was. She slid the blade back to Brynn and touched her hand. She said, "As you walk the monuments of the Gods tomorrow, you will meet someone who does not fit in, and he will tell you a place that you will journey to put this blade in its next final place where it will remain for over five hundred years untouched until it is time for it to be rediscovered again for its next journey."

Brynn smiled at Jane and said, "Thank you for the message. We'll follow your guidance."

Jane said, "That athame and I have been together once before in a past life; this blade saved my life twice. It was divine to reconnect with it for this short time, but this is the last time I will see it in my current lifetime. I have dreamt of this moment, and I have foreseen it in my visions, but just moments ago, the spirit of the athame promised me we would reconnect in another future lifetime, that I could be the one who finds it again and rediscovers its power. Oh, the adventures we have had and what we could do in the future! I can leave this lifetime knowing that a future lifetime will have it again."

They continued to talk and finish a second bottle of wine. It was one of those once-in-a-lifetime discussions that was rich, sweet, intellectual, and spiritual. When it was time to leave, they all got up slowly and everyone helped clean the table and get it ready for customers the next day. Jane walked them to the door with graciousness and hugged them both deeply. As Jane hugged Brynn she started to tear up and said, "You, my dear, we have been friends many times, and it was so wonderful to spend dinner with you once again. You are part of my soul, and we have been friends in past lives and will meet again in our next lives. Please live beautifully and free."

Brynn and Jane hugged one more time and then Paul and Brynn got into their VW and started to back up, but Jane looked frightened and stopped them. Her mood was completely different. Brynn looked at Jane and said, "You look frightened! Are you ok?"

"I just received a vision," Jane declared. "After you find a secure place to hide the athame, in the next year, please study a past life of the evil one. She was once called by legend, The Dearg Due."

Paul looked at Jane puzzled because he knew the story. "You mean the Dearg Due, Ireland's most famous female vampire?"

"Yes, you must study the tragic Waterford legend of love lost. It's the next part of your journey."

Brynn smiled. "Paul, you are lucky today, because I have researched her and written a book. I can catch you up in the next year." Brynn winked at Jane. "I will tutor him and maybe we will make a trip to Ireland next year."

Jane returned the smile and said, "Be careful, drive safe tomorrow, and carry your protection crystals with you at all times." She waved at them as they drove out of the parking lot, and she walked back into her restaurant and started to close it up.

Paul and Brynn went back to their hotel and fell asleep in bed exhausted next to each other with full trust and energy.

They woke up late and made their way down to the hotel cafeteria for coffee and a quick breakfast, knowing they needed to get to the Garden of the Gods where they were supposed to meet someone who does not look like they belong there. They checked out of their hotel and put their bags in the VW and drove to the state park to look for a person who may have their next clue.

They drove across Colorado Springs, found the park visitor center, and walked around to get their maps and get a feel for the park they were about to explore. They both wanted to hike and get some exercise so they decided to walk the Chamber/Bretag/Palmer trail, a moderate three-mile trail nearly circling the entire park, with rolling rocky terrain away from the traffic. As they parked and found the trailhead, they were amazed at how the rocks were formed and how beautiful. As they walked, they read that Charles Elliot Perkins had owned the Burlington Railroad and had purchased 240 more acres to include the Garden of the Gods for his summer home. His intent was to leave the property to the state of Colorado, but he died in 1907 before he could make it a state park. His children, knowing their father's intent, conveyed his 480 acres to the City of Colorado Springs, the Garden of the Gods. The name was acclaimed by the comment, "Why, it is a fit place for the Gods to assemble, we will call it the Garden of the Gods."

They moved through the park in spontaneous enjoyment of the beauty and magnificence of the rock formations. They spent the first hour of their hike visiting the formations with the normal tourists, taking photos along the way. Brynn and Paul continued to be amazed by how the rocks were formed and agreed that gods must have been involved in making the park. When they finished the trail, they realized that they did not meet any person with a message for them. Their steps were heavy with disappointment as they started back toward their VW. As Paul's hands touched the door handle, he noticed two people sitting on a picnic table near them with their backs to them. He felt a rise of goose bumps on his neck, and he thought he knew those two people. Brynn looked as he pointed toward the two people who were dressed formally and did not look like tourists. Paul nodded with a smile and they both started walking toward the picnic area.

About ten feet away, Paul laughingly called out, "I thought it was you!" The four exchanged hugs. Paul was surprised to see how comfortable Brynn was.

Brynn laughed at Paul's confused expression. "Hey, I was there at the big party at your inner temple, remember? Besides that, Merc and Lilith have been connected to me for years."

Paul still felt uncertain. "Ok, so are you the two we are supposed to meet?"

Merc and Lilith just laughed and Merc said, "We wanted to visit you along your current journey and to assist somewhat along the way. We might get into a little trouble, but it's just our style."

Lilith and Brynn were having a private conversation like they were old friends, quickly catching up and holding hands and like they had been friends for decades. Paul continued walking with Merc. Paul said, "Merc, we were supposed to meet someone to help us to our last location."

Merc smiled at Paul and said, "Yes, I am walking you to the person who will help you."

Merc walked with Paul down a small path away from Lilith and Brynn and said, "Paul, the clue to the final place you must hide the athame will be confirmed with a person who does not fit in to this time or state park." As they continued walking down the path farther away from Lilith and Brynn, they came upon a person standing alone touching one of the huge rocks, walking with a cane, with round blue glasses, but wearing an eighteenth-century suit with a top hat and long white hair. Merc stopped and said, "This meeting, Paul, you must do yourself. I am not supposed to be a part of this conversation."

Paul started walking toward the gentleman and looked back toward Merc, but he had disappeared. Paul continued to walk toward the elderly man, hesitant to interrupt him.

The elderly man, his back to Paul, said, "Paul, I hope you are committed to finishing your task?"

Paul, who still could not see the man's face, said, "I am committed to finishing the journey."

The elderly man, who did not fit in the park setting with his elegantly tailored suit and top hat, finally turned around and looked at Paul. He had a gray beard and tapped his wooden cane. He looked straight out of the 1800s.

Paul was confused but gave the elderly man the fullest respect. "Sir, why I am supposed to meet you today in this park?"

"Paul, we have never met before in past or current lives, but my friends have fought many battles side by side with you. I need to tell you where to bury the athame and why. Throughout the last four thousand years, the athame has been hidden and recovered repeatedly by a certain group of people. Those people are powerful, and I am here to help you create an extra security layer so the athame is secure for a long time. There is nothing but death associated with that blade and we need to make sure it is not found for at least another thousand years until the person who is destined to find does so to change the balance of power and begin a new phase of human evolution."

Lilith and Brynn near the VW were still talking when Paul walked up to the car with a look of closure. Lilith smiled. "I can tell that you have received the location by the look on your face."

Paul smiled and nodded at her. "I also seemed to have lost Merc in the walk."

Lilith smiled again. "That's just what he does, do not take it personally." She looked at Brynn. "My sweet dear, I will visit you next month, we shall have whisky at the small churchyard near Strongbows Tree in Waterford for the ceremony that must be completed. Promise me. We need to finish what we started."

Brynn kissed her on both cheeks and said, "I will be there and Paul will be there with us. He is a part of this past journey, but he does not remember it yet." Lilith and Brynn both looked at Paul and smiled mischievously. Paul just shook his head and smiled back and turned on the engine.

Brynn lounged back in her seat before flashing Paul

a brilliant smile. "So, where are we going?"

Paul said, "Well, I am not allowed to tell you, that was part of the agreement. You can always ask Lilith."

They both looked toward where Lilith was standing but she was gone or vanished. They just smiled together. "So, you are not going to tell me where we are going. You're saying I have to rely on your directional skills? We might take a wrong turn and end up in Wyoming."

Paul just laughed. "I thought you would say that but I have GPS so we might not get lost. It's only about five hours away."

Brynn chuckled, put on her sunglasses, and draped her bare feet on the dashboard. "Well, let's get going. I would like to get there before dark."

They started on the highway heading west toward the mountains. He plugged in his phone to the VW and looked up a playlist and hit play. He was guided to play a certain song as they started their drive onto the freeway bustling with truck drivers and pickup trucks. In the back seat of the convertible, there was a leather satchel full of ancient leather journals from the museum vaults and the other knives from the secure section of the museum. As they drove, the athame in his satchel started to glow revealing new text on the blade. When the song started, Paul looked over at Brynn, smiling to himself as the wind blew her brunette curls all over her face, but she was smiling and at peace too.

The song Paul was guided to play was Queen's single "Who Wants to Live Forever" and as the words were sung by Freddie Mercury there were particular lines that were relevant to their journey.

CHAPTER 27

AD 2719

Kilas was a Cardovian pilot from the outer rim. A cargo space mover in the trash galaxy called the Mantu, she would go to planets in various solar systems and look for artifact pieces to sell to the space kings and politicians who owned the universal military force in the abandoned galaxies. These so-called leaders ran the laws, whether right or wrong. Kilas had worked in the Independence and Galactic wars and had served with the current political leader years ago during key victory battles of the campaign. After wars, victors have the spoils. Kilas was offered a plum job, but since she had seen enough war and enough violence, she chose an austere, mundane job in one of the most barren and frontier galaxies.

She walked with a limp. For losing part of her leg, leadership had given her a medal. For helping win the key battle where injured, she'd been compensated with her current ship and a job. None of her colleagues or comrades knew why she wanted to work in the galactic frontier where it could be more dangerous than the crowded planets. Where the civilization lay was order and justice; out where Kilas worked there was just the law of the fittest.

Kilas was a green, muscular human. She had two robotic humanoids as workers and companions who were almost real but never aged. Their names were CRAG (Cognitive Reactive Assistant Guide) 34 and 54 but Kilas called the identical robot twins Craig and Greg. Kilas only knew the difference between them because she made them wear different work clothes and had them put a mechanic's cloth nametag on their uniforms. In the end it did not matter as long as the work got completed and the ship kept working.

She was the pilot of callsign "Regulator 4," an older cargo spacecraft but reliable and well fortified against a space fight. She named her spacecraft after a long-ago cavalry frontier trooper, a mythic soldier that symbolized the beliefs of a colony that called themselves the Regulators. On their planet, the wind blew constantly. The Regulators were hardened by the terrain and the weather and were content to work the land in its harsh conditions. Cowboys and ranch hands had found a home in one of the most desolate military units before the great war and before the great Apocalypse of the nuclear age. The Regulators were proud of their independence, and proud it was born from the harsh, isolated conditions of the human-devastated planet (whether or not they were proud of the human causes of the devastation is lost to time).

Kilas was a soldier but by academic trade was an archaeologist and always dug for historical items on the frontier of the galaxies. The items she found could bring her a great deal of trade credits with the governor of the sector, a typical bureaucratic politician.

She was war hardened from her stint in the Independence Wars, and just wanted peace in her duties as a collector in a little uncivilized corner of the galaxy. She had her simple task to explore planets and the opportunity to make extra credits with selling her finds to the governor. Her mission this year was to dig in an abandoned and infamous planet called Nebartuy and to look for magical items that had internal power.

Kilas had her coordinates loaded and her two companions working as navigator and ammunition defense weapons expert. She had a lead for power elements reputedly still on Nebartuy but that planet had been almost destroyed by nuclear annihilation in 2145 during the last war of civilization. Most of the population and ecosystems had died during the fighting or died within ten years from radiation sickness or cancer. Most of the planet's economic activity was fuel exchanges because the fossil fuels inside the crust of the planet were not affected by the radiation. Nebartuy had plenty of fuel to still be useful and had pockets of austere civilizations, despite not being officially a part of the network of human civilizations slowly rebuilding from thousands of years of war. Nebartuy was behind technologically, but still, if you wanted to find a fight that was where you would go. Kilas only wanted to look for relics and get some fuel.

Kilas received permission to enter the atmosphere for landing for supplies and refueling and a little relic searching. Her crew of two androids did everything exactly as needed for the procedures for landing onto new planets and the ecosystems and pressure changes needed for the aircraft to not burn up through the atmosphere. Kilas asked them to also have combat mode ready, which meant the full defense system and outside guns fully loaded in case they landed into trouble. Kilas went into her quarters and pulled out her multiple energy plasma handgun, her AT-56 grenade launcher, and a long-range rifle with self-guided bullets. Once her weapons were stowed about her person, she pulled out a wooden case which held an old knife for close combat, which had strange text written on it that she had found on a lost planet almost thirty years ago from a special relic buyer that Kilas often dealt with, who never sold anything but on that occasion said the knife had spoken to her to sell it to her through a message. All Kilas knew was that if the knife was by her side, she was protected; so call it superstition or magic, she always carried the knife when she left her ship.

Their final approach was well under way; the ship's visual showed miles and miles of desert and the derelict station by the sea. Kilas could see all the fuel wells receiving fuel from the ground to run the station and feed the local population of terrain beings. The aircraft was about one hundred yards in length and needed a larger landing pad. The landing guides could be seen directing Kilas to land on bay 26. Kilas landed the aircraft, successful as always with the experience of thirty-plus years of flying, fully comfortable trusting her intuition. The favorite part for Kilas was always when the exit door released gases and started to lower. She knew the first impression walking off a ship set the stage for the rest of the visit. The appearance of a strong person with confidence was always needed on a new station for help with negotiations.

Kilas wore her military-issued black leather cape with red boots slightly scuffed and worn from battle. Her holster kept her handguns and her dagger was always hidden in the base of her back in a leather sheath. Kilas had on gray pants with a red stripe down the side, also from soldiering. There were lots of veterans who continued to wear parts of their uniforms after the war to start conversation and to build understanding quickly. You could never go into any bar without finding a veteran of the wars. Most of the veterans just wanted to stop fighting and make a living and live in peace like Kilas, so wearing the old parts of the uniform usually meant quick access to comraderie and respect and information.

Kilas readied herself to exude confidence. As she walked off the platform with Craig and Greg following her, there was only an older robot half working with an older man with a stooped back waiting for clearance to fuel the ship. The entire area was empty. Kilas kept walking over to the pathway and toward the main building to learn more about the place. She received many strange looks from the different types of beings there in the hallway, but she kept walking to find an information office. Kilas walked into a room that was dusty and had "headquarters" painted in older paint on the almost broken door. She walked into the office and there was only one desk in the middle with a very large blue creature with two large eyes wearing a green cloak and a leather brown belt draped diagonally across its torso. The blue face was dominated by a large mouth with a few missing teeth that was currently smoking some wrapping paper tobacco. Kilas walked in front of the desk and asked, "Sir, may I ask for assistance?"

"Well, can you?"

"I would like get some fuel and visit your sector for special items," replied Kilas.

The creature smiled. "My name is Kobar. I run this sector. Please just let me know what you are looking for so you don't waste your time, plus we do not like strangers hanging around."

Kilas said, "I am looking for ancient relics and have my two humanoids who assist me through their radar-sensing technology. We can cover a great deal of ground per day. If we find something and sell it on the intergalactic market, there is a cut for the governor."

Kobar asked, "So you agree to share profits with me on whatever relics you find on this desolate planet? That is a good deal—what is the catch?"

"There is no catch. If I find anything, I share the profits with you. I am an honorable former soldier."

Kobar studied the tough muscular woman. Not many folks in these parts admitted being a soldier from the prior wars. She held out her hand for a deal. He knew soldiers were honorable and he felt like he could trust her. He said, "Ok, but you have to tell me what you find no matter how small and you will sell it at our outpost unless we can get a better price off-planet, but I need to know everything you find, I mean everything. There are certain items that are storied to be on this horrible planet but no one has ever found the pieces, so I am curious if you can find any relics worth any money. I will give you one week to find something." He shook her hand, sealing the deal between them.

Kilas smiled as she shook his hand knowing that he was a thief and a swindler but also knowing that he was honorable in the basic handshake.

Kilas departed his office to recon the map of the planet to see where past cities had once existed because that was the most logical place to dig. She walked back to her ship and met Craig and Greg with instructions to scan the planet history and the terrain for the most likely areas of artifacts on the planet. Craig and Greg started the computer protocols as they had done on other planets. Within twenty minutes, they had found six places that would have the greatest probability of artifacts that they could profit from. They identified three places as unlikely, one place that was not probable, and one too deep to excavate, but the last location was unique because it was on top of a mountain crest only six feet into the ground and on a pinnacle like it was meant to be found. This puzzled Craig and Greg when they brought the locations to Kilas.

Kilas grinned and then said, "It can't be, it just can't be." With deft, precise motions she sped from her captain's chair into her quarters and came out to meet Craig and Greg with a book. "We will go excavate that mountain. It is probably nothing, but it could be of legends, possibly, maybe, we just have to go see if the site is as it is told."

Craig said, "Captain, I am programmed with the entirety of galactic history and have no recall of anything buried on this desolate planet. This planet had over a hundred nuclear explosions during its last humankind warfare. The descendants of the handful of survivors have reproduced for only nine hundred years, this planet has no significant artifacts left that are worthy of your excitement, because I would know. I am programmed with all human knowledge."

Kilas just smiled and said, "There are some things you do not know because they are folklore and not in history and to put you in your place, you are only as good as your data that was put into your artificial intelligence mainframe by a human."

Craig looked puzzled and glanced at Greg. Greg just lowered his head and said, "The captain has a factual point. Our programming—even though it is extensive and has more recallability than a human—is possibly only as good as the program, and the error of humans could be in our protocol even though we have the ability to learn everything in the universe."

Greg looked disappointed at Craig. "I thought we were brothers. Why would you say that?"

Craig said, "My programming protocol prohibits me to lie. One of the reasons you can say we are always factually correct."

Greg looked up at Kilas. "Captain, it seems that I could possibly not know all the facts of the universes in the last trillion years, please educate me."

Kilas looked up at both of them. "Well, there is a legend that is unsubstantiated and can't be proven in any way but people still believe it because the story has stayed alive over four thousand years. There is a legend of a cursed and highly powerful dagger that has possible alien or unknown origins. They say it was cursed by the act of a wicked woman sticking the blade into a prophet, killing him. It spent the next hundred years playing a role in the death of innocent women before it was lost. Legends passed down among treasure hunters have always said that the last owner of the blade did not want to destroy it but wanted to bury it where no one would find it and burn all directions and swear first-witnesses to never tell, but legend says this 'Nera blade' is buried on top of one of the tallest mountains on this planet called Earth, and that it has its own energy source and is cursed to those who hold it."

Craig said, "None of that is in my data storage. Where did you get such an outlandish story?"

Kilas said, "Well, stories that become legend are told from one generation to another and repeated through the generations to not be written down, because only those people who are in the right families, inner circles, and in the right brotherhood have the privilege of knowing. Secret societies like the ancient Free Masonic followers, the secret sects of ancient religions especially the so-called Christians, the famous Knights Templar, the secret Illuminati, the Skull and Bones, and the Elders of Zion keep the folklore alive as part of their linage and secret history. My family genealogy comes from Yabu and from this planet Earth; my family history left here over a thousand years ago right after the explosions that ended most of life to migrate to another planet in the neighboring systems. Many left their home planet to start anew, and many like my family changed their names to fit into their new home planets. My lineage derived from Magnum to Magheeberg to MacGhee, to my ancient origin of MacGregor, over three thousand years ago. So in my family history, written by over ten generations, which you see on this table here, there is a story of one of my great-great-way-back-grandfathers who came upon a two-thousand-year-old cursed dagger. The family says he and his spouse buried the dagger on the highest mountain of their homelands so no one could ever find it, but its coordinates reflect exactly where we are going to see if that artifact is the historical and cursed knife."

"There is no proof it exists. We need to explore the area just so I can prove that the artifact does not exist and that folklore are just fantasies and not based on fact," Craig said.

"I will take that as an apology," said Kilas. "Get in the pilot's station and get us as close to the site as you can maneuver."

Greg said, "We are probably wasting our time because humans throughout generations can change the stories of the fables to a version that is purely fantasy and not based on any fact."

Kilas said, "That is why we need to explore the site. Let's go and stop talking about it."

Craig and Greg assumed the pilot and copilot chairs and navigated the craft to the grid that the computer radar had given them. The grid was on top of a mountain range and the radar device gave an exact location about four feet below the ground. They had to find a safe place to land the ship so that they could explore the site for the artifact. As they found a clearing almost two kilometers from the site, Kilas, Craig, and Greg left their aircraft by foot with their digging gear and radar sensors. As they started walking the mountain terrain, they noticed how the trees had devoured the land after all the Armageddon of nuclear explosions of the area almost nine hundred years ago. Nature survived, no matter what man did to it. As they flew closer, their tracking device started bleeping more rapidly and the map on their device said it was right in front of them in the most nonsignificant digging place; it was just a place between the trees on top of a hill; there were no markers and no significant navigational features to bring other people to the treasure or the "x" spot to dig for this treasure. They only knew about the location because of the new technology that was created in the last twenty years of geological explorations with the application of metallurgical nuclear navigation system to help identify small energy sources.

They landed the ship within ten meters of the identified spot and the crew exited the rear of the craft with all their equipment. Kilas walked with her handheld device identifying the energy source and as she walked toward the trees the beeps became faster until it became a constant sound and she stopped and said, "Boys, here is the spot. Please start digging."

Craig and Greg set down their equipment and started shoveling the dirt substance, forming a hole about three feet in diameter. After a few minutes one of the shovels clanked against something metal. Kilas said, "Feel for the edges. I am surprised. I actually did not think it could be there."

Craig and Greg slowly moved the dirt away to find the edges of a box. The box was a green metal with a handle on both ends. They brought the box out of the ground and put it next to Kilas. As they brushed the dirt away from the top of the box, they could see stenciled words. Kilas read the words "Property of the U.S. Government: Top Secret." Kilas smiled at it knowing that anything classified or secret would never be just buried in the forest with no instructions. She thought most highly secret objects would be sealed in vaults and safes and then she thought maybe being buried in mountains away from civilization would be safer than a vault. Over the course of generations of war, most of the treasures of the civilization were stolen or destroyed. They all stared at the box. There was a simple lock on a latch, and Kilas said, "Craig, please unlock the box and open it."

Craig took a metal bar and pried the lock open until it broke and released the latch.

They peered inside. Another box sat there, surrounded by black foam, but this box was wooden and had a carving on the top. It was long in shape and Kilas picked it up and blew dust off the top so she could read the engraving.

Since the engraving was in an ancient language, they would have to plug into their mainframe for deciphering. It was not a known language from the past two thousand years. The words were "Suil Dhe na gloir, A ghnus Dhe nan dul."

Kilas asked Craig and Greg again if they knew the language and they both looked perplexed. For the first time in over five years her AI robots did not know something. She smiled and started to laugh at her robots, who were so smart but did not know this language. Kilas opened up the wooden box and inside was an object wrapped in cloth. She pulled the object out and undid the ancient cloth and there was a knife in her hands with the same markings engraved on the blade as on the box. She grabbed the knife, and the blade started to glow and suddenly she was transported to another place. She was no longer in the woods on top of a mountain digging for a box with Craig and Greg.

She was standing near a mountain lake. She saw that someone was building a cabin on the lake because the frame of the cabin was up and the log roof was halfway done. A man stood about thirty feet from her under a tree, about to pick up a huge log over his shoulder. He had long gray hair in a ponytail with strands down his face, and he was extremely muscular without a shirt but had scars wide and thin on his back that she assumed were from battles. He had his back to her, and she watched him pick up a large log, turn around toward her, and stand up with the log over his shoulder. He had tattoos all over his back and shoulders and as he stood up straight, he walked toward her away from the shadow of the tree. As the sun shone on his skin she noticed the man was green. He looked up at her and smiled.

Chapter 28
The Answers Revealed

Three angels stood on the hill watching Kilas meet the Green Man. Each wore stylish black suits with traditional winged-tip shoes. They were muscular and fit and their black wings were partially folded.

Senoy said, "Think Lilith will be irate with us for what we have just done?"

Sansenoy smiled. "I hope she is infuriated. It is so lovely to get her all mad and watch her become who she is destined to be from the past. I am not a fan of the nice Lilith; to be frank, I miss the woman who would devastate civilization under her wrath."

The third angel, Semangel, chimed in, "We can't underestimate what Lilith will do. We did, after all, just mess up plans that she has been working on for centuries. She will be pissed at us, just like the first time she met us, when God kicked her out of Heaven. Remember that first time?"

Senoy laughed. "I do not ever want to meet that pissed-off Lilith again. I was even scared of her. Oh, how she was a scorned woman!"

"Well, I so look forward to what will come next, the adventure begins now. There is going to be hell to pay. My friends shall we have a drink?" Sansenoy pulled out a flask from his coat.

Senoy said, "Well, well, well, is that a little boom boom?"

"You know it is. Want some?"

"Of course. I think the last time we did this was in the 1400s?"

"Early 1500s, but who is counting. You know this would not feel so revengeful had Lilith not broken your heart. Lilith probably still loves you—but not after what you just did to her plan. She might have sex with you, but love is out of the picture. You are such a poor bastard; she is going to be pissed with all of us but especially you. The only good thing you did was help inspire the witches' creed, but then we crossed the line on that one too."

"So, what are we going to do with Nera?"

"I have a plan to resolve that problem once and for all. It is time to call Jamie into the process; she has been quietly waiting to participate to seek her revenge. She has also been Paul's secretary for years, so Lord knows she deserves some crumbs off the table. Yes, it is time. The fireworks are really going to happen now."

They each took a long swig from the flask that was being handed around. Each wore an identical, unrepentant smile. They all knew what they had just started ...

The End, or really until the story continues ... in the next book.

About the Authors

P.E. Berg has a doctorate in adult education and served in the government for 29 years. Paul has written military history and adult education journal articles over the past 15 years and The Birthmark Scar is his first novel. He is currently a university professor, tries to write full-time, and lives on Sentinel Hill in Kansas on his five wooded acres.

Amanda Hemmingsen: Tantra, Ayurveda, and energy healing are Amanda's 3 core metaphysical disciplines. She has a master's in English, and works full time as an editor. You can reach her via www.amandahemmingsen. com.

The Birthmark Scar is their first book of their trilogy.

If you liked this book, you might also like:

Little Steps
by James Adams
In Light and In Shade
by Patricia Irvine
Where the Weeds Grow
by Curt Melliger
Dancing with Angels in Heaven
by Garnet Schulhauser
Beyond all Boundaries Book 1-2
by Lyn Willmott
The Forgiveness Workshop
by Cat Baldwin
Dancing with Mountains
by Paul Travers
Croton & Croton II
By Artur Tadevosyan

For more information about any of the above titles, soon to be released titles, or other items in our catalog, write, phone or visit our website:
Ozark Mountain Publishing, LLC
PO Box 754, Huntsville, AR 72740
479-738-2348
www.ozarkmt.com

For more information about any of the titles published by Ozark Mountain Publishing, Inc., soon to be released titles, or other items in our catalog, write, phone or visit our website:

Ozark Mountain Publishing, Inc.

PO Box 754

Huntsville, AR 72740

479-738-2348/800-935-0045

www.ozarkmt.com

Other Books by Ozark Mountain Publishing, Inc.

Dolores Cannon
A Soul Remembers Hiroshima
Between Death and Life
Conversations with Nostradamus,
   Volume I, II, III
The Convoluted Universe -Book One,
   Two, Three, Four, Five
The Custodians
Five Lives Remembered
Jesus and the Essenes
Keepers of the Garden
Legacy from the Stars
The Legend of Starcrash
The Search for Hidden Sacred
   Knowledge
They Walked with Jesus
The Three Waves of Volunteers and
   the New Earth
A Vey Special Friend
Aron Abrahamsen
Holiday in Heaven
James Ream Adams
Little Steps
Justine Alessi & M. E. McMillan
Rebirth of the Oracle
Kathryn Andries
Time: The Second Secret
Cat Baldwin
Divine Gifts of Healing
The Forgiveness Workshop
Penny Barron
The Oracle of UR
P.E. Berg & Amanda Hemmingsen
The Birthmark Scar
Dan Bird
Finding Your Way in the Spiritual Age
Waking Up in the Spiritual Age
Julia Cannon
Soul Speak – The Language of Your
   Body
Ronald Chapman
Seeing True

Jack Churchward
Lifting the Veil on the Lost Continent of
   Mu
The Stone Tablets of Mu
Patrick De Haan
The Alien Handbook
Paulinne Delcour-Min
Spiritual Gold
Holly Ice
Divine Fire
Joanne DiMaggio
Edgar Cayce and the Unfulfilled
   Destiny of Thomas Jefferson
   Reborn
Anthony DeNino
The Power of Giving and Gratitude
Carolyn Greer Daly
Opening to Fullness of Spirit
Anita Holmes
Twidders
Aaron Hoopes
Reconnecting to the Earth
Patricia Irvine
In Light and In Shade
Kevin Killen
Ghosts and Me
Donna Lynn
From Fear to Love
Curt Melliger
Heaven Here on Earth
Where the Weeds Grow
Henry Michaelson
And Jesus Said – A Conversation
Andy Myers
Not Your Average Angel Book
Guy Needler
Avoiding Karma
Beyond the Source – Book 1, Book 2
The History of God
The Origin Speaks

For more information about any of the above titles, soon to be released titles,
or other items in our catalog, write, phone or visit our website:
PO Box 754, Huntsville, AR 72740|479-738-2348/800-935-0045|www.ozarkmt.com

Other Books by Ozark Mountain Publishing, Inc.

For more information about any of the above titles, soon to be released titles,
or other items in our catalog, write, phone or visit our website:
PO Box 754, Huntsville, AR 72740|479-738-2348/800-935-0045|www.ozarkmt.com